T0331259

PRIVATISATION AND DEVELOPMENT

Privatisation and Development
Theory, Policy and Evidence

CLAUDE V. CHANG

*Former Member of the Governing Council of the
University of Guyana, Guyana*

Routledge
Taylor & Francis Group

LONDON AND NEW YORK

First published 2006 by Ashgate Publishing

Reissued 2018 by Routledge
2 Park Square, Milton Park, Abingdon, Oxon OX14 4RN
605 Third Avenue, New York, NY 10017

First issued in paperback 2021

Routledge is an imprint of the Taylor & Francis Group, an informa business

© Claude V. Chang 2006

Claude V. Chang has asserted his right under the Copyright, Designs and Patents Act, 1988, to be identified as the author of this work.

A Library of Congress record exists under LC control number: 2006018460

Notice:
Product or corporate names may be trademarks or registered trademarks, and are used only for identification and explanation without intent to infringe.

Publisher's Note
The publisher has gone to great lengths to ensure the quality of this reprint but points out that some imperfections in the original copies may be apparent.

Disclaimer
The publisher has made every effort to trace copyright holders and welcomes correspondence from those they have been unable to contact.

ISBN 13: 978-0-815-39116-6 (hbk)
ISBN 13: 978-1-351-15136-8 (ebk)
ISBN 13: 978-1-138-35714-3 (pbk)

DOI: 10.4324/9781351151368

Contents

List of Figures

List of Tables

Preface

Timeo hominem unis libri [I fear the man of one book] – Thomas Aquinas

The 'World Development Report 2006: Equity and Development' is devoted almost entirely to issues of inequality and equity. But notions of equity and good governance are concepts that have been around for at least since the thirteenth century, rooted as they are in Thomism and more recently in neo-Thomism, the latter as espoused by Pope John XXIII in one of his last official statements *Pacem in Terris* [Peace on Earth] in 1963, some 43 years ago. No matter, it is a welcomed phenomenon not least by those who have consistently challenged the prescriptions of the IMF and World Bank (Bank) over the years.

This transformation by the Bank from structural adjustment at-all-cost in the 1980s to the point where 'reducing inequality [becomes] a question of morality' to quote James Wolfensohn, former head of the Bank, in the twenty-first century has been quite a journey for both the Bank and its clients in terms of consequences to the latter, especially the poorer developing countries whose official debts to the multilateral financial institutions have had to be forgiven in 2005.

In terms of timing, by coincidence this book – which has been in the writing for several years – details part of that journey in terms of antecedents and consequences with respect to the privatisation phenomenon of the 1980s and 1990s and should serve as a basis for a more detailed inquiry into the changed thought-processes at the Bank. It is signposted for the student of privatisation and development albeit not exhaustively so, and is mainly prescriptive in approach to allow policymakers and practitioners to guard against the several missteps in past privatisation programmes.

Claude V. Chang (2006)

Acknowledgements

This book has it origin in my first experience as an UNDP/UNIDO consultant to the Government of Guyana and is long in the writing. It has benefited from the passage of time and from ideas articulated in the several quoted references; from participation at international forums; and from interaction with grass-root operatives; from friends as well as from former colleagues at all levels of government in Guyana; and from interaction with the President and former presidents of Guyana, parliamentarians and members of the international community. I am richer for the experience and owe a debt of gratitude to all, particularly to the late President Desmond H. Hoyte for sharing his insight into the Guyana political landscape with me on the occasional personal Tuesday morning breakfast meetings and to the late President Dr. Cheddi Jagan for the vote of confidence.

There are others whose professional influences have contributed to the writing and publication of this book. I owe a debt of gratitude to Matthew Martin of Debt Relief International for the opportunity to contribute at the *Centro De Estudios Monetarios Latinoamericanos* (CEMLA) seminar: 'Financing Sustainable Growth and Development in Latin America'; and to Professor Colin Kirkpatrick for his advise, availability, and the opportunity and privilege to contribute to the DFID-funded Regulation Research Programme at the University of Manchester of which he is a co-director. I am also deeply grateful to Professor Eric Radford A.E, of St. Edmund Hall, Oxford University, for his profound influence upon my academic interests and approach to writing this book.

Last but not least are the several staff members of Ashgate Publishing whose professionalism and assistance have provided a welcomed level of assurance in the preparation of this text, in particular the editorial comments of Brendan George and his review team which serve to bring balance and coherence to the text. I am deeply grateful to all. My special thanks to Nikki Dines, Editorial Manager, for her courteous and efficient responses to my several questions and to Nicola Nieuwoudt, Desk Editor, for her professional guidance, patience and quiet efficiency.

I am, of course, fully responsible for the content of this book despite the several acknowledgements but would be remiss if I were not to express my gratitude to Bebe for her unfailing support and encouragement.

List of Abbreviations

ACP	African Caribbean and Pacific
AFDB	African Development Bank
CAP	Common Agricultural Policy
CARICOM	Caribbean Community
COMECON	Council for Mutual Economic Assistance
EEC-3	Eastern European countries of Czechoslovakia, Hungary, and Poland
EU	European Union
EPZ	Export processing zones (EPZ)
FDI	Foreign direct investment
GATT	the General Agreement on Tariff and Trade
GEC	Guyana Electricity Corporation
GUYSUCO	Guyana Sugar Corporation
GT&T	Guyana Telephone Corporation
HIPC	Highly Indebted Poor Countries
IDB	Inter-American Development Bank
MFA	Multifibre Agreements
MFI	Multilateral financial institutions
MIGA	Multilateral Investment Guarantee Agency
OECD	Organisation for Economic Cooperation and Development
OPEC	Organization of Petroleum Exporting Countries
PE	Public enterprise
PPP/C	Peoples Progressive Party/Civic government (Guyana)
PUC	Public Utilities Commission

PART I
Privatisation and Development

Chapter 1

Privatisation and Development: An Overview

The ideological context

The *raison d'être* of privatisation long found description in economic orthodoxy; it arises from the dichotomy between a capitalist world-economy and a politically-coercive economic system. The Yalta Conference (1945) inaugurated a Europe largely divided on the basis of ideology and set the stage for the 'Cold War' that followed. On one side of this ideological divide, the 'Berlin Wall' symbolised the 'Iron Curtain' that permitted entry into a socioeconomic and political system controlled by the Soviet Union with no exit, as the Hungarians found out in 1956 and the Czechoslovakians in 1968. The Soviet Union became an open antagonist to capitalism and created the Council for Mutual Economic Assistance (CMEA) as a means to promoting communism as an alternative ideology.

On the other side of the ideological divide, the Bretton Woods Agreement (1944) inaugurated a post-war economic system premised on Keynesian economic doctrine of state intervention: It defined post-war economic policies in the West for over 30 years, with the more powerful states manoeuvring for economic dominance and asymmetric advantage within a multivalent framework of international economic cooperation and development. Within this framework, the United States (US) gained ascendancy to world-economic dominance while the now European Union (EU) as an embryonic regional trading bloc in the late 1950s and 1960s received institutional support more for what it offered as a buffer against the spread of communism than for its contribution to the notion of open–market economics, earning it the dubious distinction of 'Fortress Europe'.

Within the framework of the Bretton Woods Agreement, a good many states led by the United Kingdom (UK) – who in 1945 nationalized major sectors of its economy – pursued welfare economics and state control of the commanding heights of their economies; many adopted import substitution as a means to economic development as conceived by the Latin American school (see Prebisch 1982). Outside of these economic frameworks, the oil rich states set their own national goals and objectives as a cartel; cooperating with others only when they perceived it to be in their interest to do so (see Ehteshami 2003). At the same time the US, firmly entrenched as the leading economic power, though not oblivious of the implications of the welfare state as an economic doctrine was not in the early goings overly concerned with it or the expanding influence of socialist ideology. To US policy makers, post-war economic prosperity was here to stay and would eventually serve as the incentive to others to join in furthering an integrated world economy based on the market mechanism.

Not so however. The pursuit of a welfare economic model by most Western states served to blur the capitalist-central-planning dichotomy for over 30 years. Concurrently, despite the rationalised benefits of an open economy, Latin America (see Prebisch 1984) and Asia continued on the path of import-substitution as a development strategy. Within a short time period, Japan and the Asian tigers emerged with the Asian economic model premised on market-augmentation (see Amsden 1989) and as rivals to entrenched Western interests. In addition, many newly-independent states emerging from colonialism and eager to disassociate with their colonial past in knee-jerk reaction atavistically opted for central-planning with all its ramifications – political as well as economic – as their preferred economic system. For most of the second half of the twentieth-century, then, political and economic ideology not geography defined West from East and became the dominant discourse as the world underwent a change in perspectives; made more immediate by the Debt Crisis of the mid-1980s and a US President determined to meet head-on the challenge of communism.

The changed global economic and political context

The changed global economic context following the 'thirty glorious years' of prosperity can be traced to three significant developments: First, the advent of stagflation in the 1970s which paved the way for a return to economic orthodoxy; second, the widespread collapse of economies arising from the Debt Crisis of the early 1980s which provided the justification for reining-in socialism and for extending market fundamentalism to developing countries; and third, the migration of the Eastern European countries to a market economy and the eventual collapse of the Soviet Union in 1991.

Stagflation and the shift to free-market economics

The concerns of Friedrich Von Hayek and Milton Friedman notwithstanding, Keynesian economics informed Western economic policies for more than thirty years. Both Hayek and Friedman believed in the market mechanism, with minimal government. Indeed, Hayek regarded government intervention in the economy as a threat to freedom and for most of the 1950s and 1960s was ostracised by his contemporaries for his position. Even the Conservative government of the UK pursued an interventionist policy in the face of rising prices and concurrent high unemployment in the early 1970s. It was not until Mrs Margaret Thatcher became Prime Minister in 1979 that a new policy approach based on market principles was implemented and began to yield positive results.

In the US, the tendency was also to favour government intervention though to a lesser extent: In the early 1960s, President Kennedy viewed the Keynesian Consensus as the practical management of a modern economy; for President Johnson, his successor, it was 'war on poverty' that saw a burgeoning central government and a consequential expansion in government spending on social programmes. But like the UK's, the economic downturn that followed in the 1970s was characterised by rising inflation and high unemployment, exacerbated if not precipitated by the first oil shock in 1973 and persisted through to the early 1980s. Following President Johnson, President Nixon's policies of increased spending and price and wage controls – Keynesian responses, to be sure – that mirrored the failed policy-options of the UK were similarly fated in the US, as was the succeeding Carter administration's attempt at much of the same.

The general failure of government intervention to keep the Western economies from sliding into recession in the 1970s served to vindicate Hayek and to elevate free–market economics to prominence under the conservative governments of Margaret Thatcher and Ronald Reagan. Like Ronald Reagan, Margaret Thatcher – influenced by the ideas of Hayek and Sir Keith Joseph – was convinced that big government was the root cause of the problem, and that holding down government spending by shifting to free-market economics was the solution (see Thatcher 1993, 6–15). Free-market liberalism thus replaced Keynesian economics as the determinant of economic policy on both sides of the Atlantic.

Confronting communism

At the same time, the US response to the not so nascent Soviet-type economic system was to go beyond its soft power and directly confront the challenge of communism led by an increasingly bellicose Soviet Union. To President Reagan this meant not only preserving democracy within the US but also extending it across the rest of the world (see Kaldor 2003, 1–22). To this latter end, the focus of US foreign aid changed from development-oriented to military-oriented, and from multilateral to bilateral, with conditions for political reform attached. The Bretton Woods institutions became instruments of US foreign policy in its bid to secure external leadership in pursuit of its national security and economic interests and a market-oriented economic system. In this effort the US found full support in the Thatcher Government. Hence, funding of the IMF and the World Bank (Bank) was reduced by the US and the UK in keeping with a distinctly ideological approach to foreign aid.

The Debt Crisis

What is known as the Debt Crisis began in 1982 when Mexico found itself unable to service its sovereign debt to the money-centre banks located mainly in the US. Up to 1979 both private and public financial flows to developing countries were at an unprecedented pace as the money-centre banks rich in deposits from the oil price increase of 1973–1974 found state-funded projects in the developing countries, mainly Latin American, attractive investment vehicles for the recycling of Petro-dollars. In fact, Latin America accounted for about one-half of the total Third World debt of which two-thirds were made by the money-centre banks (see Edelman Spero 1992). At the other end of the relationship, developing countries were willing borrowers, facilitated by the phenomenon of negative real interest rates.

The Debt Crisis is characterised by three discreet phenomena: external shocks, changed approaches to development aid, and the Baker Plan. These are discussed in some detail below.

External shocks

Between 1979 and 1981, the world experienced several external economic shocks which were devastating to most of the developing countries: First, the second oil shock of 1979–1980 caused the price of oil to surge above US$35.00 per barrel in 1981 and left many economies with huge external debts that became unserviceable. Second, anti–inflationary policies of the developed economies and a steep recession in 1981 and 1982 caused a precipitous drop in the terms of trade for developing countries' exports. Third, in the early 1980s the US embarked on a tight monetary policy as a means to reducing the high domestic inflation rate. This latter policy caused external interest rates to escalate to an average of 13.0 percent during the period 1980–1984, reversing the negative 1.1 percent real interest rate enjoyed by borrowers during the period 1975–1979 (see Krugman 1988, 62).

The impact of high oil prices and high interest rates on the developing countries was almost immediate when combined with the simultaneous reduction in their exports: Their combined trade deficits increased from US$22.2 billion in 1979 to US$91.6 billion in 1981; interest payments over the same period increased from US$24.3 billion to US$ 41.8 billion. By 1982, interest payments exceeded private lending to these countries by US$3.5 billion (Edelman Spero 1992, 175); it became the straw that broke the camel's back.

New approach to development aid

The plight of the developing countries was exacerbated by the change in policy to official aid. As discussed above, the governments of the US and UK saw economic recovery in terms of a return to market fundamentalism, more specifically, supply-side economics as promulgated by orthodox economists and strongly embraced by Ronald Reagan – even against the advice of White House staff – and Margaret Thatcher who was seen as equally strong-willed. In consequence, developing countries were to be made less reliant on official aid and more upon market forces, including providing commercial opportunities and incentives for investment by both domestic and foreign enterprises.

In keeping with this changed policy on foreign aid, the US and later the UK reduced their aid to the developing countries. Moreover, with a defence-oriented federal budget aimed at stretching the Soviet Union's economic system to breaking point,[1] the US bilateral approach to foreign aid became the principal means by which to influence political reforms in aid-dependent countries. The message was clear: Unless developing countries were willing to embrace democratic principles and pursue political and economic reforms, US aid would be drastically curtailed or eliminated. Further reinforcing this resolve, as noted above both the US and the UK reduced their contributions to the IMF and Bank. At the same time, aid from the Organization of Petroleum Exporting Countries (OPEC) declined precipitously and left many developing countries without access to what had become a major source of finance for most of them.

By adopting the Baker Plan – discussed below – into their lending frameworks, the IMF and Bank assumed the responsibility for ensuring implementation of an Anglo-American foreign-aid policy mandate: That developing countries must migrate to an open market economy, with opportunities for foreign investment and with reduced dependence on official aid.

The Baker Plan

With poorly managed economies, many larger developing countries – Mexico for example – found they were unable to service their external sovereign debts mainly with the money-centre banks which were equally unprepared for the crisis that ensued. As shown by Edelman Spero (1992, 181), loans by these banks were mainly to the major South American countries and Mexico and amounted to US$182.0 billion, with no loan-loss provision and with a debt exposure/equity ratio of 125 percent. It was not until 1987 before they were able to restructure their balance sheets to the point where their exposure as a percentage of their equity capital was reduced to 57 percent.

The realisation that a collapse of the Western banking system was imminent caused the governments of the lending countries to act to avert the collapse. Managing the Debt Crisis became an imperative of US foreign policy from which evolved the Baker Plan. In order to justify fundamental structural changes to the economic systems in developing countries, the Baker Plan framed the crisis as arising from inappropriate policies of the developing countries and not as arising from exogenous shocks or poor lending policies of the money-centre banks.[2] It further signalled the nature and extent of reform required by the US government which were to be administered by the IMF and Bank as loan conditions.

---

[1]   It was the opinion of President Reagan and his CIA Director, William Casey, that the Soviet economy could not support a protracted arms race and would disintegrate if pushed to the limit.

[2]   The same reasoning would be advanced in response to the Asian financial crisis in 1997–1998.

The Baker Plan focused on three goals: structural change by the debtor countries which emphasised private-sector investment; tax, labour, market and financial institutional reforms; and trade liberalisation. As observed by Secretary Baker:

'Many debtors are already taking important steps toward increasing savings and investment, improving their economic efficiency, and encouraging the return of flight capital and privatization of public enterprises. The International Monetary Fund and the World Bank have an important role to play in this process. They can assist by promoting adjustment policies and longer–term structural changes within the debtor countries' (Baker 1987, 354).

The Debt Crisis thus provided the opportunity to widen and deepen the requirement for fundamental structural change in the smaller developing countries by way of the redefined policy-prescription mechanisms of the IMF and Bank. In addition, the diffusion of capitalism and democracy became a central role of the IMF and Bank in keeping with the ideological resolve of the US and UK. The Bank's commitment to 'Programme and adjustment Sector' which included debt-reduction as a defining characteristic was increased from four percent of total commitments in 1970–1979 to 18 percent in 1980–1989 and to 23 percent in 1990–1995 (see Kapur 1997, 130). During the same period, as reported by Freedom House in its report 'Freedom in the World', the number of countries pursuing democracy as the principal form of government increased from 69 in 1987 to 91 in 1992. In 1997 it increased still further to 118. Since then, four other countries, including Afghanistan and Iraq, have been added to the list of fledging democracies.

Outcomes

In keeping with the Baker Plan – now fully incorporated into IMF and Bank lending-policy prescriptions – privatisation of state-owned and state–controlled enterprises which were either established or nationalized in keeping with the notion of state-capitalism and which were inefficient users of resources was made a reform imperative. Indeed, not unexpectedly privatisation in developing countries was viewed as a logical extension of the process that began in earnest in the UK in late 1970s.

Against this backdrop of a changing ideology in the US and UK, and the Debt Crisis, the focus of structural adjustment lending shifted from fiscal and trade policies to address balance of payments problems in the 1970s, to structural adjustment that treated privatisation of public enterprises as the dominant reform mechanism in the 1980s and 1990s.

Revenues generated by privatisation between 1988 and 1994 totalled US$112 billion, of which 40 percent were foreign direct investment (FDI) derived (see Megyery and Sader 1997, 1). However, disaggregating the data by region as depicted in Figure 1.1, it is clear that for the period 1988–1992 privatisation in the Latin America region in accounting for 67.8 percent of sales was driven primarily by debt repayment to the money-centre banks whilst the 17.6 percent attributed to Europe and Central Asia represents the early years of transition to a market economy; Sub-Saharan Africa meanwhile is shown as accounting for 0.5 percent of total sales.

Moreover, FDI as a percentage of sales was greatest in Europe and Central Asia at 55.3 percent, with Latin America and Caribbean at 19.8 percent and accounted for 96.1 percent of total FDI from privatisation during this period. Less than 1 percent of total FDI went to Sub-Saharan Africa. More detailed analysis revealed that of the US$5.869 billion of FDI flows to Latin America, US$5.0 billion went to Mexico (see Sader 1993). Based on these numbers, FDI up to 1992 had bypassed the smaller developing countries.

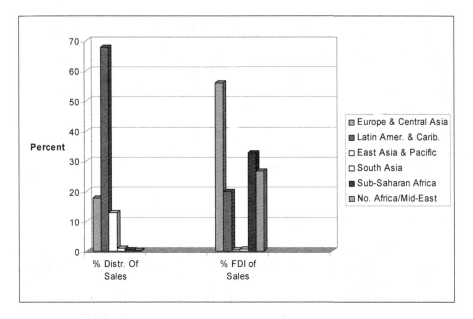

Figure 1.1   Privatisation sales and FDI participation: 1988–1992

Source: Compiled from Sader, F. (1993, 16, 22)

As noted above, privatisation in Hungary, Czech Republic and Poland (EEC-3) were accomplished primarily with private capital flows. As shown in Table 1.1, for the period 1988–1992 privatisations accounted for 73.41 percent of the total FDI flows to the Czech Republic, and 64.84 percent of the FDI flows to Poland. In the case of Hungary, privatisation accounted for 86.24 percent of FDI flows from 1989 to 1992. For all other countries in Table 1.1, with the exception of Peru (41.86 percent), Venezuela (41.25 percent), Argentina (35.55 percent) and Jamaica (33.60 percent), FDI flows were substantially for reasons other than the privatisation of public enterprises. For example, in the case of Mexico, although US$1,048.5 million of FDI flows were proceeds from sale of public enterprises, it represented only 5.45 percent of the total FDI flows to it.

Table 1.1   FDI from privatisation 1988–1992: Selected countries

Countries	US$ (million)	Percent Total FDI
Czechoslovakia*	1,882.3	73.41
Hungary**	2,295.7	86.24
Poland*	490.2	64.84
Argentina	4,022.1	35.55
Venezuela	1,512.8	41.25
Mexico	1,048.5	5.45
Turkey	373.3	10.34
Chile	254.0	14.19
Peru	139.8	41.86
Philippines	287.4	8.85
Sri Lanka	36.7	13.01
Jamaica	126.0	33.60

* Started in 1990; ** Started in 1989
Source: Compiled from Sader (1993, 60)

Shift in investor-focus

In the mid-1990s privatisation in the EEC-3 countries and Russia became the focus of Western investors arguably at the expense of FDI in the smaller developing countries as Table 1.1 tends to suggest. Indeed, the privatisation activity in the EEC-3 countries seems also to support this observation.

Hungary   By mid-1995, Hungary had liquidated 536 enterprises, fully divested 620 and partially privatized 924 of the larger enterprises. Sales proceeds amounted to US$3.5 billion for an estimated US$10 billion in assets. As noted earlier, the state maintained approximately US$10.5 billion in equity interests in 740 partially privatised enterprises. It was with respect to this retention of equity interest by the government that concerns were expressed. According to Borish and Noël (1996, 66–7), corporate governance reportedly was compromised by: subsidisation of 'loss-making enterprises'; interference with restructuring decisions, often altering or reversing them to protect jobs; and debt forgiveness by state-owned or state-controlled banks. However, the above concerns and other constraints to the process were addressed in the Law on Privatisation passed in May 1995. The planned privatisation by the government of Hungary to the end of 1997 included divestiture of: one-half of the remaining equity holdings in the 740 companies; majority holding in the broadcasting enterprise; four gas distribution companies; and five power distributing companies. Together, these properties were valued at approximately US$ 5 billion and contributed to further increase FDI flows to Hungary through the end of 1997.

The Czech Republic   In the case of the Czech Republic, the second stage of the programme saw the completion of all small-scale privatisation at the end of 1994, and 80 percent divestiture of the more than 3000 larger enterprises by March 1995. Of the 200 companies remaining to be privatised, two-thirds were partially privatised.

Poland   With respect to Poland, the privatisation process was much slower than in Hungary and the Czech Republic primarily because of the Polish government's approach to the process, which was to let it evolve rather than to force it. As a result, 135 properties were sold by the end of 1994; 25 more than the 110 targeted. However, there was no mass privatisation (400–600 were planned), and enterprises liquidated were limited to 2,289 some 800 less than targeted. It should be noted that liquidation here refers to enterprises that were divested in parts, mainly to employees.

Russia   Privatisation by Russia was by far the more dramatic however, with over 14,000 enterprises privatised between December 1992 and June 1994 (see Boycko, 1995, 105), prompting Martin Feldstein to observe:

> Russia's privatization of virtually all businesses and housing has been one of the late 20th century's most remarkable achievements anywhere in the world ... despite some economic policy mistakes and much political turmoil, the progress is enormously impressive.[3]

Later official reports would suggest a different picture, however: According to the U.S. General Accounting Office Report (2000, 90): 'no aspect of Russia's economic transition has been more controversial than the privatisation of enterprises' (Goldman, 2003). Certainly, the creation of oligarchies – the most notable being Yukos – has been attributed to the rapid privatisation in response to the political imperative. Irrespective of the outcome of the Russian privatisation programme, it clearly was in the national security interest of the US specifically and the West generally, to ensure not only the rapid ideological transformation of Eastern and Central Europe but also to counter any resurgence of Russian nationalism; the latter fundamentally more distinct from the West and arguably more problematic than communism (see Huntington 1996).

Privatisation in poorer developing countries

While many of the larger developing countries were fairly positioned to comply with the reform mandates of creditor countries and indeed proceeded to successfully restructure their economies accordingly, to most of the poorer developing countries – for the most part semi-traditional on the development continuum conceptualised by W. W. Rostow (1961) – such reforms were considered drastic if not unconscionable. Many developing country governments took the position that Washington was

---

[3]   Feldstein, M., 'Russia's Rebirth', *The Wall Street Journal*, 8 September 1997, p. A22.

seeking to impose democracy by holding development assistance hostage to political and economic reform, a take it of leave approach if you will (see Kllick 1995).

But neither Washington nor London was listening. Indeed, hardships notwithstanding and as if to dismiss the concerns of the developing countries the conservative governments of the US and UK, who were at this time becoming increasingly alarmed at the spread of socialist ideology among the newly-independent states and whose main focus was to revive their flagging economies, thought it propitious to effect a shift to market principles in developing countries, and to dismantle institutions that treat with the commanding heights of the economy as the domain of government. Hence former British colonies who upon gaining political independence patterned their economies to reflect the mixed-economy model of the UK found themselves having to re-orient their economic strategies; others who adopted a Soviet-type economic model and were deeply in debt found the transformation to a market-economy even less agreeable.

Not surprising, then, in comparison with the results from privatisation in the EEC-3 countries and Russia, the results out of developing countries, especially Sub-Saharan Africa, were less encouraging despite the increase in the number of countries pursuing privatisation programme since 1988. The number of enterprises privatised in developing countries between 1988 and 1994 totalled about 3,300 and lagged privatisation in the EEC-3 countries in terms of both number of enterprises privatised and revenues there from as shown in Figure 1.1 and Table 1.1.

Many privatisation programmes in Sub-Saharan Africa to be sure appeared to have stalled for one reason or another. In terms of enterprises privatised, the numbers were indeed telling: Between 1988 and 1992, Benin divested eight state-owned enterprises out of a total of 57, for a total of US$53.0 million; Ghana sold 34 out of 345 state-owned enterprises for a total of US$37.5 million between 1989 and March 1993, and liquidated 26 during the same period. Nigeria divested 29 out of 140 such enterprises for a total of US$110.0 million between 1989 and 1992; while Togo sold six enterprises for a total of US$28.0 million (see Sader 1993, 41–2). The combined sales proceeds for the region were less than half of Poland's which many observers sought to attribute to a lack of cooperation from governments in the region.

In comparison with other regions, fund-flows to Africa on all counts appeared to have either stagnated or failed to come close to recording proportionate increases. This and other issues prompted the Bank in 1989 to explicitly attribute the region's inability to keep pace with the rest of the developing countries to a 'crisis in governance' (Kapur, 1997, 129). But there are other contributing factors besides governance, some of which are offered below.

Size of public investment   To be sure, the ideological implication of privatisation was not lost on Africa and, in consequence, was slow to take hold because of fundamental differences in culture and mode of production. Moreover, whilst the public sector in most African countries' comprised many commercial enterprises, all without exception included almost all basic infrastructure – telecommunications, power, transport, water and sanitation – which to most African leaders represent the 'commanding heights' of their economies. Indeed, infrastructure was estimated to represent about one-third to one-half of public investment and about three to six percent of GDP during the period under review (Glen and Sumlinski 1998; see also Kessides 1993). Additionally, the capital intensive characteristics of infrastructure put them beyond the capacity of the private sector in most developing countries and endowed them with monopoly status which the Africans and others outside of Africa were unwilling to pass on to foreigners.

Commercialisation as the preferred choice   As a further reinforcement to the African position, studies conducted by the Bank and others have concluded that, because of multiple linkages of infrastructure, economic growth is positively or negatively impacted by the character and state of a country's infrastructure, control of which is best left in the hands of Africans. Hence, Africa's stance on privatisation reflected a general belief that state-capitalism in the African context meant limiting foreign influence on economic integration at the national level (Lewis 1994). Indeed, during the 1980s and early 1990s, most African countries preferred to pursue commercialisation as an alternative to privatisation, especially with respect to infrastructure (AFDB, 1999). But, the relatively poor performance of their infrastructure sectors under commercialisation in the 1980s and early 1990s prompted many African countries to implement or contemplate implementing privatisation and regulatory reforms in an effort to improve performance and to contribute to the liberalisation of their economies as a whole.

Poorly-designed approaches   Where privatisation was pursued, according to the Bank[4] the process as applied to Africa has been characterised by poorly designed approaches and a lack of prior preparation, requiring consensus-building, centralised coordination, greater legal authority for the privatising agency and transparency. Indeed, the lack of transparency is perhaps the single most important criticism that is levelled against African governments, especially when valuation are considerably below public expectations. This was the case in Côte d'Ivoire and Togo in which both governments were severely criticised for the lack of transparency in selling state-owned assets (Campbell White and Bhatia 1998; Dzisah 1996). On the other hand, The Zambia Privatisation Agency (ZPA) has been singled out as 'exemplary' for accountability and transparency (Campbell White *et al.* 1998).

Inexperience with corporate structure   In addition, West African countries have been singled-out for their '... extremely cumbersome procedures for setting up and administering corporate structures' (Vuylsteke 1988, 92). In the specific regard to infrastructure, in addition to the issues raised by the Bank, innovative operating and financing structures are typically considered essential aspects of the privatisation process given the monopoly nature of the services and the requirement for sunken capital. Moreover, the process is made complicated by issues of social obligations and the absence of market-oriented institutions. Nonetheless, the pace of privatisation in infrastructure picked-up in the mid-1990s as the experience-base

---

[4]   World Bank, 1997 Abstracts of Current Studies: 'Private Sector Development and Public Sector Management'.

was expanded and deepened, and the process approached within the broader context of modernisation and promoting economic growth.

Capital flows

With respect to private capital flows, IMF data quoted by Helleiner (1997, 4) show a marked increase in private capital flows to the developing countries and Eastern Europe, from an annual average of US$11.6 billion in 1983–1988 to US$114.3 billion in 1989–1993. In 1995, it amounted to US$ 166.4 billion. At the same time net official flows declined from US$29.5 billion in 1983–1988, to US$11.7 billion in 1989–1993. Although net official flows stood at US$27.3 billion in 1995 it represented 14.1 percent of total capital flows compared with 71.8 percent in1983–1988, thereby clearly indicating a shift from official flows to private capital flows, with negative impact on Sub-Saharan Africa. Indeed, as shown, while net official flows decreased from US$ 29.5 billion in 1983–1988 period to US$ 27.3 billion in 1995, flows to Latin American and Caribbean increased from US$5.1 billion to US$ 22.4 billion during the same period. Of equal significance was the increased flows to Asia of both FDI and portfolio investment consisting of equity and debt instruments in terms of absolute amount and as a share of net total flows which, arguably, contributed to the Asian financial crisis of 1997–1998.

  Foreign Direct Investment (FDI)   Although FDI in Africa increased proportionately to total inflows, for the reasons given above coupled with the high risk reward ratio attributed to Africa by foreign investors, it remained small in absolute size and was limited to six Sub–Saharan African countries. Also, while portfolio investment benefited from the worldwide expansion of stock–fund investment, it too remained small: at below US$120 million a year during 1990–1993 in comparison with the several (US$) billions of portfolio investment flows to Asia and Latin America as shown by Kasekende *et al.* (1997, 63). In addition to the relative small size of private capital inflows, Sub-Saharan Africa's outflows unlike other regions' were greater than FDI inflows. As revealed by the data provided by Kasekende *et al.* (1997, 63), even assuming that short-term loans have been entirely utilized to pay down long-term loans, there still remained a substantial proportion of long-term loan repayments that had to be met out of FDI flows. By contrast, Latin America's short-term borrowings were almost equal to its long-term loan repayments, whilst Asia's were greater than its long-term loan repayments. Clearly, these outflows have been a significant constraint to Sub–Saharan Africa's economic growth. What is more, the changed status of South Africa in 1994 caused that country to exert a greater pull of FDI, arguably at the expense of others in the region.

A concept unexamined

Development, according to Wallerstein (2004, 21) emerged as a concept after 1945 based on a 'theory of stages' with differences in growth attributed to distinctly different notions of efficiency and effective use of resources and with the most developed states being offered as the model for the less developed. Indeed, as regards the latter the evidence suggests that many developing countries were counselled, if they were not obliged by mid-1980s, to sign on to the binary distinction – capitalist or communist – that attended the dominant discourse of Cold-War politics. Prior to that, the dominant discourse on development centred on the perceived core-periphery relationship between the developed and developing countries, with the weak states perceived as kept in dependent economic relationships in respect to FDI and technology transfer and often exploited by the core countries for their inexpensive labour, resources and markets (see Sklair 1995; Prebisch 1982; Wallerstein, 1974).[5]

Since the theory of stages, sustainable development has been defined by the Bruntland Commission in 1987 as development that 'meets the needs of the present generation without compromising the needs of future generations' (Serageldin 1993, 6). More recently, that definition has been broadened to become 'a multidimensional undertaking to achieve a higher quality of life for all people' (United Nations, 1997) and as freedom (Sen, 1999). All have relevance to the discourse on development, particularly the notion that freedom is both instrumental as well as substantive in a world in which demography, geography and institutions converge to determine development effectiveness; all have relevance in the evaluation of privatisation effectiveness, particularly in developing countries.

In terms of socioeconomic and political system remodelling, Mrs. Thatcher sought to create a new class of voters in the UK – the 'enterprise class' as she puts it – by the privatisation of state-owned enterprises, many of which as noted above were nationalized by the first Labour government in the mid-1940s, while the Europeans sought to follow suit if only cautiously so. The vast body of analyses emanating from the dominant institutions speak to the investment opportunities created by privatisation and the beneficial impact on national income streams. The influential literature of the time exalted the virtues of privatisation based as it were in economic orthodoxy: Change in ownership was a priory enterprise efficiency and effective use of resources, with the success of the UK's privatisation programme as validation (see Vickers and Yarrow 1995).

For most of the 1980s and 1990s, then, privatisation effectiveness – evaluated in terms of development – in developing countries was a concept unexamined. Following the lead of the IMF and Bank, few scholars and practitioners of privatisation were willing to treat with the broader socioeconomic implications of wholesale structural adjustment in poor countries; fewer still to look pass the 'nomothetic pretensions' of privatisation; all deferring to other disciplines on issues of social disruption and their

---

[5] While the distinction between core and periphery has become fuzzy over the years with the emergence of the larger developing countries as rivals in an interstate system in which the rules of behaviour are becoming less skewed, control over access to certain resources or assets considered strategic is still being exercised by the developed countries. 'Resources' meanwhile has been redefined to now include financial reserves of the developing countries to be accessed to fund budget deficits on a *quid pro quo* basis.

several manifestations. Indeed, according to Eduardo Aninat, Deputy Managing Director of the IMF, the Washington Consensus, which informed policy prescriptions for much of the period, did not '... provide any important ideas for integrating the social issues we are now more concerned with into the mainstream'.[6] Moreover, privatisation was generalised to developing countries through the auspices of the IMF and Bank not only on the basis of the change in policy to development aid but also in the belief that the Debt Crisis was a sham; '... the result of an unwillingness of developing countries to service their sovereign obligations' (Bauer 1991, 61), fostering a narrowly-focused quest to establishing the market as the primary disciplinary mechanism.

The Washington Consensus replaced the Baker Plan and guided development-aid policies at the IMF and Bank, much to the chagrin of many developing countries even after two decades, as evidenced by criticisms by the host country at the Summit of the Americas in Argentina in November 2005 and the gathering of anti-globalisation factions in Venezuela in January 2006.

Criticisms notwithstanding, since the end of cold-war politics and with James Wolfensohn guiding development policy at the Bank for much of the 1990s, the socioeconomic and moral consequences of inequality have increasingly entered the consciousness of the donor community and MFI and are reflected in their policy approaches to development assistance. Indeed, Arthur Lewis' notion that inequality is good for growth – derived from economic orthodoxy – has been replaced with the notion that inequality is harmful for sustainable growth in a capitalist world-economy that is consumption derived and in which 'reducing inequality is a question of morality'.[7] These and other development issues are more fully discussed in Chapter 3.

Purpose and outline of the book

The underlying purpose of this book is best expressed in this quotation from Wallerstein (2005, 1):

'We need to confront directly how we have come to think the way we do that we can begin to liberate ourselves to think in ways that permit us to analyse more cogently and more usefully our contemporary dilemmas' (Wallerstein 2005, 1).

This book therefore seeks to interrogate privatisation in terms of its effectiveness vis-à-vis the stated goals on the one hand and more fundamentally in terms of development at the level of developing countries. It seeks to explain why privatisation was highly successful in the UK and other Organization for Economic Cooperation and Development (OECD) countries on the one hand and why it has not met with equal success in developing countries on the other. In this regard, it further seeks to unmask the procrustean proclivity of proponents in pursuing privatisation at

---

[6]   'IMF support focuses on participatory approach, 'inclusive growth', *IMF Survey*, Vol 29, No 12, 19 June 2000.

[7]   Wolfensohn, J., National Press Club Address, Washington, DC, 29 October 2003.

the level of developing countries by interrogating policy prescriptions of the IMF and Bank and contested issues vis-à-vis the conceptualised benefits and theoretical assumptions underlying them. It examines the extent to which culture and customs, indeed the mode of production, stand in determinate relationship to the goals, techniques and outcome of the process. It further examines the extent to which the socioeconomic and moral consequences of privatisation have been ignored in pursuit of the ideological imperative implicit in the Washington Consensus.

At the other side of the equation, it shows through the Guyana experience how many of the poorer countries have developed a culture of entitlement and, in the absence of a coordinated donor monitoring and evaluation framework, have become adept at the display of market institutions as part of their strategy to attract grants and soft loans while patronage flourishes as the preferred form of governance. As part of the process, the roles of the MFI and foreign investors are critiqued in context of a liberalised global financial market and the notion of profit maximization implicit in a market economy.

Many of the issues discussed in this book have found description in related disciplines; few in the vocabulary of the interconnectedness between privatisation and development. Indeed, the disconnect between orthodox economics and social consciousness continues to inform private sector reform in the twenty-first century even though the experiences of developing countries in the 1980s and 1990s suggest a causal relationship between the Washington Consensus and social inequality at the lower end of the development continuum. Hence, the purpose here is to contribute in the first instance to reflective thought that must necessarily be part of validation, the sine qua non of any theory, and in the second to provide the basis for a balanced and empirically-valid theory of privatisation.

Organization

The book consist nine chapters organised into five parts, with this introductory overview as Part I. It is organised to serve as a potential text for guiding thought towards a holistic approach to privatisation by providing in terms of the development and privatisation narrative insight garnered at the policy-making, implementation and grassroots levels. It also targets analysts and government officials who must in their respective roles pursue privatisation and development with due regard to notions of effectiveness, professionalism, transparency, and accountability.

Part II examines the relationship of the mode of production – the trinity of reciprocity, redistribution and price-determined exchange to the development effectiveness and in turn to the privatisation effectiveness. In Chapter 2, the notion of economic determinism is examined: The derivation of the capitalist world-economy is traced and contrasted with other economic systems that reflect the unequal stages of development explained in terms of the mode of production. It examines the theoretical underpinnings of privatisation in the developed countries on the one hand and the inherent constraints to its universal application on the other.

In Chapter 3, development effectiveness is evaluated in terms of freedom (see Sen 1999). The nature, cause and consequences of social inequality are examined, with any correlation between privatisation and social inequality or indeed reduction in social inequality highlighted.

The chapters in Part III examine privatisation from the perspective of economic orthodoxy: Outcomes and analyses drawn from selected reports and other published works are synthesized and presented. Attention is drawn to the relative ease with which countries with market institutions are able to seize the benefits of privatisation to their betterment within the framework of the capitalist world-system whilst the poorer more traditional societies find the concept debilitating, if not predatory.

In Chapter 4, the goals of privatisation are critiqued. Their basis is examined in terms of the underlying theory and in terms of effectiveness. The differing perspectives of the US, UK, Western Europe, the Eastern European countries of the EEC-3 and Russia are contrasted, as are the perspectives of the developing countries. The roles of the IMF and Bank are examined in terms of the appropriateness of policy prescriptions, with contrasting outcomes between OECD countries and selected developing countries offered as indicators of effectiveness. In this connection, outcomes are compared and contrasted cross-country and cross-regionally to highlight differences in privatisation effectiveness.

The techniques of privatisation are examined in Chapter 5 in context of the underlying goals of the process pursuant to the Washington Consensus. Attention is drawn to the inherent internal constraints to the process and attendant social disruption which have been made secondary to the goals of debt repayment, restitution and the creation of investment opportunities for foreign investors. The disparity in foreign investment flows is highlighted, with the opportunity for profits a priori private capital flows.

The nuances of the privatisation experience of the EEC-3 and Russian are highlighted in Chapter 6 to conclude Part III. The motives behind the privatisation initiatives of the EEC-3 countries are examined, as are the approaches and the role of private capital flows from Western investors. The Russian experience is critiqued from the perspective of dismantling a socialist economic model in contrast to the return to a market economic system of the EEC-3. The distinction is drawn between IMF and Bank controlled approaches in Hungary and Poland with the essentially mass–privatisation approach of the Czech Republic (formerly Czechoslovakia) and Russia.

Part IV consists of two chapters in which the Guyana experience is offered as a case study: Development and privatisation are examined from the perspective of the framework discussed in Part II and in terms of their effectiveness. Development is analysed in context of a highly indebted poor country in which foreign aid is viewed and pursued as an aspect of national development and a measure of performance; and where corruption is deemed endemic. Constraints to an effective privatisation programme in a small developing country in which the political will is largely constrained by Marxist–Leninist ideology and deep-seated racial distrust, and where patronage is a defining characteristic are highlighted. It draws from the author's experience and research as a United Nations Development Programme (UNDP) consultant to the government of Guyana in the early days of its Economic Recovery Programme (ERP); as a senior finance executive in the Guyana sugar industry; and as Secretary to the Treasury under the Peoples Progressive Party/Civic government (PPP/C).

Chapter 7 provides context for the case study that follows in Chapter 8. The social, economic, and political framework is critiqued from the perspective of effecting a fundamental shift: from a socialist economic model of development to a market economy and the challenges attendant on political governance constructed largely on the basis of racial arithmetic and imbedded distrust. Against this background, the roles of the IMF and Bank are examined from the perspective of policy prescription with the initial aim at recompense and thereafter to creating a vibrant private sector with the public sector as facilitator.

The privatisation of the Guyana Electricity Corporation (GEC) is examined in Chapter 8. The circumstances leading up to the abandonment of the rehabilitation project by the investor in April 2003 with the parting statement: 'The risks associated with investing in GPL make it less attractive for CDC to invest further funds than walking away'[8] are examined in depth as a case study and serve to inform the tenor of this book.

Part V offers a concluding policy perspective in Chapter 9. It synthesises the several recommendations offered in the literature and the author's own findings and experience from having been on both side of the privatisation and regulatory divide.

---

[8]   Singh, G., 'CDC open to selling its stake in GPL', *Stabroek News*, 28 February 2003; see also Singh, G., 'CDC ready to sell GPL for $1 – Investing in Guyana is not for the faint of heart says official', *Stabroek News*, 13 March 2003.

PART II
Liberalisation and Consequences

Chapter 2

Economic Determinism as Liberalisation

There is no such thing as society. There are individual men and women, and there are families
(M. Thatcher, 1987)

Introduction

The World economy derives from the interstate system institutionalised in the Treaty of Westphalia, 1648. By that treaty, certain rules of interstate behaviour rooted in a common moral grounding were established and were expanded upon over time in a visible framework of law and policy, moral argument and legal argument. Within this framework of international relations and law evolved a capitalist world-economy of multiple states turning on a self-regulating system of markets with laws of its own and giving rise to the notion of economic determinism in societal integration (see Wallerstein 2004, 2; Polanyi 1977, 47 and Dalton 1968, 70).

Within this system of price-determined exchange, the efficacy of the commoditizing of property rights is no less a condition sine qua non than the efficacy of the division of labour advanced by Adam Smith in 1776 (see Campbell *et al.*1976). And as it is with labour, the institution of property rights requires a legal system to protect and enforce such rights. It is thus within this framework of price-determined exchange of property rights and labour that privatisation has been conceived as a means to preserving and expanding the capitalist world-economy. However, the extent to which these institutions are present depends crucially on the basis of societal integration discussed below.

Given the importance of institutions to development and privatisation, it is proposed here to go beyond their mere mention and to examine their evolution as the underlying logic of a market economy; the most significant form of societal integration as conceptualized by Polanyi (1977). It is also proposed to examine the extent to which the mode of production reflects development and thus stands in a determinate relationship to the outcomes of privatisation. In this latter regard, the UK as a society integrated on the basis of the market mechanism and proven-in over time is offered as the benchmark – possessing of all the required elements of demography, geography and institutions – against which selected developing countries are contrasted.

Societal Integration: Modes of Production

Generally, societies can be distinguished by their integrating processes, their modes of production or transaction if you will. Drawing from Polanyi's (1977) conception of societal integration Chase-Dunn (1989, 15) defines mode of production as

'... the basic underlying logic which any social system exhibits'. As conceptualized by Polanyi (1977, 36) three modes of production or transactions distinguish societal integration: reciprocity, redistribution and exchange, the latter interpreted as price-determined in a market economy referred to as the economic mode of market exchange (Dalton 1968, 30); the first two often are found in a harmonizing relationship in 'primitive' societies. When viewed from this perspective it is clear that economic growth as measured in terms of GDP per capita is derived from market exchange and is influenced by demography, geography and institutions, the latter reflective of the stage of modernisation of the society or its status within the capitalist world-economy; it is arguable whether development is enhanced necessarily by the replacement of indigenous institutions in the transformation to a market economy.

Reciprocity and redistribution

Whilst the developed countries are primarily defined by transnational practices within the framework of a capitalist world-economy – discussed in greater detail below – developing countries to a large extent fall within the category of non-industrial economies in which reciprocity and redistribution determine integration or as politically-coercive economies where the mode of production is essentially redistributive in keeping with Marxist-Leninist ideology.

Where the mode of production is manifestly one of reciprocity and redistribution, resources are organised and distributed according to cultural practices agreed upon by the collective: family, village and so on. While not entirely absent in politically-coercive or market economies, reciprocity predominates in kin-based or communal societies in many areas of the world and are undertaken between groups before redistribution among members of the collective (see Polanyi 1977, 36). Hence, aspects of indigenous customs are discernible in varying degrees in many of the larger Asian and African societies, many as conflicted societies depending on the influence of European colonialization. In the case of countries who have embraced the socialist economic model – politically-coercive for the purpose of this discussion – market-supporting institutions were either absent or if inherited, as some were, compromised over time.

The case of India   India arguably is an example of a culturally conflicted society to the extent that it embodies two seemingly conflicting modes of societal integration, that is, a market economy is embedded in an essentially traditional society. Having been colonised by the British for almost 200 years, it was in many respects caught between distinctly opposing modes of production. This conflict in cultures has manifest in India's choice of production strategies since its independence: Despite its policy of nonalignment which it pursued after independence in 1948, its mode of production was patterned after the politically-coercive model of the Soviet Union and was pursued as a means to restoring national pride and customs. This policy resulted in an inward-looking India who sought to resist foreign influence on its economic development for almost four decades. It is only after witnessing the tremendous economic progress by China since the mid-1970s that India began to pursue an open-market economic system and is encouraging FDI with equal success, especially in the field of technology. But India's cast system is also seen by many observers as a source of conflict and a constraint to reducing inequality and thus its rapid transition to a modern market economy.

The case of Africa   In Africa, conquest was taken a step further: attempts to civilise Africa by the destruction of indigenous cultures and customs are still within living memory. But Africa survived partly by reason of geography: kin-based and communal societies are still present and influence economic transactions more than in any other region of the world. Moreover, many African countries have attempted to recapture aspects of their culture since breaking away from colonialism, more so since the collapse of their economies in the 1980s but not always with beneficial results: The dismantling of Western institutions have left many African countries in tribal conflict; the election of a new Muslim president in 1989 brought with it a reversion to Islamic customs in Nigeria, including the restriction on women's rights at a time when gender issues have become a major focus of multilateral and bilateral donor countries; and the general reluctance to use contraceptives has contributed to the spread of AIDS in Southern Africa, as have many other tribal notions relating to virility.

Politically-coercive society

In a politically coercive society, that is where the state stands in a determinate relationship between productive resources and society, the mode of production is said to be primarily redistributive. The Soviet-type economic system organised on the basis of central control – without which it could not exist – and on the notion of egalitarianism albeit loosely so, exemplifies such a system.

Up to 1989, when centrally-planned economies began to unravel in Central Europe starting with Hungary, the Soviet-type economic system was to be found in several countries which together accounted for one-third of the world's population (see Carson 1997, 37). If India were to be included as a centrally-planned economy, the percentage would be even greater. Indeed, India was the closest to a centrally-planned economy outside the communist bloc. Moreover, many former European colonies pursued some form of central control of the commanding heights of their economies. For this reason, a brief examination of the Soviet-type economic system would help to explain the reluctance of and or difficulties encountered by many of the smaller developing countries to converting to a market economic system.

Planning   Under the Soviet-type economic system, production priorities were formulated and set up to fifteen years out. There were other shorter plan periods: medium-term of five years, and a short-term of one year or less. Planning took the form of deciding on outputs and inputs in the production process rather than on aggregate demand. Whilst the long-term plan was broadly defined by projections of economic development, technology diffusion and resource availability, the other two plans were more focused the shorter the time-span (see Carson 1997).

Organization   With respect to the organizational structure, it was strictly a top down approach, with the Central Committee – the Politburo – and the Council of Ministers setting policy. Broad guidelines were handed down to a state planning agency made up of technocrats which was responsible for formulating detailed economic directives to be further handed down to the economic ministries. Each ministry had responsibility for a particular economic sector or group of industries. Thus detailed plans were passed down to the enterprises from the ministries via the regional and industrial authorities. This approach played to the narcissism which defined many developing country leaders of the period and continue to hold appeal to the neo-patrimonial ruler.

Sole sourcing of supplies   Unlike a market economy, firms did not compete for supplies but were instead assigned a supplier for the specific production output; suppliers also were restricted to the firm to which they were assigned; a phenomenon that was found to constrain the effective utilisation of resources in some developing countries. Output and delivery targets set by the planners were the measurement criteria of performance; not cost or other efficiency measurements. Whilst the larger industries and farms were organised and run by the state, smaller farms were organised as collectives and decentralised. In this latter organization, there were some forms of decentralised control and ownership.

Redistribution   Redistribution was determined mainly by the level of contribution to the production effort. Rationing and queuing were the main methods of distribution because demand always exceeded supply. Price was not a determinant in the distribution process nor was it a reflection on production cost at any one factory. The privileged did not receive income differentials as such but had access to special distribution centres and to a wider variety of goods and services.

Outside the Soviet Union   Developing countries which possess a significant industrial sector but adopted a Soviet-type economic system either out of notions of utopian socialism or from knee-jerk reaction on freedom from colonialism comprise the politically-coercive group outside the Soviet Union. Several developing countries in Africa fall within this group as a step back from a market economy. Many of them relied to varying degrees on central planning methods, dismantling inherited market-supporting institutions in the process, as evidenced by the wholesale nationalisation which took place in the 1960s and 1970s; many pursued 'indigenisation' as a means to narrowing the target of African economic development. And because most of them have either stagnated or collapsed since gaining political independence and have to a degree reverted to reciprocity and redistribution, market-supporting institutions must be either implemented or restored as a precondition to becoming a market economy. But as the evidence suggests, the privatisation process has been generalised to both groups despite the absence of market-supporting institutions.

Social democracies

In those economies that were not communist but were engaged in some form of central planning – usually referred to themselves as social democracies – the primary role of the state-planning function was '... to compensate for perceived market failures – in terms of growth, efficiency, and or distribution – while leaving most of the market system intact' (Carson 1997, 37). Nonetheless, the decisions taken at the state-planning level often constrain development of the private sector and provide opportunity for corrupt politicians and public officials to benefit themselves. As a consequence, in the 1970s and 1980s the non-competitive prices paid by the state-marketing boards for agricultural products in most of these social democracies caused many farmers to abandon farming and to seek work in the cities; only to be replaced with cronies brought in through the granting of privileges. In this connection, it is perhaps of some significance that the President of Guyana has resisted repeated suggestions by the IMF to fully consolidate the state planning function within the ministry of finance. Indeed, notwithstanding that the state planning secretariat is co-located within the ministry of finance and is represented as coming under the minister of finance, it is de facto separate and reports directly to the President.

Market economy

The third mode of production is a market economy situated in a capitalist world-economy in which production is determined by the price mechanism. In a market economy and therefore the capitalist world-economy, economic determinism derives society (see Wallerstein 2004, 24; Dalton 1968, 70; see also Polanyi 1944).

But as is well recognised, notwithstanding parochial interest in maintaining asymmetric advantages in international trade and commerce there are degrees of state intervention within individual market economies: from the social-welfare state of Sweden and other European countries to the US concerned with providing the civil minimum.

It is also from this gathering of interstate actors that political and economic hegemony is derived. But it is also from within this framework of multilateralism derived from the interstate system that norms rooted in moral grounding are translated into a visible framework of international law and organisations as a means to transforming hegemony from dominance to leadership. This has never before been more evident than in the early years of the twenty-first century.

Mixed economies   Social-welfare states that were predominantly market oriented were regarded as mixed-economies or market-economies depending on the influence of the state in the economy. Whilst markets have been in existence for as long as cities, because of market failures in the provision of non-competitive goods and services, the state plays a role in the distribution process. But economic orthodoxy restricts the provisions of the state to only those goods and services that are communal in nature and are considered non-rival, for example, police and fire-fighting services, parks and roads. Even so, providing the civil minimum requires intervention beyond the provision of non-rival goods and services and may take several forms. It is thus within this framework of societal integration where demography, geography and institutions assume significance that the development effectiveness of privatisation should be examined.

The role of agriculture

The role of agriculture in production is yet another indicator of the stage of growth and therefore the mode of production or transaction. Agriculture pursued as subsistence represents reciprocity and possibly redistribution; it becomes exchange when agriculture is pursued for gain (see Polanyi 1944, 41). It is perhaps instructive that while Mexico, Korea, Thailand and the South American countries are shown in Table 2.1 as shifting production away from agriculture, the Philippines, Bangladesh and most of the African countries either by design or circumstances have not.

Table 2.1   Structure of production: Selected countries. GDP distribution by sector (percent)

Country	Agriculture			Industry			Manufacturing			Services		
	1965	1989	1995	1965	1989	1995	1965	1989	1995	1965	1989	1995
Mexico	14	9	8	27	28	28	20	20	20	59	59	64
Argentina	17	14	5	42	33	30	33	20	20	42	53	65
Korea	38	10	7	25	44	43	18	26	29	37	46	50
Indonesia	56	23	17	13	37	41	8	17	24	31	39	42
Philippines	26	24	22	28	33	33	20	22	23	46	43	45
Peru	18	8	7	30	30	37	17	21	23	53	62	56
Thailand	32	15	10	23	38	39	14	21	29	45	47	50
Nigeria	54	31	43	13	44	32	6	10	7	33	25	25
Ghana	44	49	46	19	17	16	10	10	8	38	34	39
Trinidad	8	3	3	48	41	46	-	8	10	44	56	51
Togo	45	33	38	21	23	21	10	8	9	34	44	41
Bangladesh	53	44	30	11	14	18	5	7	10	36	41	52
Malawi	50	35	31	13	19	21	-	11	14	37	45	47
Benin	59	46	34	8	12	12	-	5	7	33	42	53

Source: Compiled from World Development Reports: 1991, 208–9; 1996, 210–11

Countries that continue to pursue agriculture as a means to subsistence in keeping with customs where the production process is largely determined by a combination of local customs and state intervention and not necessarily by economic considerations could be classified as falling somewhere between reciprocity and redistribution modes of production (see Dalton 1968, 128). In most such cases these smaller or agriculturally-based economies must be first brought to the point of 'take-off' (see

Rostow 1961) before privatisation can be fully effective. Yet, as revealed by the evidence these countries have been forced to privatise what many of them consider as either instruments to national cohesion or as central to their progression toward economic growth and development at their own pace. Many of these countries especially in Africa have incurred unsustainable external debts in an attempt to circumvent the influence of demography and geography while consciously or unconsciously maintaining the economy as an aspect of their society as opposed to submitting completely to the market mechanism as the determinant of society.

With few exceptions, most of the smaller economies fall within the reciprocity-redistribution classification, notwithstanding attempts to establish light manufacturing by promoting export processing zones (EPZ): evidence of straddling two modes of production, if you will. Where EPZ have been established, transnational corporations (TNC) are given special privileges in a defined area within the general economic framework of the country. EPZ have been created primarily to take advantage of the abundance of low-skill, low-wage labour found in many of the underdeveloped countries. While some countries saw this as a first step in the learning-by-doing process – it was through this process that Mauritius developed its garment industry – others rejected this stage of development as, to paraphrase an African government minister, not every country's idea of industrialisation.

Economic determinism

Economic determinism as used above suggests that the market mechanism determines the way of life in a society. Hence when left unchecked the 'invisible hand' of Adam Smith (Campbell *et al.* 1976, 477) operates outside the framework of normative behaviour, that is, it does not identify with the larger collective but instead promotes individualism within the capitalist system. Indeed, as observed by Wallerstein (2004, 24), large entities beyond the level of individual households which are income-pooling are considered dysfunctional for the capitalist system; and a capitalist system exists only when the system gives priority to the endless accumulation of capital. Thus defined, the market relies on the notion of individual preference facilitated by the finite commoditizing of the factors of production – division of labour if you will – and attributes utility to each commodity measured in terms of price. In its function as a distributive mechanism of productive resources therefore, the market necessarily requires the creation of an integrated network of political, legal and social institutions supportive of that function. As we know, these institutions are both cultural-ideological as well as infrastructural derived within the framework of the interstate system. It is in this regard that economic determinism is seen as the overwhelming influence in a capitalist world-economy; and in the liberalisation process prescribed by the Washington Consensus and promulgated by the IMF and Bank.

Property rights

As remarked earlier, one of the more important market-supporting institutions and a fundamental requirement of a market economy is the institution of property rights. Indeed without property rights there can be no exchange. In a market economy property rights include rights of individuals, firms and states to access and utilise goods and services on the one hand and to exclude others from using them on the other; to derive income from assets and the right to alter or change the form of the asset, including the right to transfer or exchange ownership in that right. Thus property rights govern behaviour among users either implicitly through customs or explicitly in the form of written rules and laws enforceable by the courts. In a capitalist society, these rights reside predominantly in individuals or class of individuals as a group, with the state maintaining ownership rights over communal property such as parks and other public places. In a communist society, as discussed above, such rights reside almost exclusively in the community or state.

Since property rights are deemed endowed with utility, they promote the notion of choice which in turn is influenced by price through the process of competition in a market economic system. Therefore, the more property rights there are, the greater the competition; and the greater and more entrenched the capitalist system in consequence. This concept clearly has not been lost on Mrs Thatcher whose understanding of the importance of property rights to a market economic system and thus to the UK arguably has led to the extensive denationalisation and privatisation in the UK.

At the level of the individual, people compete for access to property rights as well as for the utility attached to them in a capitalist world-economy. In this regard, they strive to improve their access through education and other means, some less socially desirable than others. Privatisation conducted in isolation of this understanding takes away from its effectiveness.

Where property rights exist and have been enforced for generations, privatisation for reasons discussed below has been successful, as evidenced by the experiences of the UK and other OECD countries.

Property rights in developing countries

In developing countries, especially in Sub-Saharan Africa, property rights attached to individual ownership of land have been in many cases severely impaired during the decades of 'reactive nationalism' manifesting in notions of indigenisation as evidenced by the Zimbabwe experience. In addition, as observed by Campbell White and Bhatia (1998) discrete laws prohibiting foreign ownership of land or leases were enacted by several African countries during the 1960s and 1970s; and discrete legislative acts prohibited some enterprises from participating in certain transactions. These laws in many respects are indicative of a rejection of the market economy as the primary mode of societal integration.

Whilst the majority of African countries have sought to remove these barriers to a market economy since the Debt Crisis, many such laws still remain as legal constraints to private participation. As a means to overcoming such constraints, many governments have taken steps to safeguard investors from extraneous laws. In Madagascar, for example, whilst the law prohibiting foreign ownership of land remains on the books, a clarification issued by the government in 1995 permits foreigners to lease land for a period of up to 50 years (see Campbell White and Bhatia 1998).

Beyond the issue of ownership to land, the deep embrace of a socialist economic system by several developing countries for almost a generation rendered laws supportive of a market economy a new experience for many of them. Indeed, for many of these countries with emerging private sectors, newly-established business legal frameworks would not have had the requisite experience-base to effectively and efficiently resolve issues of contract-enforceability and dispute settlement on a consistent basis. Moreover, in the case of infrastructure projects which are contract-intensive and usually involve the state or state-owned enterprise as a party, the issue of equal status under the law will likely arise from time to time until firmly established by judicial decisions. In the meantime, many government officials and politicians will tend to resort to the notion of the state as all powerful: The cancellation of the joint venture agreement between Nigeria's NITEL and Digital Communications Limited in 1995 following a dispute between the partners speaks powerfully to the need for a body of case law. The cancellation in April 1998 by Tanzania state-owned electricity corporation (TANESCO) of its contract with Independent Power Tanzania Ltd (IPTL) for the construction of the 100MW electric power system[1] is yet another example of this need. Both cases evidence the respective country's restricted approach to dispute resolution, an important concern of foreign investors.

But Africa is not alone. In Guyana, ownership to property is one of the major concerns of foreign and even local investors. The failure to privatise the Guyana National Co-operative Bank as a going concern despite its extensive customer base is a consequence of defective titles to properties pledged as security for loans and other advances: Often, the same property is offered as security to two or more commercial banks such is the deficiency of the official records and record keeping.

Since the mid-1990s, several African countries have begun the process of restoring the above-mentioned laws as fundamental to their societies. For many, it is simply a matter of removing laws restricting private participation in economic activity. For others, the process also includes removing restrictions imposed on foreign private participation and on the rights of foreign personnel. Regarding foreign investment, the issues include the right to repatriate capital and income derived from investment without hindrance, and the right to international arbitration where there are significant differences in due process. Several African countries have joined MIGA in addition to entering into bilateral country agreements with the investor home country so as to increase the level of investor confidence for FDI flows. In 1997, sixteen Francophone

---

[1]   *Business Africa*, 1–15 May 1998, (London: IC Publications Limited).

countries sought to harmonise their commercial laws through the Organization for the Harmonization of Commercial Law (OHADA) so as to portray a commitment to the concept of property rights and the development of their private sectors.

Once again, the above observations are not unique to Sub-Saharan Africa. In Guyana there are concerns for the enforceability of agreements and for due process. As discussed in Chapter 8, despite the several agreements restricting the involvement of the local Public Utilities Commission (PUC) in the setting of electricity rates, the President ordered the PUC to intervene. Also, despite a valid licence that authorised mobile telephone interconnection to the incumbent monopoly facility-based telephone network, the Prime Minister, the minister responsible for telecommunications and issuer of the licence, did not find it appropriate to enforce the provisions of the respective licences of the parties (Chang 2004, 432). In 2005, the President sought to influence the judicial process with respect to an action brought against the Guyana Sugar Corporation.[2] Four years earlier, he sought to influence the outcome of the investigations by the Central Bank in the matter respecting the collapse of Globe Trust and Investment Company Limited (GTICL).[3] These interventions by the head of government contradict the stated policy of due process and serve to alarm both foreign and local investors as evidenced in the decline in private investment and the high country risk-premium it attracts.

Transnational practices

Another dynamic of a market economy that needs to be examined is the interaction of firms and other actors operating in a virtual borderless environment, what Leslie Sklair (1995) defines as transnational practices. As defined by Sklair (1995, 6), transnational practices are distinguished by their three distinct functions: economic, political and cultural-ideological, represented by different institutions. In the case of economics, the TNC is the centre of international economic activity, whilst the transnational capitalist class is the major locus of transnational political practices. The cultural-ideological function is the responsibility of the advertising agencies and marketers of global-consumerism whose reach transcends political borders as evidenced by the increasing use of the Internet as a marketing tool.

Arising from the increase in competition for property rights or the accumulation of surplus value in the capitalist world-economy is the TNC. The TNC's primary purpose is to increase its ownership of property rights by pursuing its competitive advantage in the production and distribution of its product in the international market place. As a result, the majority of property rights reside with TNCs located in the established market economies.

---

[2]   Editorial, 'The more things change', *Stabroek News*, 17 May 2005.
[3]   Davidson, W. 'Big Fat Cats will not go free', *Guyana Chronicle*, 4 August 2001.

Darwinian conception of trade

In context of the global economic system, the notion of transnational practices becomes significant in cross-cultural-system analyses. Whereas in a politically-coercive economic system there is no competition among firms or individuals, in a market economic system competition is promoted and is fiercest the greater the degree of commoditizing of property rights. Such competition takes on Darwinian dimensions as the capitalist world-system continues to evolve to become all-inclusive. Hence, in addition to Wallerstein's (2004, 32) observation that the repeated failure of firms is a condition sine qua non of the endless accumulation of capital in the capitalist world-system, Bhagwati (1988, 38) believes that:

> ... free trade comes as one's ideological and policy preference only when one is strong and ... appeals to those who expect to emerge as winners, so it is preferred by nations that possess actual or perceived competitiveness.

With the emergence of the several Asia countries as competitive economic entities as evidenced by the more than doubling of their average annual GNP growth rate as a group (see Figure 2.1), the emphasis has shifted from winning in the 1980s to protecting actual or perceived competitiveness in the 2000s and thus evidences an increasing insecurity on the part of the established economies.

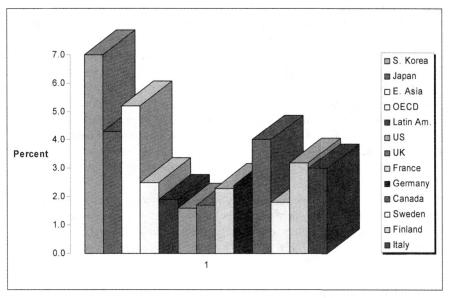

Figure 2.1   Average annual GNP growth rates: 1965–1989

Source: Data extracted from World Development Report (1992, 204–05)

This shifting perspective on trade can be appropriately interpreted to mean that protectionism will be resorted to whenever a country is unsure of its ability to effectively compete and would not be readily abandoned by those whose established trade regime increasingly depends on maintaining some form of asymmetric advantage. Thus looking beyond rhetoric, as is implied in the following discussion on first-order power it is the universality of protectionism and not predatory predilection that is the more dangerous for evil in a capitalist world-economy.

First-order power

Since the TNC has an insatiable appetite for the accumulation of surplus value, it respects no national boundary, and the existence of foreign resources or foreign state-owned property rights are seen as opportunities to increase its share of property rights outside its borders. Within the framework of transnational-capitalism, then, TNCs compete against one another for dominance, which is reflected in the competition for hegemony among the more highly developed countries. Indeed, a primary function of governments in a capitalist world-economy is to facilitate the accumulation of surplus value from trade for their respective citizens. In this connection, the TNC exerts its intrinsic first-order powers through the political process in its home-state, which it controls, to penetrate barriers to its access to foreign resources and markets. To this latter end, TNCs and other special-interest groups require a political system that supports modalities by which states interfere in international markets without which the capitalist system could not thrive and therefore could not survive. Indeed, the urgency with which political and economic alliances are being re-ordered in the twenty-first century speaks to attempts to slow if not to stem the tide of history. But the historic visit by the King of Saudi Arabia in January 2006 to China – who has surpassed the UK as the fourth largest economy in the world – followed by President Putin of Russia in March 2006 and the resultant cooperation agreements on energy are clear indications that history will not be denied. The hosting of Chinese officials by Queen Elizabeth II at Buckingham palace in 2006 is yet another indication of the influence of the TNC. The rapid growth of the Indian economy and the increased flows of FDI in consequence are further testimony to the changing tide, as is President Bush's visit to India in 2006.

Clearly, the more powerful TNCs and special-interest groups influence the political processes within their respective nation-states and in consequence have largely informed foreign policy; evidencing a special relationship between economic producers and holder of political power. This relationship becomes even clearer from examining the process in the US and the EU.

First-order power of the US

In the US, Section 301 of the Trade and Tariff Act of 1974, later amended to Super 301 in the 1988 Act, speaks to the extent to which the political process is accommodating to 'big business': The restrictions on Japanese automobile exports to the US through voluntary export restraints (VER) (see Bhagwati 1988) and sugar exports to the US from the Caribbean Basin Initiative (CBI) countries which declined by up to 84 percent in consequence of the Sweetener Policy in 1982 (see Krueger 1993; Strange 1987), stand in evidence. With respect to sugar, recall that the kingdom of Hawaii was overthrown in 1893 to accommodate US sugar plantation owners. Recall also the Helms-Burton Law passed by the US Congress in 1995 which sought to further isolate Cuba by threatening punitive measures against other OECD-member countries purchasing or using US-owned properties expropriated in Cuba. Recall further, Secretary of State Colin Powell's pronouncement on restricting the award of contracts for the reconstruction of Iraq to firms located in the 'coalition of the willing' and, in the case of non-US companies, only after they have managed to overcome certain hurdles, an off-putting experience for most non-US companies to be sure. Many observers would further point to the access of Halliburton, the US oil service giant, to the Office of the Vice President as evidencing the political reach of the TNC. Many still would point also to the then National Security Advisor, Condoleezza Rice's, pronouncement to 'forgive Russia, ignore Germany and punish France' as further evidencing the political reach of the TNC.

Further evidencing the reach of the special-interest groups in the US is the attempt to force China into revaluing the Yuan, that is, to remove it from its peg to the US dollar. According to the argument, the Yuan has become under-valued as a result of the rapid and sustained growth of the Chinese economy and, of course, as measured by the growing trade imbalance in favour of China. In this regard, recall that in the late 1980s, the US pursued a policy of letting the dollar depreciate vis-à-vis the Japanese Yen in an attempt to stem the flow of Japanese exports to the US and to reduce its trade imbalance with Japan. According to Lawrence Summers, then Harvard Professor of Economics, ten percent depreciation in the dollar does more to reduce the trade imbalance than a ten percent reduction in imports. Also, as articulated by John Connally, former US Treasury Secretary, 'the dollar is our money but their problem'.[4] Recall, however, that the Southeast Asian countries, especially Malaysia, were admonished by Alan Greenspan, the Chairman of the US Federal Reserve, for abandoning their currency pegs to the US Dollar when it was clear that their over-valued currencies fuelled currency speculation by hedge funds the likes of Long-term Capital Management (LTCM), a US-based hedge fund, and by George Soros. To his credit, Soros accepted partial responsibility for contributing to the Asian financial crisis, but correctly blamed the collapse on the inadequacy of the international financial monitoring system; LTCM on the other hand had to be bailed out through intervention by the Federal Reserve System which the US Fed Chairman sought to avert by seeking to disabuse intervention by the Hong-Kong authorities.[5]

---

[4]   'Dornbush offers advice on role of countries' exchange rate policies', *IMF Survey*, Volume 29, Number 15, 31 July 2000, p. 250.

[5]   The Hong-Kong authorities did indeed enter the market in support of the HK Dollar, threatening to use all of its US$96 billion reserves if needed.

The imposition of quota restrictions on New Zealand exports of lamb to the US and steels from Brazil and Europe further evidence the resort to non-tariff barriers, and speaks to free-trade as a concept of convenience. Indeed, the push by the US to remove agricultural subsidies and remaining tariffs on manufacture at the Doha Round Ministerial Meeting in Hong Kong in December 2005 comes from the assessment that it stands to benefit proportionately greater than the Europeans from further trade liberalisation. Moreover, past experience suggests that sanctions by the WTO for violating its rules are calculated to be less damaging to the US economy and to the political incumbent given the bureaucratic lag that attends the process and the nature and value of such sanctions when they are eventually determined and imposed.

The European Union's Common Agricultural Policy

In Europe, the Common Agricultural Policy (CAP) of the European Union (EU) is yet another example of the use of the political process to support entrenched political and economic interests. The importance of agriculture to the then European Community (EC) policy formulation was evident from its inception: The first six signatories to the 1957 Treaty of Rome regarded the integration of their agricultural sectors as essential to an industrialised EC that was seen as being dominated by the German manufacturing sector. As a result, France, Italy, and the Netherlands pushed for trade-off of their imports of German manufacture for exports of their agriculture within and outside the customs union. In addition, the consensus was that industrial competitiveness of the union was dependant upon stable agricultural prices and that efficiency gains were achievable within the community if production of agricultural products were on a comparative advantage basis. As a consequence, the CAP was agreed to in 1961 (see Koester and Bale 1990). Since then, the EU maintained a regime of subsidies, tariffs and quotas on the argument that they were General Agreement on Tariff and Trade (GATT)-compatible in keeping with Article 24 of the GATT (see Pelkmans 1992, 10); not by explicit affirmation however, but out of failure of other member states '... to censure any GATT-incompatible agreements ...' (de Melo and Panagariya 1992, 12).

The GATT-compatible presumption had been frequently cited as a counter to the 'Fortress Europe' charge levelled against the EU. In addition, although the EU readily acknowledged the discriminatory nature of its 'pyramid of preference' dictated by the politics of EU's economic integration, it has over the years sought to justify it on non-intervention by the GATT membership in the first place and in the second, by holding it out as a means to providing an incentive to other countries to pursue economic efficiency through similar arrangements (see Pelkmans 1992, 12).

Nonetheless, removal of the EU's pyramid of preference through GATT and later WTO negotiations has been a work-in-progress since the 1980s. In the case of direct agricultural support, Brazil, Thailand and Australia have been the protagonists, especially with respect to the EU's sugar regime which is deemed to be the more far-reaching of such support (see Borrell and Duncan 1992; Koester and Bale

1990; Kelly et al. 1988). Opposition to other barriers comes from US corporations as the main producers of bananas in Latin America and from local growers in the Caribbean. Within the EU itself there are calls for economic reform: The Dutch, for example, feels that European expansion has taken place on their backs, whilst the British want to free up European economies to better meet the economic challenges posed by China and an emerging India.

In 'Core Europe', attempts to eliminate the CAP are strongly resisted and have sparked grassroots reaction in France, the chief beneficiary of the CAP, as evidenced by the rejection of the EU Constitution in 2005. France's rejection of any attempt to eliminate agricultural subsidies on the scale envisaged by the UK is unambiguously evident: France's Minister of Trade, Christine Lagarde, charged that Peter Mandelson, the EU Trade Commissioner, 'had overstepped his negotiating mandate' by agreeing to expand cuts in EU's subsidies in response to the offer from the US 'to cut its farm subsidies by 60 percent and import duties on agricultural products by 55 to 90 percent'.[6] At the same time the Director General of the WTO admonishes China for not opening its markets to US exports.

Not unexpectedly, France and others EU member-states opposed to the elimination of agricultural subsidies found support in the remaining members – some have accepted the EU's offer of adjustment assistance and have existed the sugar industry – of the 19 African Caribbean and Pacific (ACP) countries that signed the ACP Sugar Protocol with the EU in 1975. But as a counter to the claim by a few of these countries that they were misled by the EU who have benefited from having a constant supply of sugar under the ACP Sugar Protocol, Mariann Fischer Boel of the European Commission responsible for Agriculture and Rural Development, was emphatic:

> ... the Protocol have been worth millions of tonnes of sugar exports and billions of euros to those countries over the 30 years of the deal's operation ... we cannot let the 35 year-old sugar regime gather dust ... if we don't decide now on a new form for our sugar regime, external forces will decide it for us, with a rather more brutal logic than we would apply.[7]

Interestingly, activism by some of the remaining ACP countries to maintain EU sugar subsidies and the ACP Sugar Protocol was pursued even though this meant excluding those poorer developing countries that stood to benefit from the EU's 'Everything but Arms' initiative. It thus evidences the extent to which vested interests not ideas have become dangerous for good or evil, and moral responsibility a concept of convenience.

---

[6]   Wright, T., 'Global Trade Talks End Early With No Progress Made', *New York Times*, 2 October 2005, p. C2.

[7]   Boel, M., 'Sugar's Role in Development Policy', German Marshall Fund, Brussels, Hotel Dorint Novotel, 30 May 2005, Speech 05/341 (10 July 05).

Multifibre Agreements (MFA)

Another example of the use of first-order power by special-interest groups, this time as a group – US and EU – against a common rival – mainly developing countries of East Asia – is manifest in successive Multifibre Agreements (MFA) negotiated in the 1970s and 1980s. The MFA restricted the East-Asian export of textiles and clothing to Europe and the US despite the prevailing notion of free-trade and studies that show the decline in revenues to be substantially restraining to development in these developing countries (see Page *et al.* 1991, 30; Trela and Whalley 1990, 25; Goto 1989).

Prior to the MFA, Japan's agreement to VER was made a condition of its membership to the GATT (see Sampson and Takacs 1990; Trela and Whalley 1990). The Japanese agreement to voluntarily restrain exports of textile and clothing caused its share of textile imports by the US to drop from 63 percent of total imports in 1958 to 26 percent in 1960 (Tussie 1987, 76). This breach was quickly filled by Hong Kong whose share rose from 14.0 percent to 27.5 percent.

The failure to successfully negotiate VER with Hong Kong and other textile and clothing manufacturers – mainly Asian – led to the implementation of a Short Term Agreement (STA) between importing and exporting countries under the auspices of the GATT in 1961, followed by the Long Term Agreement (LTA), the precursor to the MFA, in 1962. The LTA was incorporated into successive versions of the MFA beginning in 1974 and was expanded to include all exporters of textiles and clothing – including manmade fibres not previously covered by the LTA – to the US, UK and the then EC (see Tussie 1987).

Perhaps the most egregious aspects of the MFA were the inclusion of the concepts of 'market disruption' and 'Protocol of Extension' in MFA II in 1978 at the insistence of the EC (see Goto 1989). With respect to market disruption, the use of quotas was deemed essential to the 'reasonable and orderly' development of the textile trade so as to avoid disruptive effects in individual markets. Still not providing the level of protection sought by the Europeans, the concept of market disruption, despite its billing as a temporary measure to allow structural changes to occur, was broadened on the notion that:

> … decline in the rate of growth of per capita consumption in textiles and clothing is an element which may be relevant to the recurrence or exacerbation of a situation of market disruption.[8]

The Protocol of Extension provided for 'jointly agreed reasonable departure' from particular provisions of the MFA II and permitted further restriction on products deemed 'sensitive'; this clause was replaced with a 'surge mechanism' clause in MFA III, in 1982 (see Bank 1987).

Through effective lobbying of the GATT and its successor WTO by affected countries, the MFA came to an end in January 2005. But notwithstanding that both

---

[8]   MFA II, para. 4, 1981.

Europe and the US have had ten years to prepare for the removal of the restrictions on the imports of textile and clothing from countries with distinctly comparative and competitive advantage, they found it necessary to impose restrictions on quantities imported from China on the basis of the inability of their respective producers to adjust to the new reality of trade absent the MFA. As noted in an editorial of the *New York Times*:

> It is extremely frustrating that political leaders refuse to recognize that all the protection created in the last 40 years to shield American textile jobs from foreign competition have failed.[9]

The above examples of the operation of first-order power serve to fully support Wallerstein's (2004, 26) observation that the modalities by which states interfere with the virtual market are so extensive that they constitute a fundamental factor in determining price and profits.

The diffusion of democracy and transnational practices

The diffusion of individualism and materialism inherent in a capitalist world-system to developing countries is rationalised in terms of eliminating oppressive regimes, corruption and cronyism and evidences economic determinism. But, as pointed out by Thomas Donaldson (1989, 4), the concern is for '... the legitimate rights of a nation, large or small, to economic self-determination' with '... the threat posed by the hegemonic powers to national sovereignty a constant'. The involvement of the US in the removal of the democratically-elected government of Iran in 1953, Allende in Chile, Noriega in Panama, and Gairy in Grenada in the 1970s and 1980s speaks to this concern; and made more current by President George W. Bush whose foreign policy in the Middle East is perceived by some observers as one of destabilising governments in that region so as to rebuild them as democracies.[10] Recall that in the case of Iran, the US in 1996 threatened sanctions against any country that invests more than US$20.0 million annually in the Iranian oil and gas industry; China has not only invested heavily in the Iranian energy sectors despite this threat but has invited the Iranian President to attend the Shanghai Cooperation Organization Summit as an observer in 2006 against the expressed displeasure of the US.

Beyond the democratisation imperative of US foreign policy, many observers in the Western democracies see this process as the rise of transnational-capitalism, globalisation if you will, and through it transnational practices and the demise of the nation-state (see Greider 1998; Rohwer 1995; Sklair 1995). As defined by Sklair (1995), the transnational capitalist class (TCC) transcends national borders and will act through its control of the political process to protect its privileges whenever or

---

[9] 'The History of Trade Part 2', *New York Times*, 12 November 2005, p. A26.

[10] A view articulated by the McLaughlin Group, Public Broadcasting Service, 11 November 2005.

wherever there is a threat to them. Its function is to promote and protect the concept of a capitalist world-economy from which it gains significance.

By this definition the TCC also exists within the borders of developing countries and consorts with others to promote capitalism within the developing countries, even in contradiction to the popular will of the local population. For example, the middle class was deemed supportive of the overthrow of Allende in Chile and the Cuban exiles supportive of the removal of Fidel Castro. This scenario is being played out in other parts of the world: Venezuela, Ukraine, Belarus and Bolivia for example, although in the case of the South American countries there is an apparent backlash manifesting in a reversion to socialist ideology.

Also, within the broader definition of the transnational capitalist class fall the IMF and Bank in consequence of their susceptibility to the influences of transnational corporations located in countries whose contributions to these organisations allow them to shape their policies (see Donaldson 1989, 3). Not to put too fine a point on the observation, a study commissioned by the US Congress on the role of the IMF and Bank concluded that the IMF became:

> a source of long-term conditional loans that made poorer nations increasingly dependent on the IMF and given the IMF a degree of influence over member countries' policy-making that is unprecedented for a multilateral institution.[11]

The contention that the largest donors to the IMF and Bank exercise the greatest control over them is not without justification. Evidence the threat by Western donors to have the IMF suspends its loan to Kenya because of disagreement with the sacking of the commissioner of customs and excise in that country,[12] and the follow-through with such suspension by the that institution.[13] In contrast, no such action was taken against Russia when President Yeltsin sacked his entire Cabinet.

Further reinforcing this contention were the added conditions which the US Senate wanted attached to IMF loans to developing countries for its approving an increase in funding for the IMF. As reported, environmental protection and labour standards were included in the list of conditions with which developing countries were expected to comply.[14] So also were some of the proposals of the Multilateral Investment Agreement (MIA) debated by the OECD in early 1998. Clearly, the inclusion of any and all of these added conditions were designed to maintain US asymmetric advantage in the global market place by imposing first-world standards upon third-world production processes.

---

[11] 'Report from the International Financial Institution Advisory Commission presented to the Senate Banking Committee in March 2000', *US Congress*, p. 18.

[12] Holman M. and Wrong M., 'Western donors may block aid to Kenya over sacking', *Financial Times*, 29 July, 1997.

[13] Holman M. and Wrong M. , 'IMF drops loan to Kenya after row over terms', *Financial Times*, 1 August, 1997, p. 12.

[14] Rogers D., 'IMF Funds Approved By Senate', *The Wall Street Journal*, 27 March 1998, p. A2.

The Southeast Asian financial crisis

The handling of the Southeast Asian financial crisis in 1997 and 1998 also stands in evidence of the relationship between the US and the IMF. The rush to impose economic reforms that favoured the Western economies without first addressing the underlying causes of the crisis and the immediate implications of their actions have led many to call into question the credibility of the IMF as an impartial multilateral institution (see Stiglitz 2002). To be sure, many attendees – including some from the IMF and Bank – at the 10th Annual Bank Conference on Development Economics (ABCDE) in Washington, DC in April 1998 engaged in what Nobel Laureate James Tobin in his 'Plea for Humility' characterised as:

> ... triumphalism of American commentaries on the events [which were] ... interpreted to demonstrate the hollowness of the 'Asian model' of capitalism ... even though the overzealous reach of our practitioners of global finance might bear some responsibility for the crisis (Tobin 1998, 20).

It would be two years before partial responsibility for the crisis is acknowledged, albeit obliquely, by the IMF. In an address to the International Law Association Biennial Conference in London on July 26, 2000,[15] the First Deputy Managing Director of the IMF returned to fundamentals in revisiting the 'impossible trinity' of 'fixed exchange rate, an open capital account, and a monetary policy dedicated to domestic economic goals' occasioned by expansion of international trade and, as he puts it, '... an even more dramatic expansion of cross-border capital flows', the latter totally ignored in early official assessments of the crisis. Of greater significance on a going forward basis is the observation that investors and financial institution have a role to play in ensuring the smooth running of the international monetary system and to recognise that international lenders of last resort, including the IMF:

> ... have to operate with rules that limit moral hazard. Otherwise, institutions would be tempted to lend with an irresponsible lack of regard for the underlying risk, secure in the knowledge that they would be bailed out if things went wrong (p. 246).

Indeed, based on the initial reactions neither the IMF nor the Clinton administration foresaw the crisis and, therefore, sought to characterise it in terms of restricted markets and crony-capitalism in the East Asian countries[16] (Stiglitz 2002). Hence, despite the lessons of the 1980s in terms of the results of austerity policies imposed by

---

[15] 'Private sector involvement is important element in reform of international monetary system', *IMF Survey*, Volume 29, Number 15, 31 July 2000, p. 241.

[16] A perspective offered by Laura Tyson, then a member of President Clinton's Council of Economic Advisors, in November 1997, and reiterated to this author by the First Deputy Managing Director of the IMF in an informal discussion at the 10th ABCDE in Washington, DC, on 20 and 21 April 1998.

the IMF attendant the Debt Crisis,[17] and the lessons from the 'Tequila Hangover' in 1995, the policy prescriptions remained unchanged and without regard to relevancy. For example, rather than stemming the decline in the value of the Indonesian Rupiah, the closure of domestic banks as required in the IMF's loan agreement served to exacerbate the crisis by creating an immediate panic among depositors. As reported, the IMF was forced to admit that 'these closures far from improving public confidence in the banking system have instead set off a renewed flight to safety'.[18] Thus at the end of February 1998 the Rupiah had been devalued by over 80 percent and domestic inflation had reached its highest level in thirty years. Riots broke out in the country and what had started out as a currency crisis turned into a full-blown economic crisis by policy prescriptions which dispassionate analyses considered to be inappropriate.

Curiously, the Asian financial crisis had a lot in common with the Tequila Hangover of 1995: A substantial proportion of the portfolio investment flows to Asia was speculative, especially to Malaysia and other Southeast Asian countries in the early-to-mid-1990s. Moreover, in a 1996 study by Chunan, et al. (1996, 23) it was found that short-term investment flows do indeed differ from FDI in terms of their reversal properties in consequence of being more foot-loose than FDI, an observation reiterated by G. K. Helleiner (1997, 4).

Such foot-loose capitalism posed a distinct challenge to managing local currencies, and to maintaining foreign exchange reserves and real exchange rates in affected countries, especially when targeted by currency speculators. The challenge is exacerbated in countries with fixed-exchange rate regimes, as was the case of the Southeast Asian countries in 1997–1998. Indeed, as attributed to the Southeast Asian crisis, an over-valued currency also encourages external borrowings for crony-capitalism and speculation within the domestic economy. Thus, as shown by Kasekende *et al.* (1997, 63), whilst Latin America and Africa reduced their long-term bank loans by a percentage greater than their short-term inflows, Asia increased such debt by 21.7 percent during the 1990–1993 period. As a result, the Southeast Asian economies and South Korea became vulnerable to the volatility of external financial flows, both in the form of portfolio investment flows and short-term credit from foreign banks.

The above notwithstanding, the point remains: private capital flows will gravitate to those countries which offer the best opportunity to maximize profits in both the short- and long-terms irrespective of economic or social consequences. This is a function of the dynamic market forces unleashed by global-capitalism which advocates of currency speculation regard as necessary to the process of keeping

---

[17] The austerity policies designed to improve balance-of-payments adjustment dramatically reduced demand and imports and brought growth to a halt by cutbacks in investment. Moreover, devaluation made it more costly in local currency to service external debt and aggravated the problem.
[18] Sanger, D., 'IMF Now Admits Tactics in Indonesia Deepened the Crisis' *The Wall Street Journal*, 13 January 1998.

governments honest. In other words, according to these advocates the fundamentals must necessarily be present to support a currency valuation. In the case of the Asian economies, deteriorating fundamentals were exacerbated by overvalued local currencies in consequence of the peg to the US Dollar which was increasing in value in the years prior to the crisis.[19]

Furthermore, when countries' economic growth rates are dependent upon a continuous inflow of short-term external borrowings and portfolio investment, as was discovered to be the case with the Southeast Asian economies – which is represented as balance of payments deficits on current account as shown in Figure 2.2 and which correlates positively with the investment-savings gap – any slowing of such external financial flows would likely reflect in a reduction in GDP growth rates triggering a reversal of flows and a run on foreign exchange reserves. This was clearly evident to international currency speculators fresh from their victories in Mexico and the Philippines in 1995 and 1996 respectively and the savings-investment gap that was getting wider in the four countries – particularly Malaysia and Thailand – cited in Figure 2.2.

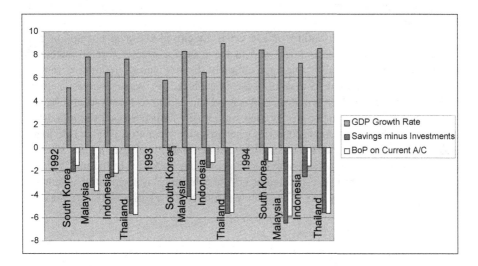

Figure 2.2   Southeast Asia selected economic indicators 1992–1994

Source: Data extracted from Park and Song, (1997, 101, 104, 106, 111)

Also overlooked in earlier analyses of the crisis is that, in addition to inadequate foreign exchange reserves and an obvious dependency on a continuous inflow of short-term capital to match domestic demand for foreign exchange, there was a

---

[19]   The reverse would be true and explains the push to get China to float the Yuan.

reduction in the amount of credit extended by US and Japanese banks to these Asian economies in the months immediately preceding the financial crisis, as was reported by the Federal Reserve Board in February, 1998. In this regard, there are parallels to be drawn from the Latin American experience of a decade and a half ago.

Equally absent from early analyses is that, in November 1995 the IMF observed that: 'Given the lack of substantial liquidity in most developing country securities markets, concerted investor movements added to market volatility'. And since institutional investors have become significant players in emerging markets, '... they may have made a significant contribution to the contagion effects observed'.[20] Furthermore, the adverse impact of a tighter monetary policy by the US in early 1994 did not go undetected. The slow down in private capital flows to developing countries in consequence of an increase in US interest rates and a loss in investor confidence by the devaluation of the Mexican peso in December 1994 were also observed by the IMF in 1995.[21]

Thus, by ignoring the lessons of the 1980s and the warning signals of the 1995 Mexican financial crisis, the Southeast Asian countries had wittingly or unwittingly set themselves up for the fall. Hence, the charges of incompetent economic management and crony-capitalism levelled against the governments of these countries were not entirely unjustified.

Nonetheless, the attributing of the crisis to closed-markets, corruption and cronyism in the affected countries and to the need for greater foreign access to these markets was a deeply-flawed perception of the IMF and its major contributors who have clearly sought to minimize the role played by Western-investor-greed and irresponsible lending practices of Western and Japanese money-centre banks. Furthermore, for Western tax-payers consumption, the 'bail-out' had been billed as a bail-out of the Southeast Asian countries when in reality the majority of the IMF loans was to service private-sector loans and investment made by Western and Japanese banks and investors, thereby raising the issue of moral hazard.[22] In Indonesia alone, private corporate debt was estimated at US$74.0 billion,[23] repayment of which the IMF sought to achieve by way of the Mexican model of the early 1980s.[24] In the case

---

[20]   'Private Capital Flows to Developing Countries Suffer Setbacks, but Recover', *IMF Survey*, 20 November 1995, 365.

[21]   Ibid., pp. 364–365.

[22]   As reported in the January 1998 issue of the Banker, US banks had begun to reduce their exposure to Southeast Asia in early 1997. This caused a shortage of foreign currency which was picked up by currency speculators who foresaw the need for a currency devaluation based on a foreign exchange shortage and an over-valued currency-peg. The resultant effect was a reversal of portfolio investment flows which can be appropriately characterised as footloose capitalism.

[23]   Ali, M., 'No Plan to Transfer US$74.0 billion Private Corporate Debt to Government', Reuters, 3 April 1998.

[24]   Under the Mexican model – 'Ficorca programme' – the government assumed the foreign exchange losses associated with the debt whilst the debtors were allowed to roll over

of Thailand, private-sector debt amounted to US$67.3 billion at the end of 1997.[25] Thus to many members of the US Congress, despite an earlier denial to the contrary by the Secretary of State, the bail-out was seen as a bail-out of Wall Street and bankers speculating in the Asian economies. Hence whilst maintaining the urgency of the bail-out in his testimony to Congress on 30 January 1998 in support of an increase in IMF funding, from US$14.5 billion to US$18.0 billion, the US Treasury Secretary characterised the bail-out as 'enlightened self-interest'.

As a final word, it is instructive to note Tobin's (1998, 18) admonishment:

> ... US history is full of insalubrious regulations designed to protect various vested interests against competition, forbidding entry into particular markets, setting prices and interest rates, distorting market outcomes by taxes and subsidies. Presumably we would like developing countries to follow our good examples and not our bad. Let us encourage them to build good national financial systems, not just open their doors ever wider.

The cultural-ideological function

As regards the cultural-ideological function, this may be either explicit as in the case of direct marketing – advertising and other promotional means – or implicit. In the case of the latter, it is the demonstration effect that operates to influence demand for foreign goods, often referred to as 'cultural imperialism'. It is the process whereby the poor in the low income countries are influenced by the consumption patterns found in developed economies, and one of the concerns of Prebisch (1984; and 1982) and others in the 1960s. In the 1990s, the trend has been for more sophisticated marketing techniques to be employed. Images – life style and personal – that appeal to the fantasies of the millions of young people in developing countries are the techniques of choice. These market-creating techniques are designed as mechanisms aided by satellite television and electronic media to effect cultural change to greater consumerism; and this according to Sklair (1995, 45–8) is because:

> Global capitalism does not permit cultural neutrality. Those cultural practices that cannot be incorporated into the culture-ideology of consumerism becomes oppositional counter-hegemonic forces to be harnessed or marginalized, and if that fails, destroyed physically.

Market-augmenting paradigm

Between a market economic system and the politically-coercive economy exemplified by the Soviet-type economic system, there is yet another economic model: One that is characteristically Asian, which Amsden (1989, 146) identifies as market-augmenting. In such an economic model the state intervenes to direct resources to particular projects it deems essential to the socioeconomic development of the

---

their debts over four years and to make payments to Ficorca, the institution set-up by the government, in pesos. Creditors were repaid in Dollars by Ficorca.

[25]   Sherer, P.M., 'World Bank's Tricky Task in Thailand: Mine Into Mountains of Debt', *The Wall Street Journal*, 1 April 1998, p. A16.

country. It secures the cooperation of its people by devising economic strategies within cultural norms. This has been particularly so in the case of Japan as a 'late industrializer' and later South Korea who adopted an almost similar economic development strategy.

In the case of South Korea, the process was one of tying subsidies to performance standards in those industries the state wanted to stimulate. It was on this notion of state intervention that the Pohang Iron and Steel Company Limited was built. This process was also responsible for the likes of Samsung (the electronics giant) and the Hyundai group. More importantly, by emphasising education as a national development priority the state assumed responsibility for laying the foundation for the successful incorporation of borrowed technology into the South Korean production processes, as evidenced by the competitiveness of their products.

The rapid industrialisation of both Japan – an OECD member – and South Korea was achieved within a market-augmenting paradigm that reflects their respective customs and culture. Theirs was an economic model in which the functions of the internal disciplinary mechanisms were partially assumed by the state, and 'getting relative prices wrong' in targeted sectors was the economic strategy of choice. Thus, in addition to ensuring access to low-interest financing by selected industries, South Korea employed a system of multiple exchange rates as a means to subsidising its traded-goods sector. Where market concepts were found to be an effective distributive mechanism, as in the traded-goods sector, they were successfully pursued. As a result, South Korea achieved GNP growth rates in excess of those of the OECD countries for the period 1965–1989 as shown in Figure 2.1 (page 33).

South Korea's rapid growth has been often attributed to its having pursued an outward-oriented economic strategy and has been proffered by the Bank as the model for other developing countries in the early 1990s. But as Amsden's (1989) research shows, in both countries – Japan and South Korea – state intervention operated to redirect productive resources to effect growth rates comparable or better than those achieved by the more technologically advanced Western economies.

As further demonstrated by the South Korean experience, market mechanisms could be successfully employed in a complementary relationship with market-augmenting mechanisms or aspects of redistribution if you will. Indeed, there could even be a causal relationship, for example, between exports of manufacture where perceived comparative if not competitive advantage is exploited to its fullest within the traded goods sector, and overall economic growth within a market-augmenting paradigm. In this regard, Amsden (1989, 154) identified strong positive externalities with respect to South Korea's ability to raise capital from its export of light manufacture; proving thereby the point that liberalisation can be pursued sectorally and can be achieved without wholesale privatisation as envisaged by the purveyors of the orthodox narrative.

This is not to say that there are no negatives in the South Korean model. Indeed, the financial crisis proved the point. As observed by Bang, (1990, 353), the financial sector failed to develop at the same rate because it was deprived of the profit motive in consequence of the government's control of interest rates. The unavoidable bail-out of the South Korean banks attendant on the Asian financial crisis speaks to this neglect.[26] Also, the power struggle between bureaucrats and politicians in the late 1990s has had a negative impact on the growth rate.[27]

In addition to South Korea, there are other examples of the effectiveness of the Asian model. For example, during the same period as shown in Figure 2.1, East Asia as a group experienced an average GDP growth rate that was more than double that of the OECD countries, and almost three times greater than that of Latin America and Caribbean. Fuelling this leap forward is the underlying cultural norms for the Asian countries to see themselves as part of a larger whole. As remarked by Dai Xianglong, the governor of China's central bank, 'Financial instability harms all Asian countries',[28] a concern that has been reiterated by US Treasury Secretary John Snow in his 2005 visit to China. Interestingly, contrary to earlier pronouncement by special-interest groups President Bush capped the issue by declaring that China was not manipulating its currency for trade-advantage reasons. Be that as it may, China's growing foreign exchange reserves of US$838.0 billion at the end of 2005 is yet another challenge to the US and EU who are clearly seeking to contain China's economic expansion and reach.

Nonetheless, as these economies mature and are incorporated into the capitalist world-economy, they will be expected to play by the rules set by the dominant members. Over-regulation, inadequate competition and capital-market rigidities if perceived by the dominant members will have to be corrected either voluntarily or by external pressures; the financial crisis of 1997–1998 speaks to such corrective mechanisms, as indeed does the relenting pressure on China to float its currency, before John Snow's visit to China that is. In that visit, contrary to expectations and clearly reflecting a growing reliance on China to partly fund the US budget deficit, the US Treasury Secretary conceded that: 'Moving toward a truly flexible exchange rate regime requires quite a large number of steps. We recognize that will take some time'.[29]

UK's socioeconomic and political structure

If the world economy came into being as a result of the Treaty of Westphalia in 1648, then nowhere was its evolution as a capitalist world-economy more firmly rooted than in the socioeconomic and political institutions of the UK. Therefore, whilst privatisation has taken place in other OECD countries nowhere was it better exemplified than in the UK where the process has been the most extensive and far-

---

[26] Schuman, M., 'Korea's Banks Take a Turn For the Worse', *The Wall Street Journal*, 15 August 1997, p. A20.

[27] Glain, S., 'South Korean Leader Struggles to Free Up A Regulated Economy', *The Wall Street Journal*, 30 March 1994.

[28] AP-Dow Jones News Service, *Wall Street Journal*, 15 August 1997, p. A20.

[29] Andrews, E., 'Snow Shifts his Demands on China', *New York Times*, 18 October 2005.

reaching: Between 1979 and 1987, thirteen new companies were created, adding over 13 billion new shares to the securities market and approximately £25 billion to the British government's coffers. Privatisation also resulted in reducing the contribution of the public-sector from approximately 11.5 percent in 1977 to between 5.5 percent and 7.5 percent (estimates vary) in 1987, (see Vickers and Yarrow 1995).

Whilst there were expressed concerns about allocative efficiency in the case of the private monopolies created by privatisation – for example, British Telecom (BT) and British Gas – and the infancy of the regulatory institution, the process was accomplished without the social and economic disruption experienced in many developing countries and in Eastern Europe. Indeed, twenty years after its privatisation in November 1984, BT is seen as having evolved into an efficient telecommunications service provider:

> prices came down, waiting lists for telephone vanished in the early 1980s and never reappeared, most faults were cleared quickly, and even public telephones began to work, once the industry regulator cracked his whip.[30]

But the UK's success with privatisation is not accidental, nor the results of trial or error but rather reflects a programme conceived entirely within a market paradigm. Since emerging from mercantilism, except for short periods of protectionism the UK has consistently embraced the concept of market economics. But its journey was as equally traumatic for it citizens as it is for the still traditional societies of the Third World. Indeed, long forgotten is that 'the road to the free market was opened and kept opened by an enormous increase in continuous, centrally organized and controlled interventionism' (Polanyi 1944, 140). The traditional fabric of society was sacrificed to the market economy on which British society now turns. The social destruction wrought by the establishing of a free labour market to support the Industrial Revolution was an inevitable consequence despite the Speenhamland Law, 1795 (see Polanyi 1944). The repeal of the Corn Laws in 1846 made it the most open of economies of the time and supported the industrial revolution that was current. As a result, market-supporting institutions were further strengthened by the process.

Political and legal institutions

In terms of governance, since the signing of the Magna Carta in 1215, constitutional government has been upheld and the notion of individual freedom protected. The English legal system has long protected and enforced the notion of property rights based on the rights given by the Magna Carta. English land law can trace its roots to Roman law and to the requirement for written conveyance back to 1677. English common law has also evolved through a system of statutes and case law over the centuries, its transformation from local customs dating back to the thirteenth-

---

[30] Foreman-Peck, J., 'How privatisation has changed Britain', *BBC News*, 3 December 2004, http://news.bbc.co.uk/2/hi/business/4061613.stm.

century. Laws relating to corporate entities – from formation to liquidation – and their transactions also have had the test of time and have been inculcated into the psyche of the British people through specialist professional institutions to which the UK can point with pride both at home and abroad.

Table 2.2   GNP per capita: Selected countries

Country	Population Mid-1989 (m)	GNP per Capita US$	
		1989	1994
Benin	4.6	380	370
Nigeria	113.8	250	280
Malawi	8.2	180	160
Bangladesh	110.7	180	220
Ghana	14.4	390	410
Togo	3.5	390	320
Peru	21.2	1,285	2,110
Jamaica	2.4	1,260	1,540
Chile	13.0	1,770	3,996
Venezuela	19.2	2,450	2,760
Mexico	84.6	1,959	4,180
Trinidad & Tob..	1.3	3,230	3,740
Hungary	10.6	2,590	3,840
Czechoslovakia	15.6	3,450	3,200
Poland	37.9	1,790	2,410
UK	57.2	14,610	18,340

Source: Compiled from WDR: 1991, 204–05; 1996, Table 1

Financial institutions

In addition to the political and legal institutions, other infrastructural institutions have been in existence long before the political decision to denationalized public enterprises in the UK. The Bank of England in addition to being the central bank for the UK has served in that role for many former colonies. London as a major financial centre is still unrivalled in many respects. The London Stock Exchange, established in 1801, has been over the decades the centre of world finance. Its motto, 'Dictum Meum Pactum' [My word, my Bond] serves powerfully as a reminder to the investment community of the importance of honour in financial transactions in as much as the scales of justice over the Old Bailey signifies the importance of the rule of law and the notion of justice under the law.

The well established financial services sector of commercial, investment and merchant banks, insurance and brokerages houses and financial advisory services have all collaborated to provide the ideal framework for privatisation. Thus privatisation in the UK was pursued within a mode of production that boasted depth and breadth of market-supporting institutions. Moreover, the UK ranks as one of the more highly industrialised countries in the world with a per capita income ten times greater than most developing countries. Hence, as shown in Table 2.2, with disposable income greater than the GDP of most developing countries – 57.2 million with an average per capita income of US$18, 340 at the end of 1994 – and a high level of financial sophistication, the absorptive capacity of the private sector was never an issue.

Institutions in developing countries

As discussed above, the UK experience with privatisation has been successful mainly because the process was conducted within a supportive ideological and institutional framework founded on the very essence of capitalism: British society and the economy became one and the same at the end of the Industrial Revolution, with economic determinism very much in evidence. Also, although the British economy was regarded as a mixed-economy in the mid-twentieth century, the public sector was at the time relatively small in terms of percentage GDP in comparison with most developing countries. Its private capital markets were therefore more than able to absorb the 13 billion new shares resulting from the denationalisation process. Moreover, British stocks are widely held overseas as a result of the level of confidence and trust foreigners have in the British system. Equally important was that, change in ownership arguably did not create any discernible negative shift in welfare.

The larger developing countries

In the case of the developing countries on the other hand the situation was very much different. The success of privatisation at the level of developing countries to which advocates often refer was mainly concentrated in the larger developing countries – Mexico, Peru, Argentina, Singapore, Malaysia, and Brazil to name a few – and was used to promote a one-size-fits-all approach across the Third World. While institutionally deficient in many respects, especially in the realm of effective governance, these larger developing countries by and large have been influenced by Western capitalism over the decades. Most of them retained many of the market-supporting institutions inherited from a colonial past and have maintained cultural ties with Western Europe. In addition, as shown in Table 2.1 whereas most of the smaller developing countries emphasised an agricultural production structure, the larger developing countries, especially in Asia, have grown their industrial, manufacturing and services sectors. As such, their economies had the absorptive capacity to support the initial phase of their privatisation programmes. In contrast to the larger developing countries, many African countries – Madagascar, Tanzania and Sierra Leone, to name a few – for reasons that may not necessarily be economic reverted to agriculture production, or at least had agriculture as their primary source of income in the 1990s.

In addition, many of the larger developing countries were able to establish their own private capital markets which operated to help finance their private-sector development. As a result, their stock exchanges have become part of the global capital-market network, and stocks of their domestic companies are widely held in comparison with the rest of the developing world. Indeed, the increasing number of US mutual funds with investments in emerging countries speaks to the growing confidence in these economies. Moreover, as evidenced by the surge in private capital flows to Asia and Latin America during the 1980s and 1990s, the integration of these larger developing countries into the capitalist world-economy has come to be viewed as a windfall for transnational capitalism in search of opportunities for profits. These 'semi-periphery' countries are not therefore the developing countries that are the focus of this volume. Their inclusion merely serves to draw attention to the development continuum and to the notion that success with privatisation is largely determined by where a country is situated on that continuum. The developing countries that are the focus of this study are those with sub-poverty income whose locus of economic activity is the family or community, essentially agrarian despite display of Western culture in the cities.

The smaller developing countries

The vast body of evidence shows many of the collapsed economies concentrated mainly in Africa are relatively small economies without established private capital markets of size to attract foreign investors and the absorptive capacity to support the dismantling of state-ownership.

In these smaller economically-backward societies, the mode of production reflected the pressures to integrate different cultural groups – displaced through the process of colonialism – within a socioeconomic framework based often on conflicting indigenous cultural practices or a specific socioeconomic dynamic in the absence of an established market economy. Public enterprises (PE) were often not organised as commercial entities per se, but as means to achieve social goals such as providing access to essential services (see Katz 1992, 6). Reflecting these social objectives, the over 3000 PEs in 31 Sub-Saharan African countries provided employment to 1.5 million workers – approximately 25 percent of the formal work force – in 1986 (see Katz 1992, 3).

Outside of Africa, in plural societies such as Trinidad and Tobago, Malaysia and Guyana state intervention was likely motivated by the need to correct perceived socioeconomic imbalances or to advance the economic and social status of a particular group (see Ralph Henry 1990, 251). Thus as shown in the country examples below, which have been chosen for both their similarities and differences, institutional infrastructure were skewed towards a state-interventionist approach rather than towards an open market system.

Nigeria

Despite early attempts to orient Nigerians to market-conforming institutions prior to its political independence in 1960, many of the colonial institutions were converted to an economic infrastructure that best reflected Nigerian indigenous society. As a consequence, within a decade of gaining independence sectional and communal interests became the main determinants of resource allocation: The prevailing mode of distribution was essentially redistributive augmented by misappropriation of public resources for private use (see Lewis 1990, 278).

As one of the largest economies in Sub-Saharan Africa, Nigeria was one of the few countries that boasted a formal private capital market in that region of the world. However, despite its early economic successes, the number of companies listed on the stock exchange was under 100, most of which were very thinly-traded. This lack of activity reflected more on a lack of confidence in the Nigerian economy than on financial liquidity. Under these conditions, unlike the East Asian and Latin American economies, the Nigeria's capital market did little to facilitate the privatisation process.

In addition to a lack of confidence in the Nigerian economy, the political structure has been found to promote sectionalism and distrust among ethnic groups, states and regions in the early years of statehood. There was also the problem of property rights. As alluded to above, attenuation of property rights in the extreme – by high taxation, licensing fees and other government controls and official corruption – was endemic and spawned the informal or parallel market in Nigeria as in other African countries. The combined effect of these difficulties, exacerbated by a per capita income of US$280, manifested in Nigeria's return to agriculture as its economic base – before opening oil production to foreign participation in the mid-1990s – where land and labour were the primary factors of production. As shown in Table 2.1 (page 26) whereas agriculture accounted for 31 percent of GDP in 1989, in 1994 it was 43 percent. During the same period, industry and manufacturing share of GDP declined by 15 percent, from 54 percent of GDP to 39 percent of GDP. Of this 15 percent decline in contribution to GDP, the manufacturing sector accounted for 12 percent whilst the industry sector accounted for 3 percent. However, as noted earlier the agricultural sector suffered from government price controls. With the removal of state marketing-boards under the Bank's structural adjustment programme, farm prices were restored to competitive levels, thereby aiding the process.

Trinidad and Tobago

Nigeria is not unique in this experience, however. Many of the conditions described above were found within and outside of Sub-Saharan Africa. Trinidad and Tobago (T&T), for example, attempted to maintain the institutions inherited on independence in 1956 but soon succumbed to the political pressures to advance the socioeconomic status of certain groups in keeping with notions of equality within a plural society. Policies that sought to be inclusive of previously excluded ethnic groups in the production activity of the country were vigorously pursued. Out of these policies grew a public-enterprise sector, mainly petroleum-based, that served to redistribute income and broaden access to productive resources and to promote diversity. However, the recession in the industrialised countries in the 1980s and start-up problems in the petrochemical industry made public enterprises dependent upon the government for support.

Buoyed by oil exports, the local currency appreciated to the point where non-petroleum output became uncompetitive – the Dutch disease effect – as labour rates were primarily determined on the basis of what obtained in the petroleum industry. Imports also increased in consequence of the strong local currency. However, with the collapse of oil prices and the austerity measures implemented in the developed countries in the early 1980s, the growth in T&T's GDP became unsustainable. GDP at market prices and real GDP began to decline from their highs reached in 1983, to their lowest levels in 1989 (see Adam *et al.* 1988).

With respect to the political and institutional infrastructure, like most of the British Caribbean countries T&T continued the parliamentary system of government inherited from Britain after independence. It also continued the legal system which followed English law. As a result, property rights based on English jurisprudence were never in danger to the same extent as they were in other countries, even in the region.

Unlike Nigeria, as oil exporter to neighbouring Caribbean Community (CARICOM) member countries T&T was a creditor nation within the Paris Club framework. Thus in May 1996 T&T agreed to a 67 percent write-off of the US$536 million owed to it by Guyana, with a 23 year repayment schedule for the remainder at prevailing market rates of interest under Naples Terms. In October 2005 following the G-8's initiative at Gleneagles in July 2005, T&T agreed to a complete write-off of the remaining 33 percent owed to it by Guyana.

In terms of private capital markets, T&T is one of the two major financial markets in CARICOM; it also has the highest income per capita in the region. As shown in Table 2.3 (page 40), at the end of 1994 T&T's income per capita was 35 percent higher than Venezuela's and more than doubled that of Jamaica's. However, like Nigeria its thinly traded stock exchange had a small portfolio of stocks: totalled 38 in 1985; and remained at that level throughout the 1990s. Also, despite its relatively high per capita income the absorptive capacity of the private sector was found to be relatively small compared to the public sector to be privatised (see Adam *et al.* 1992, 176). Hence, market-supporting institutions while better represented in T&T than in many other developing countries were still not fully supportive of privatisation on the scale envisaged by the IMF with which it had a loan facility.

Conclusion

In this chapter, the institutional infrastructure that evolved in support of the capitalist world-economy was examined from the perspective of its derivation based on a culturally-determined development continuum. As discussed, the notion of growth which emerged as a concept is based largely on a theory of stages (see Rostow 1961) by which the developed market economies are offered as the model for the less developed. Moreover, the more powerful states get to set the rules of the game, often to their advantage in what is widely regarded as a 'centre-periphery' relationship. Hence, where a country is situated in terms of demography, geography and institutions determines its ability and thus its willingness to adapt to changes, especially when imposed from the outside. Therefore, the more traditional or archaic a society, the greater is the need for a country-specific approach to privatisation.

Chapter 3

Inequality and Consequences

Introduction

Like the Cold War model of global politics that existed for forty years and derived the binary distinction between capitalism and communism and which became obsolete in 1991 following the collapse of the Soviet Union, the orthodox model of privatisation arguably has become obsolete; requiring re-description in a world in which reducing inequality has become a question of morality. Indeed, drawing from Wallerstein's (1974) conception of the modern world in which countries are shown not to be equal in terms of GDP, market institutions and other wealth-capability enhancing characteristics, evaluating the privatisation effectiveness in developing countries calls for investigations into its connectedness with development, the latter as broadly defined by Sen (1999). Indeed, as shown in Part III, while the outcomes of privatisation are almost predictable in the developed economies and serve to validate its theoretical construct, it is less certain and identifiable in the developing countries primarily because of the influence of demography, geography and institutions. Hence, the inquiry into these linkages – which are necessarily empirical and causal at the level of the developing countries – acquires significance and relevance and demands an alternative perspective.

Beyond the objective of diffusing capitalism and democracy – its ideological raison d'etre and features – and the repayment of sovereign debts, privatisation contributes to development only when increasing human capabilities is made a fundamental objective of the process by the sharing of the opportunities and benefits; and when governments are made accountable to their citizens for public funds. This long-held contention finds corroboration in the increasing focus of the Bank's lending policy on empowerment of the poor, stressing as it now does the redistribution of resources, equity, transparency and public accountability, public participation and sustainability as elements of empowerment (see Bank 2006; Narayan 2002; Bank 2000/2001, 77–81). However, lest we forget these are not new concepts (see Chang 1997) nor are they rooted in economics but rather in neo-Thomism, articulated by Pope John XX111 in his *Pacem in Terris* [Peace on Earth] delivered in 1963 (Sigmund 1988). No matter, since 2000 good governance and the development effectiveness of public funds – including foreign aid – have become of particular concern to the MFIs as evidenced by the Bank's emphasis on good governance in its Development Policy Review (DPR) on Guyana (Bank 2003). And since proceeds from privatisation however derived are public funds, the development effectiveness of such funds must necessarily be part of validation of privatisation.

Toward a 'single pillar'

A notable weakness of the DPR on Guyana is the absence of coordination in the treatment of the several issues addressed in the report. This perception is reinforced by the Bank's Operations Evaluation Department's (OED) 2004 Annual Review of Development Effectiveness (ARDE) in which it is noted that the two pillar model of the Bank '... tends to overlook the interactions between growth and social aspects of poverty reduction that can have important effects on poverty outcomes' (Bank 2005: xii).

Furthermore, according to the ARDE, 'the Bank's main analytical work has tended to focus narrowly on the social sectors, while neglecting productive sectors and governance issues' and 'needs to pay more attention to the interaction between growth and social aspects of poverty reduction ...' (Bank 2005: xiv).

The ARDE further suggests that the overlapping nature of private sector development and public sector reform would be better understood if they were associated in a 'single pillar' that is, correlated under one head. It also considered from the perspective of the development effectiveness the 'willingness and ability of each country to implement reform' and found that improvements in human development '... have been better when interventions have been linked to institutional reforms and support for capacity building'.

Hence, the prescription if you will of a single pillar is premised on the observations that, '[a] healthy business environment for private sector investment requires an effective and accountable public sector in order to protect property rights and to ensure equitable and consistent treatment under the law' (Bank 2005: xiv); that political stability is an enabling environment for success; that strong ownership of reform contributes to successful outcomes; that the executive, legislature and bureaucracy must work for common purposes; and that the administrative capacity to implement must exist. While these observations are not new it is the first time they are being perceived not as discrete issues but rather as interrelated issues requiring closer administrative coordination.

Constraints to development

The observations of the ARDE suggest a growing awareness of the interrelatedness of the issues of development which were heretofore regarded as discrete and the domain of other disciplines. Clearly, there are constraints to development; many of which are not directly related to privatisation but none the less operate to limit the pass-through benefits of it at the level of developing counties. These are reviewed in this section.

Inequality

Arthur Lewis' notion that inequality is good for growth has lost currency in an evolving capitalist world-economy that is consumption derived, for two reasons:

First, whereas inequality was thought to provide opportunities for investment – an orthodox view and hence Lewis's thesis (see Lewis 1955) – an equitable distribution of income generates greater demand for goods and services which in turn supports large scale production that leads to economies of scale and technological development. Secondly, since reducing inequality has entered the consciousness of the MFIs and donor community it has now become situated within the broader framework of growth and development and has become an indicator of development effectiveness. From this perspective, equality is good for growth or put another way, inequality constrains economic growth in a capitalist world-economy.

Moreover, detracting from the notion that growth is good for equality is the evidence which suggests that reduction in inequality has not kept pace with growth. Indeed, several cross-disciplinary reports and studies point to the increasing inequality among and within states: Whereas 20 percent of the people in the richest country had 30 times the income of the poorest 20 percent in 1960, it had increased to 74 times in 1997 (see Wermuth 2003). Poverty in rural Africa increased despite economic and social reform initiatives: The number of urban poor swelling as a result of migration to the cities (WHO 1998, 166) and per-capita income in Sub-Sahara Africa lower in 1999 than in 1970 (UNDP 1999, 3). Confirming this trend, the World Food Programme in 2005 identified thirty countries in Africa as having signed on to food aid; and despite efforts by Bob Geldof and Bono to raise Western consciousness to the plight of the poorer countries, poverty in Africa has doubled in the intervening twenty years between 'Band Aid' and 'Live Aid'.

This trend of increasing poverty has been in the making for some time now: The gap between rich countries and poor countries has widened since World War I: Declining or stagnant GNP per capita has been the trend in African countries since the Debt Crisis of the early 1980s as shown in Table 3.1.

The cumulative decline of GNP per capita in Sub-Saharan Africa was calculated to be 21 percent between 1981 and 1989 (Basu and Stewart, 1995, 139). Moreover, several of the countries surveyed were found to have suffered decline of over 40 percent in their GNP per capita during this period, requiring the funding of poverty alleviation programmes. Indeed, as shown in Figure 3.1, 76 percent of the countries in Sub-Saharan Africa were ranked 'Low Income' by the Bank, compared with 31 percent in Asia, 13 percent in Europe and Central Asia and 10 percent in the Americas. In terms of real GDP growth, African countries with growth rates above 5 percent declined from 24 in 1996 to 13 in 1998. During the same period, countries with negative real per capita GDP growth rates increased from ten in 1996 to 23 in 1998 (AFDB 1999, 3).

Outside of Africa, poverty in the 'Transition Economies' of Eastern Europe and in Russia increased during the period 1993 to 1995, evidencing what some observers characterised as an unwillingness or inability of their governments to address the issue of social inequality attendant on privatisation (see Stiglitz 2002; Grootaert and Braithwaite 1998).

Table 3.1   **Annual GNP per capita growth rate (percent): Selected countries**

Country	1981–1985*	1985–1990*	1985–1995
Benin	0.6	-2.4	-0.3
Burkina Faso	1.8	1.7	0.2
Côte d'Ivoire	-2.7	-8.3	-
Cameroon	1.1	0.0	-6.6
Congo	6.0	-9.5	-3.2
Gabon	-6.3	-18.4	.8.2
Ghana	-3.2	1.8	1.4
Gambia	-3.4	1.2	-
Kenya	-2.8	2.2	0.1
Mali	-1.2	4.5	0.8
Malawi	0.0	-2.4	-0.7
Madagascar	-2.0	-1.1	-2.2
Mauritius	2.5	8.1	5.4
Mozambique	-8.0	0.0	3.6
Nigeria	-9.1	-5.2	1.2
Tanzania	-1.7	-3.0	-0.3
Sudan	-3.0	0.3	-
Zimbabwe	2.5	0.3	-0.6

* In 1987 US dollar
Source: Stewart & Basu, (1995, 139); WDR (1997, 215)

On a global scale, income differentials between rich and poor countries are widening: In 1913 the ratio between rich and poor was at 11:1, in 1997 it had increased to 60:1 and more alarmingly, to 70:1 in 1997 (UNDP 1999, 3). The differential in outlays on education is equally telling: In 1960 the OECD countries spent 14 times more on education than the developing countries, in 1980 the differential increased to 22 times and in 1990 to 50 times (Stromquist 2002, pp. xx). It is thus not coincidental that the Bank should find itself concerned with the issues of inequality and social justice (Bank 2006): the evidence is clearly overwhelming.

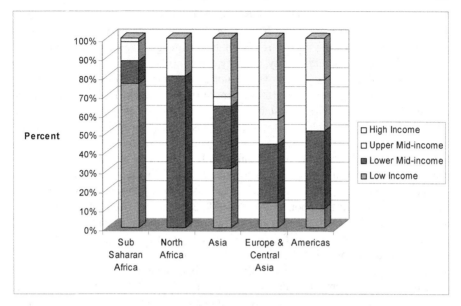

Figure 3.1   Classifications of economics by income and region

Source: Constructed from World Development Report, 1997

Correlation between income distribution and social inequality

In terms of impact, there are several studies on the correlation between the distribution of resources and social inequality from which to draw. At the developed country level, although the US spends 15.2 percent of GDP on healthcare or more than twice as much on a per capita basis than most other OECD countries, life expectancy is lower in the US than in Sweden as a result of the greater social inequality in the US as evidenced by the growing number of persons without health insurance – estimated to be 43.6 million in 2003 – and the increase in the number of Americans who are at or below the poverty line, estimated at 33.0 million in the third quarter of 2003. At the same time, the number and net-worth of wealthy Americans have grown at an unprecedented rate in the 1990s. Also, income inequality has been found to be positively correlated not only to health-related deaths but to homicide and to strained marital and family relationships in the US (see Wermuth 2003).

This ever-widening gap between the wealthy and poor in the developed countries in terms of both income and relative self-worth or social standing within the community is likely to contribute to a lack of trust and loss of social and political capital. Indeed, for the US and President Bush whose domestic focus is on creating an 'ownership society' by proposing privatisation of the social security system and healthcare, it was hurricane Katrina in August 2005 that pierced the veil of prosperity, diversity and inclusion; for France, mired in high unemployment and a conflict over farm subsidies, it was two weeks of riots by disaffected second generation immigrant youths in late October and early November 2005 and riots by young workers in protest of labour law reform in March 2006 that challenged the Republic's notion of *Liberté, Egalité, Fraternité* [liberty, equality, fraternity].

The correlations discussed above are not confined to the developed countries. Homicide in Brazil increased by 160 percent during the period 1977 to 1994 and is attributed to Brazil's economic instability and increasing social inequality (Wermuth 2003, 185). Similarly, with no safety-net for those falling through the privatisation crack, Argentina is experiencing worsening inequality and poverty. The increase in crime and homicide rates in Guyana since 2001 is similarly attributed to growing social inequality arising from social exclusion based on race and political party affiliation. In contrast, Chile has fared better: Its 'popular capitalism' approach to privatisation targeted the poor (Nankani 1988, 30); the cut back on business and upper-class privileges in the 1990s and the use of increased taxes on the rich to fund social-equalising programmes for the poor has resulted in a reduction in poverty: from 44 percent prior to 1990 to 22 percent; an increase in investment of over 25 percent in 1993; and an average growth rate of six percent in contrast to an average growth rate of two percent under Pinochet (Wermuth 2003, 188–9). Similarly, the welfare indicators of Singapore, Malaysia, Mauritius and South Africa, for example, are trending up in response to credible policies aimed at reducing social inequality.

Based on these findings, it would not be unreasonable to posit that even though the central focus of Highly Indebted Poor Country (HIPC) initiatives is poverty reduction, society-building and thus development would not be fully realised unless the broader issue of social inequality is comprehensively addressed by governments in fiscal budgets that reflect redistributive policies, and in policies aimed at improving civic involvement and empowerment. Moreover, as many African economists and observers have repeatedly stated, foreign aid rarely reaches down to the level where it is most needed because of corruption.

Governance and corruption

The issue of corruption has been studied for decades, with little progress in terms of identifying a universal causal relationship. Minogue (2004, 173), for example, has taken the position that rather than 'indulge in high-minded condemnation' of widespread and persistent corruption, the phenomenon needs to be understood as a form of behaviour and, as suggested by Brinkenhoff (2000, 241) quoted by Minogue (2004), in context of the political, institutional and social settings in which it occurs. Indeed, the Guyana experience – albeit a single country experience – detailed in Chapter 7 in part speaks directly to the need for social empowerment, specifically inclusion in the economic and political processes, as a means to reducing one aspect of corruption. But, as recognised by Minogue, corruption is multidimensional, and when brazenly pursued detracts from development and cannot be excused in toto on social grounds (see also Rondinelli *et al*. 2003, 101; Narayan 2002: xix; Hellman *et al*. 2000). In this regard, it is instructive that the Bank in 2004 estimated corruption in developing countries at US$100 billion. In 2006, the President of Nigeria estimates 25 percent of the GNP in Sub-Saharan Africa is lost to corruption. It is therefore no accident that Paul Wolfowitz, Head of the Bank, has taken the position that corruption must be vigorously stamped out in client countries. Some of the more notable manifestations of corruption are discussed below.

Clearly, having a 'monopoly on information' serves to reinforce social inequality, supports rent-seeking and detracts from good governance and therefore development (see Kaufmann 2000). Furthermore, 'high levels of corruption deter private sector investment ...' (Bank 1997, 21); and 'state-capture' – the ability of powerful firms to buy political, bureaucratic and judicial influence – is an aspect of poor governance and corruption (Hellman *et al.*, 2000). Additionally, as is well documented in studies conducted by the Bank, case-by-case discretion in the granting of investment incentives leads to state-capture and corruption and increases the country-risk premium which must be borne by the citizens. Similarly, the private-sector investor who explicitly or implicitly buys privileges and exemptions from established rules and regulations, and taxes – prevalent in privatisation agreements in many developing countries – disturbs in a fundamental way the equitable distribution of resources and reinforces social inequality.

Despite these and other well articulated findings and refrains on corruption the evidence suggests that corruption at the highest levels of government continues unabated in many countries and is particularly attached to privatisation in developing countries. Indeed, the privatisation of public enterprises, large public works projects and the awarding of contracts and the distribution of land are proven opportunities for large-scale bureaucratic and political corruption (see Rondinelli *et al.* 2003). Hence, as the 2004 ARDE observes: 'So far, there is little evidence that governance is improving or that corruption is decreasing' [and the] ... kinds of reform [envisaged] entail changes in power and influence within a country' (Bank 2005: xiv). These observations are supported by Transparency International (TI) 2005 Report. According to Peter Eigen, TI's Chairman: 'Corruption is a major cause of poverty as well as a barrier to overcoming it. The two scourges feed off each other, locking their populations in a cycle of misery. Corruption must be vigorously addressed if aid is to make a real difference in freeing people from poverty'.[1]

But the twin issues of governance and corruption have concerned academics and observers for decades: For Huntington (1968, 1), 'the most important political distinction among countries concerns not their form of governance but their degree of government'; for Migdal (1968), quoted in Turner and Hulme (1997, 48), 'there is an ongoing struggle between state and societal actors over who has the right and ability to make the rules that guide people's social behaviour; and just because state legislation exists it does not necessarily mean that it is enforced'. Indeed, some 35 years after these observations' and notwithstanding increasing attention to monitoring by the donor community, the Guyana experience stands in validation: Corruption has been deemed 'endemic in Guyana' and state discretion in implementing laws and

---

[1]   Guyana gets poor rating in corruption survey', *Stabroek News*, 19 October 2005.

regulations as seriously hampering private sector development (see Bank 2003, 28). The policy response of the government was a public pronouncement that 'public money and property must be used in the most efficient manner. Corruption must be weeded out'.[2] In practice, however, corruption has been restricted to criminal acts punishable by the courts; excluded are bureaucratic and political corruption; so too is state and regulatory capture.

Again, drawing from the Guyana experience with respect to state capture by foreign investors, the privatisation of the Guyana Telephone Corporation (GTC) and GEC (Chapter 8) are cases in point. In the case of GTC, the investor has effectively utilized its resources to maintain its monopoly position, squelching regulation and competition and overwhelming the legal and political processes to its advantage (Chang 2004; Bank 2003, 32–3). In furtherance of its control, it sought to have the US District Court block a loan from the Inter-American Development Bank (IDB) to the government of Guyana.[3] The foreign investor in the electric utility on the other hand, unable to capitalise on asymmetric advantage secured in negotiation of the several agreements with the government, sold its holdings back to the government for US$1 in April, 2003 (see Chapter 8).

Manifestation of corruption

The DPR on Guyana is clearly not a recommendation to foreign investors and must be regarded as severely critical of governance in that country; nor, indeed, are the 2004 ARDE and 2005 TI Report recommendations to foreign investors of developing countries generally. However, a refrain in reports is that governments have the power to break the cycle of corruption by promoting good governance through legislation, persuasion, and leadership at the policy-making level, and through transparency and public accountability at the execution level by recognising corrupt practices (see Narayan 2002; and Stiglitz 2002; Hellman 2000; Kaufmann *et al.* 2000). Equally instructive in this regard is Sen's (1999, 277) observation that: 'the established rules of behaviour are particularly attached to the conduct of people in positions of power and authority'.

Even when corrective measures are enacted, investors tend to be hesitant without an acceptable country-experience base upon which to rely. A 1996 survey of risk analysts, insurance brokers and bank credit officers found that, with the exception of Mauritius, Botswana and South Africa, African countries were rated high risk (with less than 50 percent chance based on the number of points allotted) for non-payment for goods and services, loans, and the non-repatriation of capital (see Kerf and Smith 1996). Again, despite measures taken in the mid-1990s to protect foreign investment, foreign private participation in African infrastructure development has been slow to develop because of pre-existing constraints in some countries and the

---

2   'Corruption must be weeded out', *Stabroek News*, 1 January 2004.

3   Atlantic Tele-Network V. Inter-American Bank *et al.*, *District Court in the District of Columbia, Case* # 02- CIVIL 1261, 7 March 2003.

difficulties experienced by others in effecting promised reforms. For example, up to 1995 the government of Ghana was unable to follow through on its promise to support collection of revenues and accounts receivable in the electricity sector. It also did not follow through with promised timely tariff approvals for both electricity and telecommunications, and the timely payment of its water bills. Senegal was found to be equally derelict in fulfilling its promises. Since then, with the assistance of the Bank, Ghana has implemented corrective measures which have allowed it to privatise its telecommunications network with foreign participation.

The removal rather than promotion or transfer of rent-seeking officials has been proffered as going a long way to breaking the chain of corruption and to establishing credibility with the public, foreign investors and donor community, as is the elimination of state discretion in the tax system. Based on a study of 53 developing countries conducted by Poirson (1998), it was concluded that private investment could be encouraged and economic growth in the area of one-half percent to one percent of GDP in the short to medium term could result from 'economic security improvement'. Citing the challenges to African countries, three priorities for African governments were identified:

- The first priority is to reduce the risk of expropriation so as to raise the level of private investment and increase the efficiency of resource allocation;
- the second priority is to reduce corruption and the risk of contract repudiation by the government in order to raise the longer-term growth prospects;
- and the third is to increase civil liberties and the quality of the bureaucracy so as to raise the private-sector confidence.

Need less to say, these priorities are not restricted to African governments. In many cases, public officials and their advisors have been found to approach privatisation as an opportunity to acquire wealth: A hallmark of the privatisation programmes in Hungary (see Csepi and Lukacs 1995, 189–190; Fletcher 1995, 113), in Russia[4] (see Goldman 2003; Rutland 1995, 301) and in Guyana as detailed in Chapters 7 and 8. As regards state discretion in the tax system, it continues unabated as a means to funding political campaigns and to wealth accumulation by corrupt politicians and public officials.

Similarly, investing in stakeholders access to information and voice in public expenditure allocation, programme implementation and in monitoring outcomes has been a refrain advanced as means to reducing the opportunity for corruption (see Kaufmann *et al.* 2000) and to enhancing the development effectiveness of poverty reduction initiatives, including privatisation. But again, the evidence suggests a reluctance of governments to shift from repression to inclusion, and away from central control and the awarding of fifes and benefices to party elites and supporters.

---

[4] Robbins, C. and Liesman, S., 'How an Aid Program Vital to New Economy of Russia Collapsed', *The Wall Street Journal*, 13 August 1997.

The debt burden

The strangulation effect of unsustainable debt in the poorer developing countries has been brought to the fore by activists such as Bob Geldof and Bono to the point of perceived embarrassment to the developed countries and the MFIs despite credible efforts at debt reduction.

With respect to debt-service costs, as shown in Table 3.2 most of the countries surveyed have external debts above their annual GNP some ten years into privatisation; many with debt service as a percent of exports above 20 percent even after rescheduling.

Table 3.2   Total external debt and debt service ratios. Selected low income countries

| Country | Total External Debt | | | | | | Debt Service: | | |
| | Amount (US$ m) | | | as   % GNP | | | as % of Exports | | |
	1983	1989	1994	1983	1989	1994	1983	1989	1994
Bangladesh	4,185	10,717	16,569	37.7	53.3	63.4	14.7	19.9	15.8
Burundi	284	867	1,125	26.2	81.9	113.8	-	32.9	41.7
Malawi	719	1,394	2,015	55.2	91.4	160.3	20.3	28.7	17.4
Guinea	1,216	2,176	3,104	69.2	85.3	94.7	-	15.2	14.2
Ghana	1,095	3,078	5,389	28.3	59.9	101.5	14.2	48.9	24.8
Madagascar	1,490	3,607	4,134	52.3	154.1	225.3	-	52.0	9.5
Sri Lanka	2,205	5,101	7,811	43.7	73.5	67.6	11.9	17.8	8.7
Kenya	2,384	5,690	7,273	43.1	71.7	112.4	20.6	33.3	33.6
Tanzania	2,548	4,918	7,441	58.9	186.1	229.5	-	16.5	20.5
Sierra Leone	359	1,057	1,392	34.5	119.5	187.3	7.2	-	-
Nigeria	11,757	32,832	33,485	17.7	119.3	102.5	18.6	21.3	18.5
Trinidad	887	2,012	2,218	10.7	53.9	50.3	2.8	12.3	31.6
Pakistan	9,755	18,509	29,579	31.3	46.9	56.6	28.1	23.2	35.1

Source: Compiled from WDR: (1985, 204); (1991, 244; 250); (1996, 220–21)

It should be further noted that:

- for the sample-countries listed above, 57 percent of outflows in 1989 was in respect of interest;
- the increase in debt between 1983 and 1989 reflected the inflows in IDA soft loans which more than doubled since 1984 whilst repayments and interest to IMF and Bank, and 'Private' transfers were substantially increased (see Helleiner 1992) ; and that,

- according to the World Health Organisation 21 countries had a lower growth rate in the 1991–1995 period than they had in 1980–1985 (WHO 1998, 166).

These and other consequences have led to the conclusion that the IMF and Bank became

> a source of long-term conditional loans that made poorer nations increasingly dependent on the IMF and given the IMF a degree of influence over member countries' policy making that is unprecedented for a multilateral institution (Meltzer *et al.* 2000, 18).

However, with a changing multilateral approach to development in the poorer countries, the high incidence of debt-service costs came under closer scrutiny. As a result, in 1997 several low-income countries received for the first time some relief under the Highly Indebted Poor Countries (HIPC) Initiative, established as a joint initiative between the Bank and the IMF in 1996. Under this programme, heavily indebted countries (with IDA concessional-terms status) whose debt burdens are deemed unsustainable and with a perceived track record of sustained economic reforms are considered for debt reduction on a case-by-case basis with the cooperation of creditors. Some 40 countries mainly in Africa have been identified for relief under the HIPC initiative. For example, in April 1997 relief of US$340 million in net-present-value terms was approved for Uganda, while Burkina Faso received US$10 million debt relief in September 1997. Similar relief was extended to Bolivia and Guyana. The HIPC programme operates side by side with the Debt Reduction Facility which was established in 1989 to provide grant funds to developing countries to buy back their commercial debts at deep discounts.

In addition to the two programmes discussed above, several developing countries benefited from the Paris Club Naples terms which provided for a 67 percent reduction in eligible debt. These included Uganda, Guinea, Senegal, Togo, Bolivia and Guyana. Other countries opted for variants to the terms which included repurchase of commercial debt at deep discounts. There was also substantial debt forgiveness in Africa, approximately US$3.0 billion each in 1994 and 1995 occasioned by the devaluation of the CFA franc. Algeria also concluded a US$3.2 billion restructuring agreement with commercial banks in June 1997.

In 2000, an enhanced version of HIPC was established in response to the increasing unsustainability of debts in many HIPCs. In July 2005, encouraged by intensive lobbying and activism on behalf of the 40 poorest developing countries the Group of Eight (G-8) developed countries at their meeting at Gleneagles, Scotland, agreed to the complete write-off of multilateral debts of 19 of the poorest countries. These initiatives and debt reduction programmes have the two-fold objective of first, relieving the pressure on these countries' fiscal budgets and second, promoting economic reforms to include privatisation and good governance.

But debt write-off on the scale authorised by the G-8 is seen by many observers as a temporary fix and an invitation to corrupt governments to incur further debts in the name of poverty reduction. Many, even within several of the beneficiary countries, have argued for increased access to developed countries' markets for their products at a fair price instead of 'hand outs' as envisaged by the United Nations Millennium Development Goals; still many more see supporting indigenous entrepreneurship not corrupt governments as the key to poverty eradication. In this latter regard, the Grameen Bank's approach to financing cottage industry is seen as exemplary. Indeed, the routing of foreign aid through grassroots non-profit organisations (NGO) has the advantage of eliminating corrupt politicians whose rhetoric is tailored for the consumption of the international community, the latter perceived as a willing victim to 'moral extortion of epic proportions, the shakedown of the millennium' (Buchanan 2002, 58).

Interconnectedness of privatisation and development

Within the broader definition of privatisation, the interconnectedness of privatisation can be readily identified and has been fully seized upon but by a handful of countries so that privatisation becomes an integral aspect of development. While the linkages are several and diverse, those that are likely to effect changes in the government income-stream require special attention.

Impact on state-funded programmes

Consider first, government-funded social services – education healthcare, and employment retraining – pursued as a matter of policy to enhance human capability and reduce relative poverty. Since these are state-funded programmes, they are likely to be impacted by any increase or decrease in the government's fiscal budget which in turn is impacted positively or negatively by privatisation. Indeed, for governments committed to poverty reduction or to redressing prior wrongs, the social consequences of privatisation and its impact on their ability to fund poverty reduction programmes, which might have to be strengthened or increased in consequence, are seen less willing to pursue privatisation on the basis of economic orthodoxy, foreign aid notwithstanding. On the basis of this reasoning the more economic-independent countries such as Malaysia, Mauritius and South Africa, for example, have conditioned their privatisation programmes on their ability to absorb workers displaced by the process.

Impact on unemployment

On the other hand, privatisation of publicly-owned commercial enterprises in the poorer developing countries often leads to a reduction in employment in an environment in which the absorptive capacity is either non-existent or minimal. For example, job losses following the privatisation of eight enterprises in Benin amounted to 36.0 percent of the number of pre-privatisation employees; in Ghana, privatisation of seven enterprises between 1990 and 1995 resulted in a 17.3 percent reduction whilst the privatisation of ten enterprises in Zambia between 1993 and 1996 resulted in a 6.7 percent reduction in employment in the enterprises privatised

(Campbell White and Bhatia 1998, 94). These workers were likely given jobs in other public-sector enterprises.

Where the policy is to have other public enterprises absorb workers laid-off by privatisation, capital additions often replace maintenance as a priority in an effort to create jobs and to keep the political base in tact. In this regard, the GUYSUCO's experience speaks powerfully to this observation: In contrast to the sugar industry in Swaziland which employs 6,000 workers to produce 360,000 tonnes of sugar, GUYSUCO employs 20,000 workers to produce 325,000 tonnes, with labour accounting for 58.8 percent of the cost per tonne sugar produced.[5] Such disparity notwithstanding, the PPP/C government of Guyana is adamant about increasing production chiefly as a means to maintaining its political base and on the belief that the donor community will be forthcoming in the funding of budget deficits and poverty-reduction programmes; it has thus far notwithstanding the evidence.

Clearly, these considerations – wholesome or unwholesome – militate against privatisation on the basis of enterprise efficiency as defined by Mary Shirley (see Berg and Shirley 1988); and indeed against the effectiveness of regulation and competition where pursuit of the political imperative is all-consuming. This said, the basis of competition and regulation needs to be examined for an understanding of their respective roles in privatisation.

Competition as first-best choice

As noted by Vickers and Yarrow (1995, 426): '... the economics of privatization cannot be separated from the economics of competition and regulation'. But as observed by Metcalfe *et al.* (2004, 59), '... the spontaneity of change that is competition is not an idea that fits easily into theories premised on the notion of equilibrium...' Indeed, competition and regulation in the provision of basic infrastructure services as the country-examples below well illustrate are often open to other considerations. Hence, the orthodox approach to competition and competitiveness, and the realist approach as touched on by Metcalfe *et al.* (2004) are usually at variance with the latter manifesting in varying degrees of pragmatism. Furthermore, between these two positions is the notion of social justice which orthodox economics must by definition ignore but which is fundamental to the concept of development and therefore to effective regulation (see Kirkpatrick 2001). Because of this, there is consensus that the interest of the consumer is best safeguarded by the introduction of competition as a first best choice as country and industry conditions allow.

Social and or natural justice

With the notion of social and or natural justice interjected in the interest of reducing inequality, competition and competitiveness have tended to be posed as questions

---

[5] Boast, M., 'Sugar will survive', *Stabroek Business*, October 2003.

and in terms of their impact on development. For example, is a firm or country truly competitive; indeed is there competition in the light of billions of dollars of subsidies expended annually to maintain perceived competitiveness? Is the developing world necessarily uncompetitive when its access to markets is restricted by protectionist regimes, and its producers forced to be price-takers? Should economic and social regulations be imposed on developing countries, couched as they are in terms of 'levelling the playing field' and 'human rights'? Are these not mechanisms designed to maintain asymmetric advantage? Clearly, the answers to these and similar questions depend crucially upon which side of the development divide one finds oneself.

In addition to fostering innovation on an on-going basis, competition is seen as offering consumers reliable and where appropriate meaningful choice in affordable services, a principle or feature firmly embraced by the Federal Communications Commission in the US and shared with developing countries. As a recommendation, entry points for competition in infrastructure services should be established with a view to fostering sustainable competition in all service areas, with safeguards against anti-competitive behaviour by the dominant service provider. In the case of telecommunications, access to advanced communications services is seen as requiring particular focus on disparity not only in the pace of competition between business and residential services but also in geographic and demographic expansion of service: The notion of universal service requires that advanced telecommunications services be available to all consumers – including residents in low-income rural and high-cost areas – at rates that are reasonably comparable to those charged in urban areas. These principles have been for the most part adopted by developing countries and are manifest in their respective telecommunications regulatory frameworks; it is their implementation that is suspect, especially in weak states, hence the need for periodical reviews.

Periodical reviews

Periodical reviews ensure that effective competition and advances in technology are not held hostage to entrenched interest but are pursued to the benefit of all stakeholders. As observed by Stiglitz (2002, 56):

> Once a vested interest has been created, it has an incentive, and the money, to maintain its monopoly position, squelching regulation and competition, and distorting the political/legal processes along the way.

Again, the Guyana experience speaks to this observation: It was not until Cel*Star became licensed to provide GSM telecommunications service to Guyana that the incumbent monopoly facility-based and TDMA service provider began to offer a similar service, and only after it was able to withhold interconnection to Cel*Star through an unrelated court action[6] that allowed it time to convert to GSM.

---

[6]   See 'GT&T Suspends all dealings with Cel*Star', *Stabroek News*, 12 November 2003.

Meanwhile, the Prime Minister who has responsibility for telecommunications and is the issuer of the licence appeared reluctant if not powerless to intervene on behalf of Cel*Star. The PUC also did nothing to disabuse the incumbent from with-holding interconnection while it seeks to upgrade its service offerings. Such inaction by a regulatory agency would hardly be deemed acceptable regulatory behaviour in the developed countries.

But GT&T is not alone in exploiting its monopoly position. The monopoly telecommunications service provider in Trinidad and Tobago, TSTT (51 percent state-owned with 49 percent remaining with Cable and Wireless on privatisation) is, in the words of its competitor Digicel, 'making a mockery of the entire liberalisation process'.[7] TSTT reportedly has claimed it will not have the equipment necessary to connect Digicel to its network until some five months beyond the proposed launch date of Digicel's mobile service. Meanwhile, like the monopoly service provider in Guyana, TSTT has engaged in a marketing blitz to sell its 'Bmobile' service ahead of the competition; and imposing penalty on customers who may consider switching to Digicel as and when it gains interconnection to TSTT's network; again, unacceptable behaviour in terms international best practice but seemingly permissible at the developing country level.

In contrast to the Guyana and Trinidad experiences, the de-monopolisation of telecommunications in New Zealand took cognizance of the importance of freeing technological development from monopoly control, as did the process in Singapore. In addition, monopoly service providers in several African countries – South Africa, Botswana, and Mauritius for example – were disabused of the practice of exploiting their monopoly positions, and were required to subscribe to the concept of universal service, as opposed to universal access, as reflected in their operating licences and in their compliance.

Regulatory and legal framework

In developed countries, the social justice imperative implicit in regulation is designed to deal with asymmetries arising from the incompleteness of the self-regulating mechanism in a market economy. Hence, absent competition or where market-dominance by a single player is overwhelming, regulation is seen as the next best choice.

As to what should inform an effective regulatory and legal framework, the British Government's guide is instructive. Clearly, the objective of regulation is unmistakably perceived as one of protecting the consumer from the abuse of market power without inhibiting future investment or innovation by the service provider, and to promote mutual trust and cooperation among stakeholders (see Kirkpatrick, 2001). To this end, public comment and participation have been included as integral aspects of the regulatory rule-making process. Moreover, a partnership arrangement

---

[7]   See Plummer, R., 'Caribbean phone wars hit Trinidad', *BBC News*, 11 January 2006, http://news.bbc.co.uk/go/em/fr/-/2/hi/business/4583432.stm >, accessed 11 January 2006.

among government, provider, regulator and consumer is perceived as essential to the sharing of the benefits among stakeholders and in this regard contributes to the privatisation effectiveness. But this policy approach would likely narrow the number of potential investors to only those who are genuinely interested in participating in the development of the host country: the withdrawal of a bidder in the privatisation of Ghana telecommunications in the absence of a limited period monopoly evidences investor-expectation.

Also, as is increasingly being recognised a regulatory framework that fosters competition as first-best choice and to addressing issues of market failure and income distribution on an on-going basis for monopoly service-providers is preferable to heavy-handed regulation. The regulatory frameworks of Singapore[8] and New Zealand provide for competition to be phased-in with a concurrent phasing out of regulation as the former takes hold – 'light-handed' regulation, if you will. In such a framework notions of equity, equality of opportunities and social justice – the empowerment response – have been considered equally with the economics of regulation and necessarily reflect privatisation not merely as a reform mechanism but rather as a contributing asset to development.

By implication, periodical review of and amendment to privatisation agreements in keeping with changing economic, political and social conditions have been made as much part of the process as the setting of tariffs, with regulation for entry, exit and price kept to a minimum. In this latter regard, asymmetric advantage becomes less of an incentive in privatisation negotiations which in turn reduces the opportunity for rent-seeking by public officials. While this is policy in Singapore and developed countries, it is less so in many developing countries and even when written into law is rendered ineffective through state- or regulatory-capture.

The importance of an independent regulatory agency is a refrain in the literature on competition regulation. Emphasised are: the regulatory agency should be separate from and not accountable to any of the service providers; it must be shielded from any political control or interference, and must be seen to apply regulation in an open, consistent and predictable way without fear or favour.

Despite these well-publicised tenets, regulation in backward and rent-seeking states continues to be displayed as aspect of the rational-legal but with politicians as regulator, granting privileges and exemptions from established regulations and local laws ad hoc.

The rules of the game

For most developing countries, learning the interplay of the rules of the game is as much part of the process as establishing the rules themselves. Public-sector managers are thus expected to understand the changing roles of government in a market economy: They will need to find effective ways to forge a partnership relationship

---

[8]   See Government of Singapore, Info-Communications Development Authority of Singapore Act 1999 (No. 41 of 1999), 3 December 1999.

with private-sector managers to ensure access to rather than delivery of services. In this regard, reorientation of public officials to the idea of being facilitator to the various stakeholders and to replace dictate with consensus on common action to their mutual advantage are stressed as necessary steps to the conversion process. The investor in such an environment is made equally responsible for the development effectiveness of privatisation.

In theory, once these new roles are understood by the participants – service provider, government and consumer alike – the necessary regulatory safeguards and the means to enforcing them will be better received by stakeholders and should reflect in a lower country-risk premium, with attendant increase in investment. In practice, the strategic investor with cooperation from willing rent-seeking officials will often seek to influence the framing of the rules of the game to its benefit; hence the observation that the asymmetric advantage of the monopoly provider is often greater in developing rather than in developed countries.

Full cost recovery

In most of the literature, the issue of cost recovery has been approached from the perspective of the investor, that is, what it would take to attract investment, mainly foreign, in developing countries; but cost recovery also has economic and social consequences for the host country as discussed in this section.

Clearly, the debt-repayment/debt-servicing imperative of the 1980s and early1990s has done much to retard economic growth and development in the HIPCs as evidenced by their debt-sustainability ratios that entitled them to special treatment. While many have benefited from the HIPC Initiatives, countries with a per-capita GDP of less than US$365.00 have found privatisation of basic infrastructure services on a full cost-recovery basis untenable. With a per capita GDP of less than US$365.00 the majority of the population would be below the poverty line and would not be able to support full cost recovery. Under these conditions or where income inequality is endemic, redistribution issues as suggested by Juskow (1998) have been approached through the budgetary mechanism rather than through the regulatory process. As a result, many countries that have undertaken privatisation under such dire economic conditions were forced to add to their external debt to subsidize cost recovery; however, many found too great the challenge of translating such borrowings to the benefit of lower-income consumers.

Other constraints to cost recovery

In addition to low per-capita income, there are other constraints to full cost recovery even when cost-covering tariffs are authorised. Two such constraints are operating inefficiency and labour redundancy.

Operating inefficiency

The low level of operating efficiency has often been cited as a constraint to effective cost recovery. This is well illustrated by the dilemma of the African railway systems. Government subsidies and cross-subsidisation from freight haulage kept passenger fares at politically acceptable low levels but also served to make African exports more expensive in consequence of the inherent inefficiencies attendant on such practices.

Consider the case of transport in Africa. Increased fares were often resisted by passengers who resorted to alternative modes of transportation. For example, in an attempt to become commercially viable, the Kenya Railways Corporation (KRC), increased passenger fares as part of its mandate under a performance contract. The result was a decline in passenger traffic by more than 35 percent (see UNDP 1995, 174). A more drastic approach was adopted by Uganda Railway Corporation which suspended passenger service in September 1996 (see Williams 1997). Moreover, the raising of freight rates was resisted by those government departments which were major users of rail transport (see Geggie 1991). However, in the case of the Cameroon railways which was privatised in May 1998, except for passenger service on a few lines which remained subsidised by the government, the concessionaire was allowed to set cost-covering tariffs for both freight and passenger services. But the issue in terms of effective cost recovery is not only whether raising passenger tariff results in a reduction in the number of railway passengers but rather the entity's responsiveness to the changing structure of demand: It took Togo nineteen years to effect closure of two short lines (see Geggie 1991).

Labour redundancy

The impact of labour redundancy is, again, best explained with reference to the railways in Africa. Whilst line-closure is often an effective cost-reduction measure, African railways have been a major source of employment for workers displaced from agriculture or other sectors. In consequence, labour redundancy has been shown to be a major constraint to cost recovery by railways in African. For example, the Tanzania railway system was found to employ twice as many workers as an efficiently run railway system in Europe. Despite the relative higher employment costs, however, Tanzania Railways was placed in a profitable position during the period 1989–1993 by the setting of cost-covering tariffs and the reduction in the number of its excess freight wagons. In contrast, the Tanzanian-Zambian Railway (TAZARA), whose main existence was as an alternative to the railway network of apartheid-South Africa in the transportation of mainly Zambian imports and exports, was plagued with excess rolling stock relative to its demand for freight services, poor maintenance and excessive bureaucratic control. Moreover, labour redundancy in TAZARA was exacerbated by declining demand for freight haulage attendant the demise of apartheid. In addition, because of its poor quality of service TAZARA was by-passed in favour of road haulage despite the relatively higher costs of the latter.

Beside Kenya and Tanzania, there are other railway systems that have attempted to become competitive through restructuring. For example, the concession agreement for the Cameroon railways called for the termination of 450 employees at an approximate cost of CFA3.0 billion. The concessionaire had agreed to contribute CFA500 million to defraying the cost of termination. In addition, the operator was allowed to set cost covering tariffs for all services except on two lines, which for social reasons continued to be subsidised by the government. In Guyana, the railway system was scrapped and was replaced by road transport.

What is said of the railways can be applied to other infrastructure service or, in the case of Guyana, to the sugar industry which employs almost three times as many workers to produce one tonne of sugar in comparison with Swaziland.

Investor expectations and asymmetric advantage

Without prospects for full-cost recovery, the monopoly service provider will be unwilling to commit to service expansion or upgrades requiring huge amounts of sunk-capital or even to provide service to low-income areas; new investors would not participate without a limited-period monopoly clause if the market were deemed too small to justify the investment, as was the case in the privatisation of the Ghana Telecom.[9] But where subsides are paid directly to the service provider, unless these are tied to specific programmes to serve the poor and disadvantaged the more affluent members of society would tend to be disproportionately benefited. This is more so where subsidies are paid merely to make-up agreed earnings requirement as was done in the privatisation of the GEC.[10]

Empirical evidence further suggests that where foreign investor perception of risk is high, their participation in privatisation requiring sunk-capital is usually on the basis of terms and conditions that allow them to recover their capital over the short-term. As a result, many countries have privatised infrastructure services such as telecommunications and electricity on the basis of an agreed rate of return (ROR) and other income-generating schemes for the strategic investor, often in joint-venture partnership, only to find it politically difficult to support cost-covering tariffs in keeping with the privatisation agreements. Drawing upon the Guyana experience once more, the foreign investor in the privatisation of the telephone utility in 1991 required: a guaranteed minimum after-tax ROR (not return on equity) of 15 percent applied on the assets of enterprise; a twenty-year period of exclusivity; and an Advisory Service Contract at a tax-exempt fee of six percent of gross revenues (see Chang 2004, 420). These terms have been questioned some 10 years into the agreement in the light of current national needs, changing technology and, of course, on the notion of natural justice.

---

[9] See Eade, P., Telecom leads the way, *Euromoney*, N335, March, 1997 Issue.

[10] See Section 3.4 Shareholders Agreement between the Government of Guyana and CDC/ESBI, December 1999.

From like experiences elsewhere one is apt to conclude that developing-country governments cannot be trusted to live up to legally-binding agreements. However, in most such cases cost-recovery as proposed by the investor often masks the seizing of perceived asymmetric advantage by the strategic investor in negotiations with an ill-informed government team or one that is disposed to rent-seeking. In the privatisation of the GTC for example, whilst a minimum ROR was required by the investor, no maximum was set and thus evidenced a flagrant deviation from international best practice. This open-ended approach to cost-recovery allowed the investor to generate substantial revenues from switching audio-text services through the Guyana facilities – allegedly an undisclosed intention of the investor at the time of negotiations – without having to either account for the revenues or directly share the attendant financial benefits with the host country (Chang 2004).

Another example of questionable approach to cost recovery is one that ignores the capitalisation of the enterprise and the cost of capital in the determination of tariffs: a feature found in privatisation agreements in several developing countries. But in rate of return regulation as practiced in the developed countries, the generally-accepted practice is to set tariffs based on the weighted average cost of capital plus operating costs: the US experience with rate of return regulation provides the authority. Where international best practices are ignored, the privatisation effectiveness is less than optimal; and in turn operates as a constraint to development.

Yet another concern centres on the issue of defining allowable operating expenses. Once again, the US experience is replete with regulatory decisions from which to draw. To be sure, any US strategic investor comes armed with full knowledge of the limitations imposed by US federal and state regulations in instances where the investor is seeking an authorised rate of return rather than face the vagaries of open competition. Even where a price-cap approach is implemented, only those operating expenses deemed necessary to the provision of the service are considered allowable; moreover savings are shared with the consumer on the basis of the RPI-X formula. Yet, at the developing country level there is evidence of transfer-pricing, cross-subsidisation, accounting irregularities not unlike those that plagued WorldCom, Quest Communications, Global Crossings and Enron, and the expensing of expenditure that would not get pass regulatory scrutiny in developed countries. These irregularities detract from a systematic approach to cost-recovery and further detract from international best practices, confidence-building within the host country and development.

Clearly, cost-recovery that is not unambiguously defined is fundamentally flawed, and not only takes away from the integrity of privatisation agreements but also creates suspicion of and hostility to the foreign investor. There is also a greater likelihood of over-building on existing technology since efficiency of the enterprise becomes secondary to the opportunity to exploit asymmetric advantages secured from a relatively ill-informed government negotiating under difficult circumstances.

Conclusion

In this chapter the issues of the development effectiveness of privatisation have been approached somewhat prescriptively based on the several well-informed reports and studies by the IMF and Bank and others, and on empirical evidence collected by the author and the author's own experience with competition and regulation in the telecommunications industry from both side of the regulatory divide. It thus provides a basis for evaluating the goals, techniques and outcomes of privatisation detailed in the ensuing chapters.

PART III
Privatisation and Development at Cross Purposes

Chapter 4

Goals of Privatisation

Introduction

Given the failure of Keynesian economics to provide solutions to the stagflation phenomenon of the 1970s, and the mindset of President Reagan and Prime Minister Thatcher to pursue free-market economics and to counter a bellicose Soviet Union, the goals of privatisation were premised on market fundamentalism. The Debt Crisis provided the opportunity to extend systemic economic reforms to developing countries pursuant the Baker Plan which mandated among other adjustments the creation of investment opportunities for Western investors while raising cash to service external debts (Baker III 1987). These mandates became fully incorporated into the lending policies of the IMF and Bank in the mid-1980s.

For most of the period since 1979 then, notions rooted in economic orthodoxy were held out as immutable truths, particularly the idea that big government was the problem and that the private sector is necessarily more efficient than the public sector, stages of growth notwithstanding. Equally compelling was the Reagan administration's bent on not only preserving democracy within the U.S. but also extending it across the rest of the world (see Kaldor 2003, 1–22), an idea reiterated by President George W. Bush with respect to the Middle East and beyond.[1]

As with the discussion on the underlying institutional infrastructure, the goals of privatisation are examined from the perspectives of developed and developing countries for contrast and comparison. However, before selected country-specific perspectives are examined, the theoretical rationale is analysed so as to provide a backdrop to the discussion on the differences in goals.

Theoretical conception

As noted in Chapter 1, the belief that government has grown to unmanageable proportions was premised on the need to reduce the constraints to economic growth and to provide opportunities for the private sector within the state. It was thus based on the notion that in terms of access to savings government has a crowding-out effect. Therefore, while there are other arguments for the reduction of government, the crowding-out effect is examined here as being the most significant.

Taking the national income identities to include foreign trade and the concept of 'zero-sum of sector balances' advanced by the New Cambridge approach that

---

[1]   Televised national broadcast of speech on 6 November 2003.

identifies budget deficit (surplus) with balance of payments deficit (surplus), then in equilibrium:

Taxes (T) + savings (S) + imports (M) = private investments (I) + government expenditure (G) + exports (X); which can be rewritten as:

$$(T - G) + (S - I) + (X - M) = 0.$$

The underlying assumption of this equation is that because what is not consumed is invested, surplus in one sector becomes the liability of the other sectors which when added together should equal zero in equilibrium. It follows that any government budget deficit (surplus) must be reflected as an imbalance in either of the other two sectors or both. That is: $(T < G) = (S - I) + (X - M)$. Thus, when there is a government budget deficit $(T < G)$, it must be financed by either private savings or imports, or a combination of both.

As an aside, the ever increasing US deficits and external debt speak powerfully to the validity of this equation. With national savings rate in negative territory in 2005 – the first time since the Great Depression – there is clearly a greater reliance on foreign capital to finance both private and public sectors. In the words of Martin Wolf, 'America is now on the comfortable path to ruin'.[2]

Crowding-out effect

From the perspective of the private sector, such a relationship operates to crowd-out private investment by keeping interest rates for domestic funds higher than they would have been had the government not had to access the market for private savings.

Domestic borrowing by the government is carried out by the issue of debt instruments such as bonds or by the intermediation of the banking system. In the neoclassical model, given the underlying assumption of full employment, fiscal policy cannot alter the level of real output and leakages, that is, savings (S), taxes (T) and imports (M) are equilibrating for given values of income. Thus government borrowings from the sale of bonds affect the interest rate and price level but not real income. Higher interest rates translate into higher costs and, therefore, lower profits to the private sector.

Crowding-out also occurs when, in order to finance the fiscal budget deficit, the government resorts to increasing the money supply, that is, monetising the deficit. By monetising the deficit the overall price level is increased to the point where, despite the increased price level people still prefer to hold a proportion of their assets in money. The movement into bonds resulting from portfolio rebalancing that is likely to occur from the increase in the money supply reduces the interest rates. The

---

[2]   Wolf, M., 'America is now on the comfortable path to ruin', in *Financial Times*, 18 August 2004, p. 17.

reduction in interest rates stimulates aggregate demand, thereby increasing the price level.

Generally, in keeping with the notion of rational expectations the theoretical relationships noted above will obtain up to the point where hyperinflation is perceived or where individuals and firms recognise a deliberate policy of sustained inflation. Nonetheless, the increase in prices will necessarily require an increase in savings for a given planned level of investment, thereby creating a crowding-out effect.

Crowding-out also occurs as a result of the reduction in private consumption attendant on the increase in the price level. It therefore follows that a smaller government will have less need to resort to monetising a budget deficit or sourcing it externally unless, of course, such budget deficits are for reasons other than national economic goals. Therefore, based on the static neoclassical model where full employment is assumed an increase in the money supply will be absorbed by an increase in the price level. However, in periods of less than full employment monetising the fiscal budget deficit will be less successful and crowding-out likely will not be an issue.

Another cause of crowding-out is an overvalued real exchange rate caused by a deficit in the balance of payments on current account. The real exchange rate (RER) is defined as the ratio of the price of non-traded goods to the price of traded goods, that is:

$$RER = \frac{\text{Price of non-traded goods}}{\text{Price of traded goods}}$$

Non-traded goods are domestically produced goods and services consumed in the home market. Traded goods are goods produced for exports and compete with non-traded goods in the domestic market when the RER is overvalued; that is, less will be exported relative to imports in consequence.

Hence, an expansion in the money supply to finance government fiscal budget deficits is likely to cause an expansion in domestic demand for traded goods resulting from the increase in the price levels. An increase in imports results in a loss of exports revenue as a consequence of the loss in the competitiveness of the domestic industry on world markets. Also, imports become relatively cheaper because of the increased domestic cost of production reflecting the increase in the general price levels. There is therefore a loss of domestic production to imports. Freeing up resources to the private sector by reducing the demands of government as, for example, by shifting the burden of healthcare and retirement onto the individual is an attempt to effect a change in these relationships.

Where the overvaluation is perceived as severe, currency speculation becomes a major challenge in a liberalised world economy, as was the case in Indonesia and other Southeast Asian countries in the mid- to late 1990s. For example, the balance of payments deficit on current account of these countries almost tracked the differences between savings and investment in almost all cases (see Figure 2.2 page 43). Also, the balance of payments deficit on current account as a percent of

GDP for Thailand, Malaysia and Indonesia were generally greater that their real GDP growth rate; that is, even after adjusting for inflation, inflationary pressures were still coming from the deficits on current account. In the case of Indonesia, the Philippines, Thailand and Malaysia – whose currencies were all pegged to the US Dollar – persistent low inflation in the US served to exacerbate over-valuation in these countries – as evidenced by their persistent deficits on current account and high domestic inflation rates – (see Park and Song 1997) thereby inviting speculation on the eventual devaluation of their currencies.

Empowering the individual

In addition to reducing or eliminating the crowding-out effect, reducing the size of government operates to empower the individual. That is, the individual will be given greater freedom of choice in how income is spent as fewer taxes are required to be paid to the government. This argument, the hallmark of Reagan's conservatism of the 1980s, has been revived by George W. Bush in his quest for an ownership society. As discussed in Chapter 2, this is also an objective of TNP: A reduction in the size of government arguably serves to transfer property rights back to individuals in the form of lower taxes. And since these individuals are generally those with discretionary income, savings likely would increase, given a relatively higher propensity to save at a higher level of income. Such savings would further stimulate private investment resulting from an expectation of lower interest rates, thereby adding to the competitiveness of the TNC. It is this theoretical conception of savings and investments that underlies Arthur Lewis's thesis that inequality is good for growth.

Because income is substantially lower in developing countries than in developed countries, the propensity to consume is greater at these lower income levels, that is, very little would be saved. As such, increases in income levels – access to property rights – resulting from reduced government spending provide marketing opportunities to the TNC. Thus, from the perspective of promoting the endless accumulation of capital and hence the capitalist world-economy, reducing the size of government through privatisation becomes an obvious policy prescription even for poor countries. But despite these rationales, government in the US has grown in terms of both size and budget primarily because of the influence of constituencies.

Improve efficiency

Other conventional arguments for privatisation are based almost exclusively on improving the efficiency of the enterprise. Public enterprises (PE) are by and large deemed to be inefficient because of: Information asymmetries; organisation paralysis and policy drift; and X-inefficiency resulting from poor management.

Information asymmetries

Information asymmetry arises in the public enterprise sector primarily because of different objectives between principal (the government) and agent (the manager of the enterprise) and an inadequate monitoring system. While conflicting objectives between owners and managers exist in private enterprise, they essentially are limited, and usually are mediated by a Board of Directors. Board resolutions set the objectives for the private firm; it is management's job to execute in an efficient and effective manner, usually measured in terms of earnings per share. In the public-enterprise sector on the other hand, conflicting objectives are accentuated. The level of discretionary powers of the PE manager is often restricted by the interplay of politics and the multiplicity of objectives of the principals. For example, operationally an enterprise might be part of the portfolio of a particular operational ministry but because the ministry of finance has access to PE's cash flows the enterprise is quite often subject to the decrees of the ministry of finance: a case in point being GUYSUCO which comes under the ministry of agriculture but which is subject to decrees of the ministry of finance. What is more, in the comparison between private firms and PEs, the former are driven by the profit motive whilst the latter by social costs and benefits considerations (see Henry 1990, 250). This often results in conflicting signals from the principals to managers who try to be as efficient as their counterparts in the private-sector. At the same time, there is the conflicting perception that the focus of the bureaucrat is on complying with procedures and political requirements rather than on operational efficiency. Evidence the observation by the Bank:

> The reluctance on the part of bureaucrats to devise efficient monitoring and incentive systems is believed to arise in principle from their desire to maintain ambiguity so that they can retain control, evade accountability, and possibly form coalitions with PE managers to secure better pay, power, and prestige (Galal 1989, 5).

Organisation paralysis and policy drift

Researchers have found a systemic deficiency in the operation of PEs in the form of organisation paralysis and policy drift. Organisational paralysis occurs when a recommended action that is potentially unfavourable to the politician is deferred or when the personal agenda of the bureaucrat is allowed to be part of the equation. Policy drift occurs when the government does not find favour with the proposal and thus overly extends the decision-making process to be effective. The extensive revision to proposed legislation on government procurement and investment incentive in Guyana, for example, speak to the issue of policy drift.

Under the above operating conditions the PE manager is often not motivated to be performance oriented. One of the goals of privatisation, therefore, is to clarify objectives of the enterprise and to improve the policy-management information network. By this means, clearly defined objectives set by the governing board will be relayed to the enterprise manager who will then be held responsible for performance.

This in turn gives rise to a chain of accountability based on appropriate performance measurements for effective monitoring. In practice, the Chair of the local board – often representing the political interests of the government – seeks to micromanage the enterprise in furtherance of personal or political objectives.

With commercial PEs, the recommended objective is profit maximization similar to that of a private firm. But such an objective necessarily requires that the enterprise be free from non-operating burden. It also requires that the management be given full control of the enterprise resources so that it can achieve the objectives set by the principals. The manager must also be able to freely hire or fire workers and to set competitive prices. The role of the principal also should be clearly defined and be restricted to setting policies. Without these clearly defined principles a profitable and efficient firm is made inefficient and unprofitable through the politics of state control, as experience has shown with industries nationalized pursuant political objectives. This is especially the case where large investments in plant and equipment replacement are required but are not provided for under a system of government budgeting. Indeed, the Third World is full of plant and equipment rusting away in consequence of inappropriate policy options.

Whether or not it is necessary to change ownership to implement the above reforms has been extensively debated, even among the Bank's staff. Evidence the observation that: '... experience suggests that the issue of ownership, although important and a major determinant of economic performance, might not always be the most important. Often, the main issue is the existence of a competitive market rather than private ownership' (Israel 1990, 6). On the other hand, the Guyana experience with commercialisation of GUYSUCO suggests that unless there is strong contract-management a politically-appointed board will have its way most of the time; more so when political support is derived in the industry. Moreover, collusion between the board and the union that is affiliated to the ruling political party is an inevitable hindrance to operating efficiency as the Guyana experience evidences.

X-inefficiency

Inefficiency at the enterprise level is believed to exist because of the existence of X-inefficiency in any business enterprise. According to X-inefficiency theory, because of the separation between ownership and management, objectives will tend to vary between the two.[3]

Whilst owners are interested in profit maximization, managers may not fully subscribe to the goal of profit maximization as the only purpose of their being. Therefore, short of replacing the manager, which can be costly to the enterprise, owners are prepared to allow their managers a certain level of discretionary powers. In the exercise of such discretionary powers it is likely that a less than maximum

[3]   See Liebenstein, H., (1960, 'Allocative efficiency vs. X-Efficiency', in *American Economic Review*.

effort will be devoted to profit maximization. As a consequence, output will be less than optimal, thereby giving rise to X-inefficiency.

It is argued in the literature that, depending on the level of incentives offered to managers, a certain degree of X-inefficiency can be overcome. This argument has given rise to production incentive bonus and stock options as part of a system of incentives in the private sector. Moreover, it is argued that product market competition can be used as a means to reduce managerial slack and X-inefficiency where there exists among competitors a common exogenous cost element that is measurable and upon which a system of incentives can be based (Vickers and Yarrow 1996, 66), as in the case of pollution control in electricity generation, for example. It is similarly argued a system of incentives and performance monitoring can be devised for the PE manager who can then be compensated based on performance. In the case of the Guyana sugar industry, the contract manager indeed was offered a production incentive bonus over 250,000 tonnes of sugar produced in the initial contract; its current agreed compensation is now entirely based on production levels achieved and reflects the control of the incumbent ruling PPP/C government.

Competition

Competition has been identified as central to improving efficiency at the enterprise level. In the case of the public enterprise, however, the PE manager is perceived as less motivated to be efficient than his private-sector counterpart partly because of a lack of competition and the absence of the discipline of the financial market: Most PEs operate in sheltered markets and has access to government funds and to foreign credit at below domestic market rates; the exception are PEs in countries whose governments are restricted by their loan agreements with the IMF and Bank as in the case of countries that have accessed funding under the Poverty Reduction Growth Facility (PRGF) programme or has been designated an HIPC. Additionally, there is no threat to the PE of either being taken-over or liquidated for poor performance; a motivation to be efficient in the private sector. Thus, it is a widely held belief at the Bank that efficiency gains are possible when PEs are made to operate in competitive or contestable markets.

Contestable market

A contestable market exists where entry or exit is not constrained by the requirement of sunken costs (such as factories and manufacturing plants), as opposed to fixed costs. In such a market, any opportunity for profit will be taken advantage of by firms as new entrants whose average costs are less than the prevailing market price (see Baumol *et al.* 1988). Similarly orthodox economics suggests that these firms will exit as quickly as they enter when their average costs are greater than price: Market share is taken away by an existing firm whose marginal cost of production is less than the average cost of its competitor and below the market price for the product.

Under these operating conditions the commercial PE will be forced to be efficient or be liquidated. In practice, however, as has been evidenced by the National Express experience in the UK, deregulation has not always resulted in a more competitive environment. 'The incumbent may retain significant market power, arising, in particular, from technical, financial and brand-name advantages which may deter entry or make the experience of entrants unappealing' (OECD 1992, 36).

In the case of National Express, new entrants to the express coach service were deterred by the incumbent adopting an aggressive pricing policy and effectively utilising its national network and marketing prowess attendant its dominant industry position. In contrast to the National Express experience is the US telecommunications giant AT&T: Despite its brand name and other intrinsic advantages, it struggled to survive in a highly competitive environment characterised in part by predatory pricing and was eventually acquired by one of its off-springs, SBC Communications in late 2005. Evidence also the bankruptcy of MCI, the advocate and eventual victim of competition in the telecommunications market that was dominated by AT&T until the 1984 Consent Decree with the Justice Department.

Implicit in the notion of subjecting the PE to competition and to the setting of performance standards is the ability of the PE to manage costs. However, as is well established in the literature, PEs are rarely free to operate as would be a private firm in a competitive environment. More often than not as mentioned in Chapter 3, PEs are often used as means to redress social inequalities. Patronage, over-staffing, price distortions and extraneous financial burdens are common findings in studies of the commercial PE (see Chapter 3, 92). If, therefore, the PE is to become efficient and to effectively compete in a competitive environment it first must be freed of these extraneous burdens.

Reducing the budgetary burden on the state

Whilst some PEs have been assigned financial burdens by the state, others have been found to be a burden on the government fiscal budget. The contention here is that the flow of government subsidies to inefficient PE is a constraint to economic growth. As discussed in Chapter 3, by reducing subsidies to these inefficient enterprises, the tax burden will be reduced or the savings put to more productive uses, assuming a balanced budget. Because of the current emphasis on reducing the size of government by policy makers, many would prefer the first. This was especially so in the early 1980s in the US and the UK. For example, a popular theory of conservative economists and governments in the 1980s was the regressive nature of taxation. As depicted by the 'Laffer Curve',[4] after a certain level of income any further increase in the marginal tax rate will result in a reduction in taxable income. This argument

---

[4]   The 'Laffer Curve' was developed by Arthur Laffer who contends that increasing the marginal tax rate serves to deter people from seeking additional taxable income. In other words, taxation becomes a disincentive to increasing or even maintaining a level of earnings. The curve thus assumes a concave relationship to the 'X' axis.

was used by the Reagan administration in the US as the basis for reducing both the marginal income tax rates and the capital gains tax; it has been revived by the Bush administration in 2000 in an attempt to reduce the cost basis of the private sector and to increase its access to capital.

With this brief discussion on the theoretical basis as background, the underlying reform perspectives of the US, UK and their influence on restructuring and privatisation in Western Europe, the EEC-3 and Russia and on developing countries are critiqued.

The US perspective

In the US, the growing concern among conservatives over the number and size of social programmes attendant on President Johnson's 'war on poverty' arguably fuelled the clamour for a return to market fundamentalism under President Reagan in the 1980s with privatisation as a central strategy. Reagan had long opposed large-scale social programmes and in consequence broke with the Democratic Party in the early 1960s. As the Republican Governor of California in 1964, he was the first to introduce the concept of cost recovery at state universities.

As an aspect of market fundamentalism, then, privatisation in the US was pursued from the perspective of the need to 'reinvent government' and to aid the competitiveness of the private sector in ways discussed above. Increasing individual freedom of choice, reducing the public provision of goods and services, and introducing competition through deregulation and the de-monopolisation of monopoly service providers were the preferred strategies (see Starr 1989, 52); so also was contracting-out of services that were deemed more efficiently provided by the private sector. Tax reduction was also made an important plank of supply-side economics that informed President Reagan's economics agenda. Adam Smith's invisible hand was thus invoked to support the dismantling of social programmes that were perceived as bordering on socialist ideology. These arguments have been revived by President Bush in 2000 in support of his tax-reduction policy which Democrats view as favouring the wealthy. Moreover, as pointed out by many observes in the US, it is the first time in recent history that tax cuts are proposed concurrently with conducting a war.

Deregulation

The deregulation of airlines in 1978, followed by deregulation of interstate transport, telecommunications and energy sectors in the 1980s and 1990s, and the introduction of competition in these industries evidenced the process of reducing the role of government and the introduction of competition, as did the privatisation of airport services. Not privatised were public transport systems, even though Amtrak, the national railway service, has been a drain on public resources.

The privatisation process slowed somewhat in the wake of the California energy crisis in the late 1990s which many analysts attributed to market imperfection and to the need for some form of regulatory oversight. The bankruptcies of Enron Corporation and WORLDCOM Inc. speak to the opportunity for abuse of market-power in the absence of close regulatory oversight in the telecommunications and energy sectors; the bankruptcies of several of the major airlines speak to the destructive forces of unsupervised competition and, according to Alfred Khan – who was responsible for the deregulation of airlines in the US – to the need for some form of regulatory oversight in the sector, as opposed to unbridled competition envisaged in the 1980s. Moreover, with the bankruptcy of United Air Lines (UAL), Delta, US Airways, and Northwest Airlines – a consequence of deregulation – the Pension Benefit Guarantee Corporation, a federal agency, has assumed the pension obligations of these airlines; in exchange it is being awarded stock in the companies. Also, as a consequence of the terrorist attack on the US on 11 September 2001 there has been recoil from privatisation of certain security-sensitive services considered strategic to national security such as, for example, airport security.

Increasing freedom of choice

Weaknesses notwithstanding, increasing individual freedom of choice continues to be the underlying argument for privatisation in the US, especially in the provision of primary and secondary education, Medicare benefits and social security retirement benefits. Indeed, a stated objective of President Bush is to create an 'ownership society' not unlike Mrs. Thatcher's 'investor class' of some 25 years earlier (see Thatcher 1993; Moore 1986). But despite the strong arguments offered in support for having 'private accounts' as a choice in the social security retirement programme, President Bush's proposal has met with nation-wide opposition. Evidently, opponents view the move as an attempt to reduce future social security retirement benefits and to transfer the risk to the individual. In addition, the theoretical basis for choice expressed in terms of scarcity is seen by some observers as falsely-based (see Polanyi 1977, 24).

It should be noted here that increasing freedom of choice in the US context refers not to a person's ability to choose – a function of increasing capability – but rather to increasing available options to the individual although, to be sure, the two tend to be complementary even for a highly developed economy.

Contracting out

In addition to reducing the tax burden, there is a growing belief that the government should contract out the provision of certain public goods and services to the private sector. As discussed in Chapter 1, proposals for the private provision of education, Medic-care, management of prison facilities and other such services in the US were premised on the notion of the relative efficiency of the private sector. Many of the services presently offered by the US government are regarded as excessively costly in consequence of the bureaucracy they attract and the problems of management discussed above. As argued by proponents of contracting out, by out-sourcing these services, resources will be more efficiently utilized and cost contained if not reduced, thereby reducing the budgetary burden on the state. As a result, contracting out has been pursued by all levels of government on the presumption that it is more efficient because it exposes the service providers – workers in this case – to the rigours of the marketplace in addition to shifting the managerial decision-making process to managers motivated by the need to make a profit.

Contracting out does not however relieve the government from the responsibility of making the decision whether to have the service or not, how much and for whom; these are political decisions. Indeed, the proposal to incorporate private individual accounts as part of the proposed reform of the US Social Security system is an attempt to combine contracting out with transfer of responsibility from the government to the individual.

In addition to the inability to shift responsibility, there are non-economic issues associated with this type of proposal. For example, as widely reported in the US news media on 15 August 1997, inmates from several US states prisons who were sent to a privately-run prison facility in Texas were physically abused by the guards of the private contractor, and have had their civil rights violated. This incident serves as a reminder that privatisation decisions require consideration of factors other than economics. This is especially so in societies where individual rights are held in the highest regard. Evidence also that, in consequence of the 11 September terrorist attack on the US, the federal government has assumed responsibility for airport security previously contracted out on the basis of the inadequacy of the service performed by private contractors and its responsibility to the citizens of the US.

Although extensively pursued as a method of privatisation in the US, contracting out is not unique to the US; many countries especially the developed countries have resorted to contracting out as a means to keeping a lid on costs but as noted above at an increase in political risk.

The UK perspective

In terms of goals, there is consensus among observers that the UK's privatisation programme was first and foremost driven by Mrs. Thatcher's embrace of conservative economics doctrine at a time when Western economies were stagnating in an era of high interest rates, high inflation and high unemployment. Secondly, the challenges associated with the government's ability to borrow on the open market without crowding-out the private sector and with funding investment in the nationalized industries were equally persuasive in a period of high interest rates and global recession.

In consequence and in contrast to the privatisation process in the US, privatisation in the UK was premised on the idea of subjecting state-owned enterprises to the rigours of competition for the betterment of employees, managers and consumers and to reduce reliance upon the state (Moore 1986, 93). To this end the UK privatised most of its state-owned enterprises between 1980 and 1987 by means of public offer of shares, utilising the well-established financial-services infrastructure.

Creating a new enterprise culture

For Mrs. Thatcher, it was propitious for transforming attitudes: creating a new 'enterprise culture' based on wider participation in the private ownership of the country's productive resources; to create a new class of voters. In terms of economics, as stated by John Moore, Financial Secretary of the Treasury, the goals initially were to subject state-owned entities to the rigours of competition for the betterment of employees, managers, and consumers, and to reduce reliance upon the state (Moore 1986, 93). This was generally interpreted to mean: improving internal and allocative efficiency; reducing public sector borrowing requirement; reducing constraints to employee betterment; and widening share ownership to the public and to employees.

To be sure, as noted earlier, the sale of public assets brought in £25 billion to the Treasury, and provided a handsome profit to the original purchasers of fixed-price share offerings. Many issues gained more than 50 percent prior to the stock market sell-off in 1987, indeed, some the next trading day after issue. Rolls Royce for example gained 70 percent on the next trading day. Privatisation also served to reduce the power of the trade unions by transferring public-sector employees to the private sector and through the creation of a 'people's capital market'. These moves followed the sale of public housing in 1979, which was well received by voters who were able to identify themselves as beneficiaries.

With respect to the notion of internal efficiency, the smaller privatised enterprises were already operating in a competitive environment prior to divestiture. However, with respect to the state monopolies, these were turned into private monopolies to the extent that they remained in tact subject to regulation. Internal efficiency was left to be derived from competition among their suppliers and from a regulatory regime that stressed financial and operating discipline (Moore 1986, 97). It is thus in regard to these monopolies that there is disagreement. Whereas the expectation was a dividing-up of the larger monopolies, at least along regional lines, the enterprises were privatised as single units. This was because both management and employees reportedly were against the splitting-up of the entities.

The failure to pursue internal efficiency through the introduction of competition has served to support the contention of the political motives of the programme. In addition, many observers held the view that the regulatory regime adopted was an inferior disciplinary mechanism in comparison to the discipline of competition. Failure to encourage competition in the large privatised monopolies has reportedly resulted in over-charging for some services, especially in the area of telecommunications. Hence, privatisation of telecommunications and utilities did very little to support the argument for efficiency gains at the enterprise level in the initial years.

A case of political opportunism?

In many ways the attendant political opportunities presented by privatisation were not lost on the Thatcher government in that they were ably capitalized upon to influence electoral outcomes in a particular direction. Indeed, the beneficiaries from the sale of public housing in 1979 and from the sale of shares at below-market price arguably showed their gratitude by electing Mrs. Thatcher to a second term in 1984.

The sale of public assets at below market valuation to be sure provided a handsome profit to the original purchasers of fixed-price share offerings. Many stock issues gained more than 50 percent prior to the stock market sell-off in 1987, indeed, some the next trading day after issue: Rolls Royce for example gained 70 percent on the next trading day (see Vickers and Yarrow 1995) Also, by transferring public-sector employees to the private sector and the creation of a 'peoples' capital market' privatisation did indeed create a new capitalist class, an stated objective of Mrs Thatcher (see Thatcher 1993). At the same time, it served to reduce the power of the trade unions, the backbone of the Labour Party.

The combination of benefiting a particular class at the expense of the nation, and the weakening of the trade unions in the process are perceived by some observers as a politically informed privatisation programme. According to Dobek (1993, 64):

> when considered in context of electoral politics, Thatcher's privatization program was a case of a politically-driven campaign aimed at enlarging the electoral base of the ruling party at the expense of the opposition.

As a consequence arguably, support for privatisation declined from a net high of 21 percent in 1981 to 4 percent in 1987 (Crewe 1989, 249). At the same time, support for the trade unions increased from 56 percent in 1979–1982 to 70 percent in 1987–1988.[5] However, public support for the unions has fallen steeply since 1988.

When viewed from the perspective of the political opposition, notwithstanding the raising of £25 billion Sterling for the UK Treasury, the process was seen more in terms of being politically propitious, for transforming attitudes, creating a new 'enterprise culture' and a new class of voters based on wider participation in the private ownership of the country's productive resources. But despite its early conservative political underpinnings, privatisation continued under the Labour government as evidenced by the government's announced plans in 1998 to sell US$4.9 billion of state assets.[6]

Politics notwithstanding, the goals of the UK's privatisation programme were achieved within the existing political environment of the time. Despite objections from trade unions and others who saw the process as asset stripping, or found the process deficient as it relates to state-monopolies, the programme was largely successful. The re-election of Mrs. Thatcher to a third term served to validate her policies. More importantly, however, was the fact that the goals of privatisation were

---

[5]   Gallup Political Index 337, September 1988, 14.

[6]   Bray, N., 'Britain's Labor, Miming Tories, Unveils 3-Year Privatization Plan', *The Wall Street Journal*, 12 June 1998, p. A9.

well within the absorptive capacity of the economy and were implemented without the social disruption that attended the process in developing countries. Hence, 42 businesses employing over 900,000 workers were privatised by 1990; and by 1997, coal, railways and nuclear power plants were firmly situated within the private sector. British Telecom (BT), privatised on 20 November 1984 has proven criticisms to be premature: According to Foreman-Peck:

> prices came down, waiting lists for telephone vanished in the early 1980s and never reappeared, most faults were cleared quickly, and even public telephones began to work, once the industry regulator cracked his whip.[7]

The Western European perspective

The economic and political benefits of privatisation as evidenced by the UK's experience were also not lost on the Europeans. The Western European programmes also sought to widen the ownership base through public share-offering in the enterprises privatised coupled with regulation in the case of monopoly service providers. As a result, despite problems with the privatisation of *Groupe des Assurances Nationales* (GAN) and the failure of the *Renault* privatisation to provide quick profits to investors, France has been second only to the UK in privatising.[8] France also introduced the concept of privatising on the basis of securing core investors or strategic partner as in the privatisation of *Compagnie Financiere de Suez; Paribas, Mantra; and Banque du Bàtiment*. The privatisation of France Telecom was also a major project for France.

The privatisation of Germany's *Deutsche Telekom* in November 1996 and the privatisation of Italy's telecommunication network Stet in 1997 served to widen the process in Western Europe.[9] Other important privatisation undertaken in Western Europe included the public share-offering by Spain's *Empresa Nacional de Electricidad* SA that brought in approximately US$7.2 billion, the biggest ever undertaken by Spain. Prior to that, in January 1997 the Spanish government taking advantage of the stock-market euphoria of the time raised 607 billion pesetas from the sale of 21 percent of *Telefonica* in the secondary market.[10]

Clearly, the wholesale privatisation which took place in the UK in the 1980s could not be accomplished with equal rapidity and success in Western Europe. Although both Western Europe and the UK pursued social-welfare as policy, it is well recognised that whereas, the UK's experiment with social-welfare really began with the nationalisation of the commanding heights of the economy in 1948, in Europe the

---

[7]   'How privatisation has changed Britain', *BBC News*, December 3, 2004, http://news. bbc.co.uk/2/hi/business/4061613.stm.

[8]   'Privatization in Europe: Is the price right?', *The Economist*, 23 November 1996. p. 87.

[9]   'Privatisation: A sorry way to sell the state', *The Economist*, 18 January 1997. p. 72.

[10]   Vitzthum, C., 'Endesa Share Offering Outcome May Set Tone of Spain's Privatization Effort', *The Wall Street Journal*, 5 September 1997, p. A7C.

concept underwrote modern European socioeconomic structure. Hence, in the case of the UK's programme, it was clearly a case of returning to market fundamentalism, reversing nationalisation if you will. In this regard, it was as easy for the UK to be in lock step with the US in terms of embracing market fundamentalism as it was for both France and Germany to proceed cautiously in their respective welfare states. This contrast is no more evident than in Prime Minister Blair, as Chair of the EU in the second half of 2005, calling for reform of the EU's CAP in support of the US proposal to end farm subsidies, and France's President Chirac's reluctance to end farm subsidies. At the same time, it is a credit to privatisation in Europe that *Deutsche Telekom* announced in early November 2005 a proposal to retrench 32,000 employees over three years in consequence of 'fierce competition in the sector'.

The Eastern European perspective

As noted earlier, the theoretical basis for privatisation as originally conceived received a dramatic boost when Hungary, Poland and Czechoslovakia – now Czech Republic – (EEC-3), encouraged by the prospects to joining a prosperous EU, and in the case of Hungary and Poland, by substantial debt forgiveness, opted to return to a market-economic paradigm following Gorbachev's call for *glasnost* and political reforms in 1987. Gorbachev initiated the process of restructuring – *perestroika* – as an aspect of modernisation of the economic system on an individual country basis in the region in an atmosphere of *glasnost* and *demokratizacya*, (Gorbachev 1987, 163) and thus unwittingly paved the way for full conversion to a market economic system by most of these countries. They were later joined by Russia on the dissolution of the Soviet Union in 1991.

In terms of approaches, Hungary's privatisation programme preceded the Czech Republic's and Poland's, and was the most market-oriented of all EEC-3 programmes. Nonetheless, they all followed a stepped-approach, with Hungary and Poland being guided by the IMF and Bank throughout the process. The Czech Republic and Russia in contrast went the way of broad-based ownership mainly through distribution as discussed in Chapter 6.

In terms of number of transactions, Hungary outranked both Poland and the Czech Republic with 140 enterprises privatised between 1989 and 1992 and continued its programme well into the late 1990s. Poland was second with 67, while the Czech Republic, preferring to take a less aggressive approach to the process and seeking to be more inclusive of the local population, was third with 55 entities (14 in 1991 and 41 in 1992). The Czech Republic was also not in search of debt-forgiveness from Western creditor-nations and thus pursued a more broad-based approach by means of the voucher system.

In terms of sales proceeds, Hungary's sales revenues totalled approximately US$2.5 billion; the Czech Republic's, US$1.9 billion; and Poland's US$714.0 million (Sader 1993, 21).

Transition to a market economy

The ease with which the EEC-3 effected the transition to a market economy should surprise no one. The three countries were established market economies prior to their forced entry into a central-planning economic system in 1948. Indeed, as part of the Austro-Hungarian Empire the EEC-3 countries were examples of European capitalism: commercial code, business law and other laws supportive of individual property rights and a market economy were established institutions. But with the liberation of Eastern Europe by the Soviet army and the subsequent agreements among the victorious Allies at Yalta, these countries came under the Soviets sphere of influence: nationalisation, collectivisation, and central economic planning, were enforced by Soviet tanks in Budapest in 1956, and in Prague in 1968, and by puppet governments in East Germany and other Eastern European countries.

Staying in contact with the West   Another factor contributing to the ease of transition of the EEC-3 to a market economic system was the unbroken trade links with the West, especially with West Germany. Trade with the West more than tripled in most cases after 1970, especially with West Germany in consequence of Bonn's Ostpolitik and the growing discontent with Soviet repression (see Rutland 1997, 301). As conceived, Bonn's *Ostpolitik*, was essentially one of reducing its dependency on the Allies for its security, preferring economic engagement with the Eastern European countries, especially East Germany with which reunification was an ever present desire of the Bonn government (see Joffe 1989, 119). Hence, for most of the period between Prague Spring (1968) and Gorbachev's *Perestroika*, the EEC-3 countries were reminded of their economic heritage through this contact with the West.

Developing countries' perspective

A discerning feature of privatisation in the developing countries is that the goals set depended to a large extent on the contribution of the public-enterprise sector to GDP and the level of external debt. With respect to the first, according to Galal (1991: ix), the contribution to GDP by state-owned enterprises varies considerably: Excluding China, it averaged 3.0 percent in Asia, 17 percent in Africa and 12 percent in Latin America in the late 1980s. In the case of Africa, the percentage contribution varied from a high of 40 percent in the Sudan and 37.8 percent in the Zambia, to a low of 8.1 percent in Kenya and 6.8 percent in Liberia (Nellis 1986, 7). As to the level of external debt, Table 3.2 (page 64) shows that whereas, in 1983 external debt for the listed countries were with few exceptions below 50 percent of GNP, by 1994 such debts more than doubled in both absolute amounts and as a percentage of GNP. Thus, the common theme that runs through the literature with respect to the goals of privatisation is the need to reduce the size of the state and the external debt burden.

As a primary instrument of economic reform in developing countries, privatisation benefited from the phenomenon of the Debt Crisis and an increasing debt burden, with the UK's programme as the benchmark, country condition notwithstanding. Hence, privatisation prescriptions to developing countries reflected a bias for traditional economic results and were vigorously pursued by the MFIs as mandated by the Washington Consensus, particularly the creation of investment opportunities for Western investors and the servicing of external debts owed mainly to Western money-centre banks and institutions. Privatisation was therefore not an option but a requirement; often under the IMF's Enhanced Structural Adjustment Facility (ESAF). Indeed, for those countries that sought debt relief under Paris Club[11] arrangements, an important condition to participation was that the debtor country must undertake restructuring measures, including privatisation. Hence privatisation in developing countries took on two distinct characteristic: 'market supremacy with an ideological fervor' (Stiglitz 2002, 73) and conversion to democracy.

Fundamental structural reform

With the Washington Consensus as doctrine, privatisation was pursued from the perspective of fundamental structural reform guided by the IMF and Bank whose rigidity reflected the switch in policy in keeping with the Baker Plan, the forerunner to the Washington Consensus. The standard IMF and Bank prescription therefore was for liquidation of non-viable state-owned enterprises and sale of those that were deemed better run by the private sector; rehabilitation and restructuring were restricted to only those state-owned enterprises 'whose performance is critical to the success or failure of other actors in the economy' (Galal 1991, 1). Moreover, the belief that the necessary institutions will as a matter of course follow the establishment of property rights and that any attendant negative fall out should be short lived served to reinforce a one-size-fits-all approach to the process in developing countries.

Further justifying the IMF's aggressive approach to privatisation in developing countries was the belief that, '... theories that place entire causal weight on external factors' have neglected to consider exacerbating forces within developing countries (Husain 1994, 5). As a result, of the 147 Bank-supported public enterprise reform projects at the end of June 1989, 67 were under structural adjustment, 36 of which were in Africa. Also, of the total projects, 80 were located in Africa (see Galal 1991, 14). In addition, there were 74 Bank projects with divestiture component: 45 were located in 22 African countries, 18 in nine Latin American countries (including five in Jamaica) and seven in four Asian countries.

The automatic resort to privatisation under IMF loan agreements and Paris Club arrangements has led to the observation that 'the ability of international institutions to push privatisation increases directly with the borrower's level of desperation' (Babai 1988, 269). Indeed, the roles of the IMF and Bank were widely perceived as

---

[11]   The Paris Club is mainly made up of the governments of OECD countries for the purpose of avoiding default of loans made by member-states to the severely indebted low income countries.

imposing restructuring policies in order to ensure repayment of Third World debts to the commercial lenders.

To be sure, many of the debt-restructuring and rescheduling have been with the primary purpose of repaying old debts and commercial bank loans. Where proceeds from privatisation were found inadequate, soft loans were made available as shown by Helleiner (1992). Even then, as shown in Table 3.2 (page 64) external debts more than tripled in absolute terms as well as a percent of GNP for most of the countries cited.

Moreover, as further shown by Helleiner (1992) since 1984 the inflows in International Development Association (IDA) soft loans more than doubled on an annual basis while private debts were being repaid at the same time, significantly so between 1984 and 1987, thereby correlating positively with the changed status of the money-centre banks in 1987 (see Chapter 1 page 7) and with the increase in external debts of the developing countries.

Clearly, a conversion from commercial loans to IDA soft loans was taking place. In addition, net outflows to the IMF and Bank began to increase in 1987 as repayments and interest more than doubled on an annual basis since 1984. At the same time, private capital flows were largely being directed to the Asian and Latin American regions in consequence of the liberalisation of the global financial markets and the greater potential for profits in these regions.

As noted in Chapter 1 (page 10), despite pressure from the IMF and Bank, except for privatisation in the larger developing countries of Latin America and East Asia, the process had not met with equal success over the years. The number of enterprises privatised in developing countries between 1988 and 1994 totalled about 3,300 with revenues of US$112 billion derived mainly from privatisation in Latin America.

Reform or asset-stripping?

The privatisation imperative conditioned upon the poorer developing countries, mainly African, fostered the perception among many of their leaders that privatisation programmes were essentially 'asset-stripping', favouring foreign investors, and as in the eyes of the former President of Tanzania, 'looting public resources'.[12] Many of these leaders point to the fire-sale prices at which their country's assets were sold to foreigners. At the same time, as is well documented in the literature, endemic corruption in developing countries also served to exacerbate the perception of asset-stripping, not by politicians but by citizens: Investors eager to acquire productive assets at below market valuation or to regain access to previously confiscated assets willingly accommodated rent-seeking local public officials. In the cases of re-privatising confiscated assets, the MFIs have been known not only to turn a blind eye to some level of corruption but also willingly address the concerns of the foreign investor. In consequence, public officials and politicians have become

---

[12] Africa Information *Afrique*, http//www.Achrive/newsletterslafrica_information_afrique_net/Tanzania/1995/950816.tan.Public Firms.

adept at 'gaming' the process, with the spoils shared among conspirators; a practice that has alarmed the IFI and the international donor community, resulting in a greater coordination among donor agencies in monitoring the utilisation of donor resources.

But foreign investors were not the only beneficiaries from the privatisation of the period. The creation of oligarchs in Russia evidenced the scramble by local speculators to acquire property rights in previously state-owned enterprises. In Guyana, local investors also took advantage of the sale-of-asset approach and acquired commercially-viable enterprises at below market valuation. Indeed, in the latter case, notwithstanding expressed concerns over earlier privatisations, Guyana Stores Limited was privatised on the basis of a substantial cash deposit in US dollars brought in from the US in a suitcase by the local purchaser, with no questions asked as to derivation; the unpaid balance of the purchase price is yet to be collected by the Guyana government at the time of writing.

Conversion to democracy

With respect to political reform, as is increasingly recognised in the literature the lending policies of the IMF and the Bank have more boldly incorporated issues of governance in recent years notwithstanding that their respective Charters require them to be politically neutral and to refrain from interfering in the political affairs of member countries.[13] To be sure, loans by these institutions have come to be premised on the notion that social and economic progress is not possible without effective and reliable public-sector institutions. According to James Wolfensohn, former President of the Bank, '[h]istory has repeatedly shown that good governance is not a luxury but a necessity. Without an effective state, sustainable development, both economic and social, is impossible'. Evidencing the emphasis on political governance, the number of countries pursuing democracy has been increasing since the late 1980s.

Other goals

Outside of the goals implicit in IMF structural adjustment loans and Paris Club membership, there are explicit operational objectives of privatisation. The theoretical rationale for these objectives has been discussed above. In order to achieve these objectives a combination of reform policies (including divestiture) were proposed and implemented with varying degrees of success.

Where reforms were implemented, increased profitability at the enterprise was the result, as in Thailand and Turkey, or losses reduced, as in Mauritius, Niger and Mali. However, even within the Bank there were concerns that 'the argument that the size of the public sector needs to be drastically reduced has been taken too far, without really analysing the full consequences of the shift. Often the dismantling of some functions implies the establishment of others' (Galal 1991, 3). Indeed, because

---

[13] See Article III, Section 5b of the *World Bank's Articles of Agreement*.

the public enterprise sector in many developing countries plays a significant role in societal integration, economic reforms mechanisms have led to social disruption not catered for in the Washington Consensus. The above points are made clearer by further pursuing the contrasting experiences of selected developing countries.

Selected country experience

The country experiences discussed below reflect the differences in goals and indeed outcomes even among developing countries.

Nigeria

Like most newly independent African states, Nigeria pursued control of the 'commanding heights' of its economy as policy not long after its independence. Fuelled by windfall oil revenues starting with the first oil-shock in 1973, it became the largest state-owned economy in Sub-Saharan Africa: 35 percent of GDP came from the public sector made up of 275 federally owned enterprises and 600 states' enterprises. Of the federally-owned enterprises, two-thirds were in commercial ventures that many observers believed would have been better left to the private-sector. In addition, Nigeria, like most Sub-Saharan Africa countries had focused more on 'indigenization' than on the changing politics of international economic relations of the late 1970s and early 1980s. Added to the endogenous factors were consequences arising from exogenous factors – falling commodity prices, and high interest rates – which were not anticipated and, therefore, were not protected against out of inexperience as an independent sovereign state.

For Nigeria, then, with a bloated public sector and an industrial sector operating at about 35 percent capacity (Lewis 1990, 278) the goals of privatisation were not to enhance employee opportunities for greater benefits or consumer surplus, nor indeed to widen or deepen the base of local shareholders. Rather, they were dictated by the failure to develop the disciplinary mechanisms necessary to effectively manage a modern economy in good times and bad and, of course, endemic corruption. With a public sector that was incurring an estimated net annual outflow of about US$2.0 billion (Lewis 1990, 279), the goals of privatisation were simply to rationalise the sector. Such action would significantly reduce the public sector claims to 40 percent of the government's non-salary budget, and thereby free up resources for debt servicing, a primary objective of the Baker Plan. In this connection, unlike most other developing countries undergoing structural adjustment, Nigeria decided in 1985 not to avail itself to an IMF structural adjustment loan and to pursue its own reform program with the assistance of the Bank.

The conditions under which the goals of privatisation were pursued in Nigeria were, however, very different from those of the UK. In addition to a deteriorated infrastructure and a private sector that was suspect in terms of its absorptive capacity and willingness to undertake risks, its agricultural sector was also in shambles.

As noted in Chapter 1, world commodity prices were the lowest since the Great Depression and extensive drought in the region had taken its toll. Furthermore, Nigeria had incurred a huge external debt burden which had to be serviced. As shown in Table 3.3 (page 87), Nigeria stock of external debt grew from US$ 11.7 billion in 1983 to US$ 32.8 billion in 1989, an increase of 180.3 percent. As a result, debt service as a percent of exports increased from 18.6 percent in 1983 to 21.3 percent in 1989, despite restructuring and rescheduling; it reached US$ 33.48 billion in 1994. In addition, interest payment as a percent of outflows was 78.5 percent in 1989. Thus, whilst the need for reform was greater than for most countries, the costs of reform were even greater in terms of economic consequences and social disruption. Nonetheless, Nigeria's record on privatisation in Sub-Saharan Africa has been better than most, having sold 29 out of 140 PE for US$110 million between 1988 and 1992. And even though one of the 29 sales accounted for US$50 million or 45 percent of the total sales proceeds, Nigeria has been rated by the Bank as one of the countries that is moderately successful with privatisation (Megyery & Sader 1997, 6). Indeed, in 1994, although the stock of external debt increased to US$33.48 billion, it declined as a percentage of GNP from 1989 level. Indeed, Nigeria was one of the few countries that experienced a reduction in both the debt-GDP ratio and the debt-service cost-export ratio. Despite these positive indicators, as reported in the Economist, the Nigerian government took a defiant stance to further privatisation. One minister has been quoted as saying: 'We have so much oil, that we can do without your money and your advice'.[14]

South Africa

Although not considered a developing country in the ordinary sense of the term, the South Africa experience stands out as a unique example of how inherent structural impediments to social, economic, and political inclusion can be overcome by refocusing national energies to nation-building objectives within the existing framework of market-supporting institutions: Black Africanism in this instance was not described in terms of tearing down of otherwise functional institutions. How this was achieved bears examination if only as a potential model for those who still find the concept of inclusion a challenge.

Reconstruction and Development Programme

After decades of apartheid rule, South Africa came under a democratically-elected government headed by Nelson Mandela for the first time on 1 May 1994. At the outset, the focus was not on retribution but rather on reconciliation, reconstruction and development. Hence, in the same year the government set up the Reconstruction and Development Programme [RDP] Fund pursuant to the RDP Fund Act, 1994. Under the administration of the ministry of finance, the goals of the RDP Fund were

---

14   'Nigeria: Privatisation? Forget it', in *The Economist*, 18 January 1997.

to get key programmes started; to have the goals of the RDP reflected in the budget; to encourage institutional reform; and to facilitate the restructuring of the public sector; all with a focus on redressing the social outrages committed under apartheid.[15]

On 26 July 1995, the Cabinet of the newly elected government appointed a committee to devise a growth plan for the country's economy. The mandate given to the committee was to determine the status of the economy up to 1994, identify constraints to growth, and to arrive at a plan that would grow the economy through policies that reflect the diversity of the country and encourage full participation by all South Africans.[16] This led to the approval of a set of RDP projects by the government. The underlying objective of the RDP was and continues to be to bring about national unity within South Africa through an all inclusive programme of economic and social reforms.

On 8 May 1996, the Constitution of the Republic of South Africa was adopted and took effect on 3 February 1997. It reflected the goals and aspirations of a nation reborn in the spirit of '… peace, national unity and the invisibility of the Republic'.[17] In 1997 the government's budget fully reflected the goals of the RDP as an integral aspect of government policy. As such, the RDP continued to define the country's economic and social development and its institutions into the twenty-first century.

One of the underlying objectives of the RDP was to accelerate the growth rate of the economy, to an annual rate of about 6.0 percent; and required as a strategy improvement in the country's competitiveness in the global market. This required the South African currency to be devalued – which occurred in February 1996 – and provided a window of opportunity for producers of traded goods, notwithstanding the resultant increase in import prices for capital goods and intermediate inputs. At the same time, control of inflation required that government expenditure be reduced and interest rates kept high. By April 1996, the interest rate was raised to 16 percent from 12 percent in 1993. It was achieved in a stepped-process: One percent in September 1994, followed by three additional increases of one percent. As reported by the South African government, 'the maintenance of positive real interest rates over the past few years have not only brought inflation down to single-digit levels, but have also, with the exception of recent developments, reduced the volatility of a number of financial variables'.[18]

---

[15] Government of South Africa, 'Financing the RDP', http://www.southafrica.net/economy/finance/rpd.html.

[16] As part of the evaluation process, it was determined that the then current rate of growth of 3.0 percent was inadequate to provide a level of employment that would be needed for the projected increase in population. It was determined that South Africa would require to grow its economy at about 6.0 percent annually if unemployment was to be reduced from its high levels, and poverty substantially lowered.

[17] Government of South Africa, Constitution of the Republic of South Africa 1996, 2.

[18] Government of South Africa, 'A Review of Economic Developments Since 1994', http://www.css.gov.za/economy/finance/app1.html.

Other monetary policy reforms included relaxing exchange control and abolishing the 'financial rand'[19] in 1995 and the acceleration of the Reserve Bank's withdrawal from the forward exchange market.[20] Sterilisation of large capital inflows since mid-1994 enabled the government to maintain some control over the Rand's tendency to appreciate in real terms, a tendency that was observed in 1995 in consequence of short-term capital inflows. The bank's gold and foreign reserves holdings were increased by Rand 9.1 billion during 1995.[21]

In addition to monetary policies implemented since 1995 in pursuit of the objectives of the RDP, the government took steps toward trade liberalisation. The lifting of trade sanctions that were imposed by the OECD countries against South Africa enabled the African National Union (ANU) government to relax its restrictions on imports. Quantitative restrictions were replaced by tariffs; existing tariff structure was rationalised by the elimination of almost half the number of tariff lines; phasing out of remaining tariffs began in 1995; import surcharges were completely abolished in October 1995; and the general export incentive scheme was completely phased out in 1997.

In an effort to rebuild its economy, tax incentives, including an increase in depreciation allowances, were offered to existing manufacturers. Beginning 1 July 1996 manufacturers were allowed to write-off plant and machinery over three years. This new tax provision applied to new plant and machinery placed into service between 1 July 1996 and 31 September 1999. In addition, manufacturers were allowed to depreciate manufacturing buildings over ten years. As an added boost to foreign investment, the non-resident shareholder tax was abolished effective 1 October 1995.[22]

Further reflecting the objectives of the RDP, a tax holiday scheme was introduced based on the nature of the projects. The main criteria for its duration were the level of domestic value added; foreign exchange conservation; labour absorption; and regional location, identified as 'manufacturing development zones'.[23]

Privatisation

An important aspect of the RDP was the privatisation of state-owned enterprises. As part of the evaluation and recommendation process with respect to privatisation, six sectoral task groups were set up to devise a set of guidelines with respect to the restructuring of state-owned enterprises. Proposals for privatisation were to identify the modality chosen from a list that included either full or partial privatisation,

---

[19]   The financial rand was one of a two-system exchange rate regime employed by South Africa to distinguish between non-resident and resident foreign exchange transactions.

[20]   The Reserve Bank returned to the forward exchange market as a market-maker after the rand was depreciated.

[21]   Government of South Africa, 'Exchange Rate Development', in A Review of Economic Developments.

[22]   See Government of South Africa 1995 Budget.

[23]   Government of South Africa, 'Memorandum on Tax Incentives for Investment'.

strategic investors, sale of concessions and private-sector contracts based on the groups' analysis of how best to achieve the government's stated objectives. Private-sector input was an essential aspect of the process, and in September 1995 a set of guidelines was approved by the government.

In keeping with expected recommendations from the task groups, state-owned enterprises were divided into three main categories: Category 1 comprised those enterprises that were considered essential to 'providing basic needs' and included all essential infrastructures. Category 2, included enterprises that, although had some significance to public policy or public interest, were not considered essential infrastructure. Category 3 included those enterprises that had no justifiable reason for being included in the public sector. On this basis, privatisation became an integral aspect of South Africa's reconstruction.

The main objectives of the recommended restructuring programme were:

> .... the facilitation of economic growth, to fund the RDP, to create wider ownership in the South African economy, to mobilise private sector capital, to reduce state debt, to enhance competitiveness of state enterprises, to promote fair competition and to finance growth and requirements for competitiveness.[24]

These policy-objectives were common to all infrastructure reforms within South Africa but played out differently based on the specific requirement and importance of the sector. For example, in the case of the water sector resources were diverted from other government expenditure programmes which were in existence prior to the adoption and implementation of the RDP. This was an explicit policy decision as a way to partially fund the infrastructure restructuring programme[25] which was conceived as promoting economic activity and increasing employment in outlying cities and towns previously neglected under apartheid.

Trinidad and Tobago

There are parallels that can be drawn between T&T and Nigeria: Both were unable to control the effects of the sudden windfall of oil revenues; both expanded their respective public-sector enterprises by the bounty; and both suffered from the collapse in oil prices in the 1980s. However, unlike Nigeria, the development of T&T's public-sector was motivated by the legacy of slavery and indenture labour under colonialism. But in seeking to put into operation its policy of inclusiveness as opposed to indigenisation, T&T grew its public-sector out of proportion in relation to its private sector. Hence by 1985, PE accounted for approximately 16 percent of GDP, 13 percent of formal sector employment and 26 percent of national capital investment (Adam et al. 1992, 182). In addition to the large capital outlays, the

---

[24]   Government of South Africa, 'Privatisation', http://www.southafrica.net/economy/ profile/private.html.

[25]   Address by The South African Minister of Finance on 18 February 1997.

government also heavily subsidised its public utilities which were accumulating substantial operating deficits.

With the collapse of oil prices in the mid-1980s, the state enterprises became dependent on government transfers. In this regard, T&T was no different from Nigeria, or any other developing country for that matter. By 1985 T&T found itself facing macro-economic collapse like many other developing countries of the period.

Like Nigeria, T&T was equally reluctant to rationalise its public sector, preferring instead to restructure and to force internal efficiency by reducing subsidies to those enterprises that were capable of effecting internal economies. By 1986 subsidies to the state-owned enterprises had been halved from their 1984 levels. However, a change in government in 1986 saw the articulation of a new, more pragmatic PE reform policy.

The primary objective of the new policy on public-enterprise reform was the rationalisation of the public sector through privatising those entities that could be more efficiently operated by the private sector and liquidating those that were deemed incapable of becoming viable enterprises – the standard IMF and Bank approach if you will. In addition, the services sector was to be rationalised, and the restructuring of strategically important enterprises which were to remain under state ownership were to be undertaken (Adam et al. 1992, 186). This programme was very similar to the one developed for Jamaica, and in effect was in keeping with the Bank's new approach to privatisation. Despite these efforts at reforms, T&T found itself in the 'debt trap' like many of its smaller contemporaries. As shown by Adam *et al.* (1992, 178) T&T external debt grew from US$887.0 million in 1983 to US$2,012 million in 1989, an increase of 126.8 percent. As a consequence debt service as a percentage of exports increased from 2.8 percent in 1983 to 12.3 percent in 1989. Interest payments accounted for 68.0 percent of outflows in 1989. As such, T&T was also borrowing to service its external debt.

Based on national income aggregates, the performance of T&T's public enterprises appeared to have improved following the reform programme instituted by the National Alliance for Reconstruction (NAR) government. At the end of 1994, GDP recovered to US$ 4.8 billion, although still considerably less that the US$ 6.2 billion achieved in 1980. However, despite the recovery in GDP, between 1989 and 1994, as shown in Table 3.2 (page), T&T's external debt grew by 10.2 percent to US$2,218 million. More troubling was the debt-service cost-export ratio which increased from 12.3 percent in 1989 to 31.6 percent in 1994.

Notwithstanding T&T's struggle to regain its former income per capita levels, a significant feature of its public-enterprise reform programme was that it was applied slowly enough to be encompassing of all state-owned enterprises. It was also implemented with due cognizance to the need for diversity in a multi-ethnic society.

But T&T was not unique in this approach, nor did the goals of privatisation remained focused on debt repayment that characterised the process in the 1980s. Indeed, in Africa build, own and operate (BOO) predominated in the telecommunications and electricity sectors, with management contract and concession as the next best, whilst divestiture was de-emphasised (see AFDB 1999). Even when divestiture was pursued, it was on the basis of joint venture with the government retaining an interest either in reserve for local investors or as a means to having a say in the future direction of the enterprise, especially if it were a monopoly. Botswana, and Mauritius, being regarded the more politically stable countries in Africa evidence successful BOO and, indeed, set the standard in Africa.

Malaysia

Malaysia offers yet another example of pursuing privatisation premised on benefiting a particular population group. Also, Malaysia's privatisation was not limited to raising cash or to the infusion of private-sector efficiency. A wider distribution of the country's wealth was a goal of the government's programme, especially as it affects the 'Bumiputera'.[26] Hence, in the case of the divestiture of the Malaysian International Shipping Corporation Bhd (MISC) there was a pre-placement of 29.4 percent of the shares with Bumiputera institutions. In so doing, the technique of having a collective investment programme for the underprivileged was employed. In addition, a block of shares – 3.5 percent – was reserved for employees, with the remainder offered to the public. Even in the public offering, 30 percent of the shares were reserved for Bumiputera institutions. In adopting this method of divestiture of MISC and indeed many other state-owned enterprises, the Malaysia government outwardly acknowledged the need to respect and protect the ethnic diversity of the country.

The targeting of Malays and Bumiputera institutions was not free of controversy. In addition to questioning the choice of candidates for privatisation, Tan Wooi Syn (2004, 374) raised the issue of patronage becoming a key feature of the process. He further pointed to weak institutions and '… a highly centralized and autocratic decision-making process which was in reaction to increased factional rivalries within the ruling Malay party'. The failure of the government to act against non-performing privatised companies such as MAS that had to be resold to the government in 2000 was cited as evidencing an ill-thought out privatisation programme (Tan Wooi Syn 2004, 372). Be that as it may, such a critique could be viewed as evidencing presentism to the extent that the financial difficulties faced by MAS in 2000 were universally applicable to airlines around the world in consequence of higher fuel costs. This is not to deny that MAS was inefficiently run or that its privatisation was tainted by corruption.

Conclusion

In this chapter the goals of privatisation have been critiqued from the perspective of both developed and developing countries. As shown, the goals between the developed

---

[26]   Refers to indigenous Malay people.

and developing countries were largely determined by the emphasis of repaying external debts and re-orienting to a market economy; demography, geography and the absence of institutions notwithstanding. In the case of the developed countries as exemplified by the US and UK experiences, the goals were to effect a re-orientation of the public provision of goods and services away from the state. How these goals were pursued will be analysed in the following chapter.

Chapter 5

Techniques of Privatisation

Introduction

A critical component to a successful privatisation programme is the strategy or techniques employed. There are basically three approaches to the privatisation process: Deregulation, that is, the removal of government controls over the private provision of goods and services and contracting out – both of which have been conducted to a large extent in the US, with the latter now routinely practised at all levels of government – and the rationalisation of the public sector so as to maximize the benefits from a more efficient and effective use of resources under a market economic system as envisaged by orthodox economics. With respect to the latter, privatisation may take one of several forms and is largely dictated by the goals of the programme.

As discussed in Chapter 4, abstracting from the EEC-3 and Russian privatisation which were premised on notions of complete transformation of whole societies, the goals of privatisation varied considerably between the developed and developing countries; and even among developing countries based on their respective indebtedness to the developed countries and on their form of governance. As such, the techniques adopted reflected these differences. In addition, the privatisation process was an evolving one even in the developed countries and to some extent reflected aspects of political expediency. In other cases the approach was one that was best suited to the government's perception of an effective strategy. In the case of the US, for example, the process as discussed in Chapter 3 was mainly one of deregulation with reducing the size and cost of government provisions in deference to the private sector a goal of President Reagan. In the case of France, for example, unlike other countries, proceeds from the sale of PE were not included in the general budget, but were used to either reduce the public debt or to prepare other state-owned enterprises for privatisation.

Theoretical framework

As would be expected, the various techniques of privatisation are rooted in the business practices of the capitalist world-economy and radiate from the developed countries to the developing countries as the model. The techniques adopted are a function of the goals discussed in Chapter 4 which in the case of developing countries are usually prescribed by the IMF, tempered by the condition of the enterprise to be privatised, the absorptive capacity of the domestic capital markets and the perceptions of foreign investors (see Poirson 1998; Servén 1997; Vuylsteke 1988; and Nankani 1988).

The existence of the necessary institutional infrastructure discussed in chapter 2 is a fundamental theoretical assumption. As such, prior to 1989 and before the EEC-3 countries began their transition to a market economic system privatisation took the form of one or a combination of the following well-established business financial techniques: divestiture of ownership, joint venture with the private sector, lease or management contract. These are examined and are related to the existence of the necessary institutions.

Divestiture

However rationalised, divestiture of public provision of goods and services is the shrinking of those public goods and services and is the preferred mode of privatisation in policy recommendation by the IMF and Bank, especially in the wake of the Debt Crisis. More often than not, then, divesture refers to the sale of enterprises in which the government has an ownership interest either in whole or in part, with the adopted method of sale reflecting the underlying goals of the divestment. Thus, divestiture of a PE may be by way of:

- public offering of shares;
- private sale of shares;
- infusion of private capital;
- sale of assets;
- reorganisation into smaller units; and
- management/employee buy-out.

These techniques are embedded in the business culture of a capitalist world economy which as discussed in Chapter 2 evolved over the centuries. Their effectiveness therefore assumes the existence of the necessary ideological and institutional framework of a market system on the one hand and the absorptive capacity on the other.

For divestiture to be effective, the public must have the confidence in the government's willingness and ability to protect their rights against any and all prior claims upon the assets of the enterprise where there is uncertainty surrounding ownership. It further presumes the existence of a credible legal system.

Public offering of shares

The public offering of shares is the technique of choice where the goal is to promote wide-spread ownership of an enterprise utilizing the capital market. As implied, the institution of property rights is central to the concept and requires the economic, legal and regulatory infrastructure of a capitalist economic system. Hence in addition to the institution of a credible financial market such as the London Stock Exchange, public offering of shares must comply with internationally accepted norms of legal and financial disclosures. For example, because the share price reflects both assets and liabilities of the entity, it is crucial to the integrity of the issue that all liabilities be fully disclosed; hidden charges or claims go to the integrity of the issue and the credibility of the government. In this connection the process turns on the integrity of the institution and on established rules and regulations governing public issues of shares.

Where such infrastructure exists, the public enterprise could be converted to a public limited company, normally referred to as a joint-stock company, in which a secondary distribution of shares is made to the public at large. This may be a partial offering or a full offering of all of the shares. In a partial offering the government retains an interest in the enterprise, either to be sold at a later date, or to retain control of the enterprise.

The shares may be offered at a fixed price or tender offers solicited. In the case of a fixed price offering the public is made aware of the value or cost of the shares, which may be priced substantially below market valuation, as was the case in the UK privatisation. Below-market pricing strategy is usually adopted when the goal is for wide public participation. In this connection, the fixed price methodology adopted by the British government set the standard which other OECD countries followed. For example, the offering of Deutsche Telekom shares in November 1996 was considered a success because the market price of the stock rose 19 percent on the first day of trading, indicating that it was offered at below market valuation..

In contrast to the British and German experiences, after a very good start in the late 1980s, the French privatisation programme was plagued with difficulties revolving around, among other things, the pricing strategy. It appears investors had come to expect below market valuation pricing and regarded anything close to valuation as a reflection of a 'greedy state'. Moreover, there appeared to be an expectation among observers that the share price of the privatised entity must keep up with the general market even years after divestiture, as evidenced by their reaction to the shares of Renault, divested in 1994: In November 1996, according to the Economist, Renault shares under-performed the French bourse by 41 percent, suggesting a dissatisfaction with the initial offer price.[1] On the other hand the under-pricing of other enterprises in the portfolio could be regarded as a political ploy by the incumbent government.

Invitation to tender   With respect to the invitation to tender methodology, unless it matters not whether the issue is fully subscribed, it is used only where the nature and performance of the enterprise commend it or where the government is seeking a strategic partner. It does not escape any of the guarantees required of a public offer.

Underwriting the offer   Where the goal is about raising cash, the issue may be underwritten by investment bankers, or syndicated group of investors, either local or foreign. By underwriting the offer, the government is assured of the sale at the agreed

[1]   'Privatisation in Europe: Is the price right?', *The Economist*, 23 November 1996, 87.

price, less expenses. On the other hand, where the object is to benefit a particular sector of the population – ethnic minorities, employees, or other preferential group – the price may be substantially below market price with restrictions attached. For example, blocks of shares may be reserved for these groups and or restrictions, usually quantitative, imposed on others. Another technique would be to provide other incentives to the targeted groups that would ensure their participation, for example, discount vouchers to employees and pensioners and their families (see Vuylsteke 1988).

Presumption of market liquidity   In addition to the legal and regulatory framework required for a successful public offering of shares, there must be available liquidity in the local market, a presumption of a market economy. If the goal is to have broad-based ownership, the government may assist by providing loans to the targeted groups. Whilst this technique allows for the sale of the shares, it does not guarantee a market. A fundamental requirement of a market is that there must exist at any one time an acceptable number of buyers and sellers for the commodity. Nonetheless, a public offering does provide the basis for an equity market.

Core investor group   There is also the perception in capitalist economies that a core investor group in any joint-stock company would facilitate efficiency of the enterprise. The rationale being that such a group provides the financial discipline, experience and direction to the company, and stimulates the competitive juices within. It is for this reason that the French has incorporated this strategy into their privatisation programme, as in the divestiture of *Compagnie Financiere de Suez*. In this case, a core group of shareholders was pre-selected and offered 36.9 percent of the shares prior to the public offering of the remainder. Other evidence was found in the privatisation of *Paribas, Mantra,* and *Banque du Bàtiment*. At the developing country level, such a group often seeks control of the enterprise.

The importance of timing   Irrespective of the pricing methodology, sale by public offer has the advantage of reaching the investment public at large and of increasing the wide-spread ownership of shares. But more importantly, timing of the public offer has proven to be the most significant determinant of success or failure of a sale by public offer as evidenced by the oversubscription to the offerings by Spain and Brazil in the late1990s. Recall that in the case of the privatisation of TELEBRAS, the oversubscription amounted to millions of dollars to the government.

Private sale

A private sale is essentially a negotiated sale between the government and a private purchaser. It is a preferred method in cases of weak public enterprise; where the objective is to secure strong owners capable of effecting a turn-around of the enterprise. Thus the purchaser is selected on the basis of prior experience, financial stability and management skills. This has been a common method employed in the poorer developing countries. As with a public offering, full disclosure of all assets and liabilities is a requirement because the purchaser generally accepts the enterprise as a going concern. This technique suffers from a lack of transparency relative to a public offer and the price set is open for dispute, more so than with a public offer. Nonetheless it is used in the absence of an equity market or where the size of the enterprise does not warrant the cost of a public offering. Also, as used by the French, it is a means by which to establish a core of shareholders known for their expertise in the field.

At the developing country level, the expertise of the private investor in search of opportunities to maximise profits could result in asymmetric advantage based on such expertise, and to agreements that no longer serve the needs of the country as in the case of the privatisation of telecommunications in Guyana (see Chang 2004).

Infusion of new capital

The infusion of new private capital is yet another technique of divestiture. With such new capital, the capitalisation of the entity is altered to reflect the change in the composition of ownership. The new offering could, for example, be made to raise funds for major rehabilitation and refurbishing of a public enterprise. For example, in the case of telecommunications in Ghana, a 30 percent interest in the restructured Ghana Telecom was sold to Telekom Malaysia as a strategic investor with management control for US$38 million with build-out condition of 225,000 new lines within 5 years.[2] The privatisation of most electric utilities has been premised on the need to infuse new capital for rehabilitation and expansion (see Covarrubias 1996; World Bank 1994; Sader 1993; and Vuylsteke 1988). This method dilutes the state ownership and provides funds for specific purpose. In its pure form, it does not raise cash from the sale of equity as does a secondary offering to the public or a private sale. It is, however, an available mechanism to reduce the size of the public sector and to transfer the cost of rehabilitation and expansion onto the strategic investor. The draw back, as shown in Chapter 8, is that the objectives of the government may be at variance with that of the investor who may not find the conditions conducive to making additional investment.

Sale of assets

The sale of assets is a technique of last resort. It is used when the enterprise cannot be sold as a going concern either because of the condition of the enterprise or because of its nature. It is also used as a method of restructuring prior to a public offering or negotiated sale. For example, assets of a public enterprise technically could be sold – transferred – to a public company which could then be sold by way of a public or private offer of shares. On the other hand, it could be a means to rationalising the entity and selling its assets. Many state-owned enterprises were so rationalised in the hay day of privatisations.

---

[2]   Alde-Loha, A., (1997), 'A Leap of Faith', *Project and Trade Finance, No 167,* (London: Euromoney Publications) March 1997, 33.

Purchasers in this case do not assume any prior liability. However, there could be prior claims to the assets if such assets were used to secure loans or were not fully owned. The method would be a sale by public auction or competitive bid. In the case of competitive bidding, transparency is a concern. Full information must be made available to the bidding public and strict selection procedures should be pellucid and be followed as part of the process. Failing any one of the requirements would likely result in a credibility problem for the government.

Once again, indemnification by the government would be expected by the purchaser. It is partly for security investment reasons that developing countries were encouraged to join the Multilateral Investment Guarantee Agency (MIGA) as a way of signalling their willingness to protect FDI in their respective states. Following the Bank-sponsored seminar in Hong Kong in September 1997, the majority of developing countries signed on to MIGA; many have enacted legislation and have adopted reform in keeping with investor's expectations.

Reorganisation into smaller units

As has been found, most public enterprises are large with multiple products or services; others are deemed natural monopolies, although some monopolies are the results of restrictions imposed by the government. For example, price regulation may operate to make it uncompetitive for a private company to enter the market. Or, in the case of imports high tariffs or quantitative restrictions may operate to block foreign competition. Evidence of such practices abounds in both developed and developing countries except that there is a greater focus of attention on those in the developing countries. Nonetheless, where the PE has grown too large to be sold as a single unit or where operating performance varied among the several operating units, reorganisation into several units could facilitate privatisation. This was done in the case of telecommunications in Brazil.

Where reorganisation has taken place the profitable or better performing units could be sold either by way of public offer of shares or by private sale. The weaker units could then be strengthened by the infusion of new capital as an aspect of the privatisation strategy. This latter approach, as noted in Chapter 8, requires mutual respect and trust between the parties, with neither seeking asymmetric advantage, which is often short lived.

The case of telecommunications in the US   There is a perception among some observers that, in the case of electric utilities and telecommunications enterprises greater efficiency is possible from competition introduced through the splitting-up of the entity into several operating units. Indeed, the break-up of AT&T by way of the 1984 Consent Decree was premised on this assumption; but, the evidence suggest a less clear outcome as it relates to the provision of basic wire-line telephone service for several reasons. In the first place, wire-line service is capital intensive and operates on the basis of increasing marginal cost. Secondly, the local-service market is clearly not contestable to the extent that it is facility-based; wireless technology has made this less of an issue over the years, however, but even for wireless telephone service, franchises operate to restrict new entrants. More significantly, however, is the fact that the telecommunications industry has been consolidating over the decades prior to the AT&T divestiture of its local-service operating companies. The process continues to be a dynamic one even after divestiture with re-consolidation a decided option. The latest merger – an ironic one, to be sure – was the acquisition by SBC of its former parent AT&T in November 2005, thus placing SBC firmly back in interoperable telecommunications services at the national level; 'Humpty Dumpty' it seems is being put back together in one form or another. It is equally ironic that, the company – MCI – that started the push for divestiture and competition in the 1980s was forced into bankruptcy by competitors in 2000 and was acquired by Verizon in late 2005.

Management/Employee buy-out

Management buy-out is typically characterised by a core group of managers acquiring a controlling interest in the enterprise. It is more often than not leveraged with the assets of the acquired company being used to secure financing for the buy out. Because the source of repayment is a major consideration to the financiers, cash flow assumes greater significance in a management/employee buy out. In the case of a public enterprise the process could be aided by the government assuming the liabilities of the enterprise and further discounting the book value of the assets. It is thus a means of rewarding a particular group, in this case, managers and or employees. It is also a method likely to be criticised by taxpayers and voters as showing preference to special interests.

Joint venture

Beyond divestiture joint venture is yet another technique of the privatisation process and has become the preferred method of many developing countries in that it allows the state to retain an interest in the enterprise. Technically, to the extent it dilutes state-ownership it is a form of divestiture. It could be achieved by way of infusion of new private capital as discussed above or by private offering of shares or a combination of both. The government could be either a minority or majority owner. Management could also be by the minority private owner if agreed to by the government.

The danger for the minority private owner is that politicians will likely continue to influence policy and operations in pursuit of their political agendas. Even when the government is a minority partner it often seeks to influence outcomes irrespective of cost to the majority partner, as evidenced by the case study offered in Chapters 8.

The exact structure of the joint venture will depend on the intention of the government. In developed countries joint venture has been used a means to attracting management skills as well as new capital and has been very successful in transforming state monopolies to vibrant competitive enterprises. In developing countries, it allows the government to appear in control of the direction of the country in the face of conditionality-based lending and to continue with patronage in the appointment to boards and arguably management. Often, the management skills of the external partner are made secondary to the will of the political directorate;[3] relegated to the 'show and display' status, if you will.

Lease and management contract

Another popular alternative to divestiture is the leasing of public assets to a private operator. This arrangement provides the government with a lease income while the operator benefits from the use of the assets. Usually, lease payments will be due and payable whether or not the operator makes a profit. By the same token the government will have no claims to the income derived from the use of the assets other than applicable taxes. Depending on the nature of the asset the government might impose restrictions as to use. Also, the lessee will likely be responsible for maintenance and protection of the leased assets.

In the case of management contract, this technique has been used where the government does not want to part with ownership in the enterprise but wants to make the enterprise efficient or to satisfy a loan condition. This is often the case where the enterprise is a significant natural monopoly or where ownership matters in the socio-political context of the country, as is the case of the GUYSUCO.

Whatever the rationale, there are certain defining characteristics of management contracts. First, authority is derived from the contract. Secondly, the management firm has no financial exposure from the operations of the enterprise, that is, fees are payable irrespective of whether or not the enterprise is profitable. Thirdly, the state retains control and responsibility for the enterprise. Fourth, the compensation package usually includes a production incentive which is conditioned upon the achievement of a predetermined output level or financial performance. Finally, the management firm is usually allowed to hire and fire to achieve objectives set jointly between the government, usually through an intermediary Board, and the management firm.

Whilst the enterprise is likely to benefit from independent professional management, the cost for such management is a short-term burden on the enterprise and is often a factor of some significance. Moreover, management service contracts have been used at the developing country level as means of restitution of assets confiscated through nationalisation, a phenomenon of the 1960s and 1970s in newly-independent states.

Broad-base ownership schemes

After the experiences of the EEC-3 countries and Russia with mass privatisation in 1989–92, the Bank's perception on privatisation changed somewhat to accommodate broad-base ownership. The contrast in performance between the regions became very glaring, especially in terms of private capital flows, and could no longer be ignored.

---

[3] See Williams, N. 'Baksh blasts management of water utility', in *Stabroek News*, 28 June 2003.

Moreover, the process had everything to do with development and very little with economic orthodoxy, that is, enterprise efficiency was not of primary concern. As a consequence, discounted public offerings, collective investment programmes and voucher-based systems became part of the privatisation vocabulary of the Bank in the early 1990s.

In the case of discounted public offerings, as outlined above the UK's privatisation programme was essentially premised on a strategy to expand share-ownership. Also, even though a voucher system was used by South Korea in the early 1980s, it was discounted as an appropriate privatisation technique for developing countries by the Bank. This was because while both techniques served to create broad-based ownership, they did not address two of the requirements of the Baker Plan: reduce the external debt and provide opportunities for domestic and foreign private-sector 'strategic investors'. Thus the focus of privatisation as a means to raising cash was consistently maintained, with broad-based ownership being relegated to a secondary position.

From both a country and indeed a long-term perspective, however, broad-based ownership appears to have several advantages:

- It provides the nucleus of a capital market and related institutions where none exist. As shown in Chapter 2, the invisible hand of the market cannot effectively operate without the necessary ideological and institutional infrastructure. The commoditizing of the public enterprise and the transferring of related property rights to the general population provide the basis for a capitalist society.
- It avoids concentration of economic power in the hands of a few local elite families or dominant firms, as has happened in the case of Chile where approximately 20 major industrial and banking groups control the economy (see Berg and Shirley 1988, 8).
- Moreover, personal savings and investment are likely to result from broad-based ownership over time as a result of trading in organised markets.
- In those economies that are not of the Soviet-type, the voucher system creates the foundation for future public offerings and for the formation of collective investment programs – mutual funds, investment or unit trusts and other trust funds.

Collective investment programme

Variants of collective investment programme have been used as a mechanism to increase broad-based ownership in countries such as Zambia, Bolivia and Malaysia, to name a few. As such, the dynamics of the various schemes are examined.

To begin with, collective investment programmes provide an intermediate step in the divestiture phenomenon. Rather than divest national assets to foreigners or to a small group of domestic investors, assets of public enterprises or shares in them are transferred to one or several of these investment trust funds. As the institutional infrastructure is established and the general population becomes more informed in the ways of capitalism and are able to take part in the process, property rights to these assets are released for public purchase.

Investment trusts

Investment trusts as a variant of collective investment programme are also simpler to administer as they do not require the issue of vouchers. For example, Zambia's investment trust fund was created by the transfer of government-owned equity in state-owned enterprises; Malaysia's unit trust fund and Bumiputera Investment Foundation were also created from shares allocated by the government. In the case of Bolivia, pension schemes were funded from the earnings of shares in PEs. Moreover, as part of the process trustees could be appointed from the private sector and be active in the management process.

A defining characteristic of investment trusts is the inherent security offered to participants. In the case of pension schemes, for example, participants will not have access to the fund until after retirement, or in the case of illness as provided for in the trust deed. For protection of the beneficiaries, trading is usually restricted: Where the fund is an open-end unit trust, trading is permitted in the secondary market. In closed-end funds, which investment trusts are, trading is not permitted. However, these funds could hold shares in several different traded companies and so take part in the wider secondary market on behalf of their members.

Privatisation trust funds

With privatisation trust funds assets are transferred to these funds pending restructuring by the government. In this type of funds assets are transferred by the government and are collectively owned by and for the benefit of current and future citizens.

Private-sector management could be an aspect of the scheme through the function of the trustees. However, because these funds remain in the control of the government they tend to lack credibility and are looked upon as means to avoiding explicit divestiture. Like investment trusts funds created by the government, the transferring of assets operate to reduce the size of government. The process does not raise cash, however, as would a private or public sale of assets.

Voucher system

Because the voucher system has been widely utilized in the EEC-3 countries and Russia, an in-depth examination of the concept is deferred to Chapter 6.

Country experience

As shown above, techniques of privatisation are rooted in corporate financial practices typically found in a capitalist world-economy. They have guided the merger-acquisition-divestment processes in the private sectors of the major developed countries for centuries, and are regarded as standard. Where the required institutions are absent or are in their infancy, alternative mechanisms have been employed. How these techniques have been applied to privatisation in developed and developing countries is examined in terms of the privatisation effectiveness as defined necessarily in context of the socioeconomic and political framework discussed in Chapter 2.

The UK experience

The UK experience is included here as the benchmark against which all other experiences are measured in terms of techniques and outcomes. Indeed, it was upon the UK's experience arguably that attempts to construct a privatisation theory based on orthodox economics were made although, to be sure, the US perspective was informed by notions of market fundamentalism, as discussed in Chapter 4. Moreover, with disposable income greater than the per capita income of most developing countries (see Table 2.3) the UK represents absorptive capacity at the upper end of the growth-development continuum.

As would be expected then, the strategy employed by the UK was largely dictated by the goals that were set within a well established ideological and institutional infrastructure. The existence of one of the most sophisticated capital markets in the world provided the British government with a variety of options. In terms of share distribution, with London being one of the major capitalist centres in the world there was very little debate as to method. Thus many of the enterprises privatised were by way of public offer of shares, utilizing existing institutional infrastructure. Hence, for most of the enterprises privatised shares were offered to the public at prices determined by financial valuation rather than economic, despite recommendations for the latter.

The pricing methodology was reflective of the political and social goals of the programme. To be sure, many of the public offerings were well below market valuation as evidenced by the market price of the stock on the following trading day (Vickers and Yarrow 1995, 177); but it is not the purpose here to debate the case for or against a particular method of pricing of the shares.

In addition to the capital gains to be had from subscribing to the issues, there were other benefits which, in the case of British Gas, Vickers and Yarrow (1995, 176) estimated to be worth a post-tax return on investment including dividends of more than 20 percent in the first six months. Equivalent benefits were also offered the subscribers of TSB and British Airways.

The windfall that attended the privatisation did not escape the investment public. For example, although 40 percent of British Gas was available for subscription by the general public, the 'claw back' provision had to be invoked against the allotments to institutional investors because of over-subscription by the public. In the case of British Airways, the issue was over subscribed by 32 times the original offer to the general public. A comparison with under-pricing of new issues on the London stock market led to the conclusion that '... there is good reason to believe that the Government could and should have sold the shares in a way that led to smaller initial price rises than those that occur in private issues' (Vickers and Yarrow (1995, 178).

When the government tried to privatise by invitation-to-tender, however, the issues were under-subscribed, some grossly so, as in the case of Britoil which was under-subscribed by 70 percent. Other under-subscribed issues included Cable and Wireless in 1983 and Enterprise Oil in 1984.

The failed experiment with tender-offer as a method in many ways provided the government with further opportunities to target particular interest groups in future privatisation. Where the concerns were for the retention of shares by the original subscribers, free bonus shares were offered to the original subscribers as an incentive for them to keep their shares for a prescribed period.

Employee leveraged buy-out

The public offering of shares, however, was not the only method employed by the British government. The sale of National Freight Company Limited was an employee leveraged buy-out. In that case, 80 percent of the shares issued by a management/ workers consortium were taken up by employees, pensioners and their respective families. The government facilitated the buy-out by writing-off some of the outstanding debt of the enterprise and provided a loan of £51.0 million against the sale price of £53.5 million. In addition, £47.0 million was paid to the company's pension fund to rectify its under-funding. Although not specifically stated, it is assumed that funding of these initiatives came from proceeds from earlier privatisation.

Citing the nine-fold increase in pre-tax profits – from £4.3 million in 1981 to £37.0 million in 1986 – the employee buy-out of National Freight has been hailed as 'one of the greatest successes of the privatization program' (Vickers and Yarrow 1995, 164). Other management/employee buyouts included Victulatic Company, a subsidiary of British Steel Corporation, in 1983; Vosper Thorncycroft Shipyard in 1985; and Vickers and Cammell Laird in the same year. To facilitate the employee buy-out of the shipyards, workers were offered interest free loans of up to £500 each. Also, after the restructuring of British Leyland, Leyland Bus and Unipart were sold as a management buyout.

Reorganization

In addition to the above techniques, other techniques of divestiture were utilized although not to the same extent as with the public-offer of shares. For example, both British Leyland and British Rail were reorganised prior to divestiture. In the case of the latter, British Rail Investment Limited was formed to acquire some of the non-rail businesses: Hotels were sold to private parties by public tender; Sealink was sold through competitive bidding; and British Rail and Hovercraft Limited was merged with a Swedish firm. British Leyland was similarly reorganised: Jaguar – now US-owned – was sold as a public offering of shares whilst Leyland Trucks was a joint venture with DAF of Holland (see Vickers and Yarrow, 1995).

Regulation before competition

In contrast to the divestiture of commercial manufacturing enterprises, the British government chose to maintain the structure of state monopolies and to employ a regulatory regime as the monitoring mechanism. Many have argued that this was against the recommendations of the consultants to the government, whose criterion for privatisation was '... the present value of aggregate net value to UK consumers' (Kay et al. 1986, 6). According to detractors to the UK programme, the private monopolies would be less efficient than if they were broken-up into smaller units and were allowed to compete with one another as was done, for example, in the case of AT&T in the US. But as noted above, the removal in 1987 of most of restrictions on the 'Baby Bells' and the intensity of global competition in the world telecommunications arena have validated the retention of the structure of BT. Moreover, the concept of RPI-X regulation (retail price index, minus a value of X) adopted by UK regulators was thought to be superior to the 'rate of return on assets' method of the US in that it forces the enterprise to be efficient; and indeed was adopted as the basis for regulating telecommunications in many developing countries.

Had BT not retained its structure it would not have been able to effectively negotiate mergers with other service providers outside the UK. Its structure allowed it to acquire properties as far away as New Zealand. Moreover, increasing deregulation of the industry in the US has provided the impetus for mergers of several of the separated units and the re-emergence of multi-service providers. Thus whether or not the break-up of AT&T has served to increase the aggregate net value to US consumers is still debated today. These arguments notwithstanding, because the British government was seen as giving in to the pressure by management and union to privatise BT as a private monopoly without restructuring, a credibility gap was deemed to exist at the time.

With respect to other monopolies in the UK, in direct contrast to BT stand the electric utilities which are considered natural monopolies by reason of their capital intensive nature, at least in the transmission function. However, because these are organised as regional or local entities rather than as two or three larger entities, they have become prey to predatory acquisitions from the outside. The transmission and distribution assets of many of them have become attractive targets for creating extensive networks supportive of large scale generation. The several acquisitions by US utility holding companies speak to this trend. As part of a larger corporate structure after acquisition, these smaller entities have operated to the benefit of the shareholders of the US-based TNC in their endless accumulation of capital. To this end, with decades of highly intensive regulatory experience behind them, US utility holding companies saw a window of opportunity to exploit the thinness of the UK regulatory experience.

Another example of failure to split-up what many regarded as an unnatural monopoly was the divestiture of British Airport Authority (BAA). The entity was divested as a single unit, despite the diversity of its business and the extensive contracting-out of most of its services to the private sector. Furthermore, less than 10 percent of the work-force was actual employees of BAA. The sale of BAA was thus regarded as a means of raising cash, with little regard for the notion of competition.

As with BT and British Gas, management opposed the splitting-up of the enterprise and the government appeared to have relented. The expectation of UK observers, on the other hand, was for a stimulation of competition from the regional airports by the splitting-up of BAA and the ending of British Airways monopoly at Heathrow.

While the above represents examples of failure to introduce competition due to pressures from special interest groups, there is evidence of reorganization prior to the offer for sale. As mentioned above, both British Rail and British Leyland were restructured prior to divestiture. But despite these efforts to appease public criticism, the UK privatisation programme continued to be viewed as designed to benefit particular interest groups, although in regard to the public offer of shares, anyone was entitled to subscribe. Still, as stated earlier, the voting public had become wary of the process, as evidenced by the reduction in voter sentiment in the poll taken by British Public Opinion in October, 1987.

Developing country experience

In the case of developing countries, notwithstanding that the Bank avoids any direct reference to IMF loan conditions or indeed Paris Club conditions, its privatisation strategy recommendations were primarily geared toward external debt repayment. In this regard, the Bank functioned as agent of the creditors in the dismantling and sale of PEs in these countries. In other words, privatisation was an involuntary reform mechanism for those developing countries seeking debt relief (see Berg and Shirley 1988). But many developing country governments, especially in Sub-Saharan Africa, were less than willing to part with their source of power, preferring restructuring – commercialisation – to divestiture. In response, the Bank adopted a sector-wide approach to PE reform in the late 1980s. This entailed restricting rehabilitation and restructuring as a reform-approach to only those PE 'whose performance is critical to the success or failure of other actors in the economy'(Galal 1989, 1). Liquidation of non-viable enterprises and the sale of those that were deemed better run by the private sector were to be emphasised. The theoretical foundation for this approach was stated by Mary Shirley of the Bank:

> The efficiency of an enterprise – public or private – is highest when the enterprise strives to maximize profits in a competitive market, under managers with autonomy, capacity

and motivation to respond to competition, and when enterprises that cannot compete go bankrupt (see Galal 1989, 2).[4]

The message was clear. The Bank had become impatient with the progress and outcomes of the privatisation programmes, especially in the smaller developing countries. As a direct result from the approach articulated by Mary Shirley, the number of Bank projects with divestiture component totalled 74 at the end of June 1989. Loan distribution to these projects is as shown in Table 5.1 below, which is by region and the number of countries in each region.

Table 5.1   Bank projects with divestiture components

Region	Countries Number	Projects Number	Loan Amount US$ million
Africa	22	45	1,687.1
Latin America	9	18	1,965.1
Asia	4	7	870.0
EMENA*	3	4	830.0

* *Europe Mediterranean and North Africa*
Source: Compiled from Galal (1991, 56)

Of the US$1,965.1 million to Latin America, US$500.0 million went to Mexico and US$402.0 million to Venezuela. In the case of Asia, of the US$870.0 million, US$500.0 million went to the Philippines with US$220.0 million to Pakistan. Turkey, Morocco and Tunisia made up the EMENA countries. Using the number of projects as a criterion, privatisation in developing countries was largely driven by the need to remain in the Paris-Club membership and by the loan conditions of the Bank.

Sub-Saharan Africa: General

In Sub-Saharan Africa, developing countries on the whole had fewer options than those available to the developed countries for the reasons discussed in earlier chapters. In contrast, privatisation in EEC-3 countries and Russia were less problematic than privatisation in the poorer developing countries: Western investors eagerly supported the integration of these economies into the capitalist world-economy if only because of geography.

---

[4]   The inconsistency of the Bank's approach is glaring when contrasted with what obtains in developed countries, a case in point being AMTRAK in the US. Additionally, subsidising cotton and textile manufacture in Europe and the US, and cost-inefficient farmers at the expense of developing countries evidence a bias against developing countries.

In addition to the ideological and institutional constraints, the lack of liquidity in the domestic financial markets of most African countries and the poor condition of the enterprise operated to limit public offering of shares as a privatisation method. Moreover, many African state-owned enterprises were found to be years behind in their record keeping, thereby making any rendition of historical data suspect. As a consequence, public offering of shares in Sub-Saharan Africa had largely given way to other techniques, despite partial success with share-offering in Kenya and Zambia, to name a couple. For example, of the 11 enterprises privatised in Togo prior to 1995, five were by sale of assets, two were by new private investment and the remaining four were leases to private operators. In many cases the enterprise had to be completely rebuilt, as was the case of telecommunications in Guinea.

With respect to private sales, all liabilities of the enterprises were retained by the government. This was primarily achieved through the process of liquidation of the enterprises, much in keeping with IMF's prescriptions. In other cases such as Guinea, for example, private sales were combined with new equity contribution as the main strategy. A consequence of this approach is that the liabilities assumed from private sale served to add to the budgetary burden of the state and therefore takes away from the development effectiveness of other budgetary programmes.

Where lease was pursued as an option, lease revenues often fell short of the debt service obligation with respect to the initial investment in the enterprise, as was the situation with Togo. As shown in the African Development Report 1999, the majority of African countries opted for Concessions and de-monopolisation/BOO as the preferred method of privatisation (see AFDB 1999, 142, 145, 149, 154 and 156).

Nigeria

As with the UK experience, the privatisation techniques adopted in Nigeria were largely dictated by the goals of the programme. However in the case of Nigeria, as indeed in most other developing countries, the goals were first and foremost the repayment of sovereign debts which stood at US$35.0 billion in 1995, although debt service cost as a percent of export was one of the lowest in the region at 12.3 percent (Bank 1997, 246).

Goals notwithstanding, since its inception in the early 1980s, Nigeria's privatisation had been challenged by controversy and ethnic issues: The Buhari regime of 1979–1983 resisted the pressure to privatise, preferring to pursue commercialisation as a reform mechanism. This was perhaps motivated by the ethnic division of Nigeria and the division of wealth between the Islamic North and the Christian South, the latter being the more capitalist (see Lewis 1994). Thus, while Nigeria is one of the few Sub-Saharan African countries to have had a functioning capital market at the time, privatisation by public offering of shares was resisted because it was viewed as a way of further enriching the Southern capitalist class (see Zayyad 1996).

Commercialisation was continued as policy by the Babangida government despite the privatisation rhetoric: In 1988, the government released a list of 71 PEs to be privatised. These were mainly public commercial enterprises to be either sold or commercialised. Many of the sales that took place during this period were transfers to other government-owned entities pending the appropriate time and conditions for public offerings, which failed to materialise as a result of renewed flows of oil revenues. Thus, in the case of telecommunications, performance contract was the method of choice, with the goal '… to ensure that the increased autonomy [arising from its separation from direct government control] is not misused … to install an attitude of accountability [and] … to ensure that NITEL adheres to well defined performance objectives'. Joint venture was also pursued between NITEL, the wire-line government-owned monopoly, and Digital Communications Limited. This joint venture failed following the political unrest of 1993. In addition the Bank cancelled its US$225.0 million loan for telecommunications projects. The EC also cancelled its grant of 10 million Ecus for the training of NITEL's staff. In consequence of the poor state of telecommunications services, private branch exchanges were established by the larger private-sector companies in Nigeria.

Like many African countries of the period, Nigeria pursued indigenisation as policy: The Nigerian Enterprise Promotion Decree of 1989 and the Exchange Control Act 1962 constrained growth and investment. These were repealed by the 1995 Budget and by the Nigerian Investment Promotion Commission Decree No. 16 of 1995. While this latter Decree permitted investment by non-nationals, investment in petroleum enterprises was restricted. However, such restrictions have since been removed and foreign investments have poured into Nigeria's petroleum industry.

South Africa

Unlike Nigeria, South Africa as noted in the previous chapter pursued privatisation with the reversal of past social injustices and exclusions in mind. Its privatisation programme focused on the expansion of basic human services – water and sanitation, electricity and telecommunications – and economic growth and thus speaks directly to the inter-connectedness of privatisation and development. Indeed, in this case the techniques adopted were positively correlated to the development effectiveness, especially with respect to water distribution, the basis for which was written into the South African Constitution as Principles 12, 13, 14 and 25.[5] In the case of telecommunications, licenses were granted based on conditions that served the RDP; specifically, holders were required to 'contribute to the provision of community services, job creation, phones for under-serviced areas and … making shareholdings available [to] black groups'.[6] Hence, in the case of South Africa, privatisation

---

[5]   See also *White Paper on Water Policy 199*, Government of South Africa, http://www.polity.org.za/govdocs/white papers/water2.html.

[6]   See Government of South Africa, *Telecommunications Green Paper*, July 1995, http://www.polity.org.za/govdocs/green-papers/telcomms.html; see also Government of South Africa, *Opening Address 1997 Budget*, http://www.southafrica.net/government/speches9.html; USAID RTR Program News Letter, http://rtr.worldweb.net/05-27-98.html.

effectiveness was evaluated in terms of development and thus shifted the evaluative framework away from debt repayment.

South Africa's approach to privatisation was mainly one of divesture with a strategic partner, with investment and employment conditions attached, and in encouraging private-sector investment in other services essential to increasing its economic competitiveness. In this regard, reform in telecommunications and ports offer an insight into South Africa's approach to privatisation programme.

Although divestiture with a strategic partner was the main approach, de-mono-polisation featured prominently in the restructuring of the telecommunications sector, with Build, Own and Operate (BOO) as the mechanism of choice, especially in the provision of mobile telecommunications services.[7]

The formation of Telekom S.A. Limited (Telkom) in 1991 marked the separation of telephone services from post and broadcasting and from public funding to full cost recovery. In addition to Telkom, there were two other major network providers operating as cellular telephone service providers: Vodacom and Mobile Telephone Network (MTN). Telkom had a 50 percent interest in Vodacom. The ownership of MTN was entirely private-sector derived, and at the time was divided up among Cable and Wireless (25.0 percent); M-Cell (29.5 percent); SBC Communications (15.5 percent); Transtel (20.0 percent; and Naftel (10.0 percent). Both Vodacom and MTN competed directly with Telkom for customers. The Telecommunications Act, 1996 that followed the change in government in 1994 codified the government's policy with respect to social redistribution; economic development; and human development, including gender issues as they pertain to the provision of telecommunications services in South Africa. It embraced the principle of private-sector participation in the provision of such services, as reflected in the acquisition of a strategic partner and in its stated goals of promoting broad-based ownership of the monopoly network operator.[8] In this regard, the Telecommunications Act incorporated aspects of the RDP, and adopted a phased-in approach to reform of the telecommunications sector.

South Africa also took to reforming its ports with the lifting of trade sanctions attendant on the change in government in 1994. Ports were considered part of the general transport system within the country. Thus, its reform was part of the reform proposal for the whole transport industry based on the recommendations of a task-team on transport. One of the recommendations of the task-team was to focus on internal restructuring of certain enterprises, including Portnet (the administrative name of the ports), so as to improve their efficiency and effectiveness prior to privatisation. Thus, unlike other infrastructure reform projects, ports in South Africa were not looked at in terms of redressing social ills principally, but rather to encourage greater private-

---

[7]   See Government of South Africa, *Cellular Telephone Networks,* http//www. southafrica.net/economy/telecom/celtel.html; see also Sergeant, M., *Ring the Changes,* http// www.southafrica.net/news/ring.html (accessed 20 August 1998).

[8]   Government of South Africa, *White Paper on Telecommunications Policy 1996,* http:// www.polity.org.za/govdocs/white papers/telewp.html.

sector participation in the provision of some services, and to re-attract freight traffic to and from the region through South African ports.

Sri Lanka

Privatisation in the poorer more traditional developing countries in general and prior to 1990 was primarily based on the experiences of the larger developing countries even though 'the 'whether' and 'how' to privatize, more often than not, ought to be interconnected decisions and, probably more so than they have been in a number of economies' (Vuylsteke, 1988: xi).

Vuylsteke's observation notwithstanding, the Bank's approach to privatisation throughout the 1980s continued to be one of liquidation of non-viable enterprises and to sell to the private sector – domestic or foreign – those that were commercially viable. This disconnect between theory and reality was quite evident in the more traditional type of societies where state-owned enterprises were instrumentalities of governance, as in the case of Sri Lanka.

In Sri Lanka, the multiple types of public enterprise – five were identified by consultants – and the close control exercised by the government made rationalisation of the public sector difficult. In addition to the extensive political interference in the management of state-owned enterprises, the private sector was mainly family-based and lacked the diversity of ownership found in, for example, Latin America or Singapore. Hence the procedure adopted was to convert state-owned enterprises into public companies with the government as the majority shareholder.

After setting-up of the usual evaluation and oversight committees, the Committee of Development Secretaries, the equivalent to a privatisation committee, arrived at a list of four categories of state-owned enterprises. These were:

- PE to be retained because of their strategic importance;
- profit making enterprises;
- enterprises in need of rehabilitation to be made profitable; and
- enterprises to be liquidated.

The techniques employed were complete or partial transfer of ownership; joint venture and management contract (see Nankani 1988, 117).

The results were mixed: Of the enterprises privatised, only three – the tile factories – were sold to the private sector and reflected the desire for concealment by the families that composed it. The lines of communication between the private and public sectors were bound-up in rent seeking. In other attempts to divest by competitive bidding, the inclusion of conditions, such as retention of workers, for example, resulted in bids that could best be characterised as confiscatory: about 20 percent of government valuation.

In the case of the State Rubber Manufacturing Corporation, attempts to enlist employee participation were met with disappointing results. Of the intended 40 percent of the restructured company stock available for employee and public participation, only 1 percent was subscribed to by employees. In all cases of failed attempts was the evidence of government interference either in the process or in wanting to retain control of the enterprise (see Nankani 1988).

The above notwithstanding, Sri Lanka had some success through management contracts, the most notable of which were the National Textile Corporation, Cement Corporation, and Lanka Cement. The success of management contract as a method of privatisation was derived from the explicit authority of the contracts. Whilst some of the negotiated terms with the expatriate management were criticized ex-post, they were nonetheless legally enforceable and, therefore, served to restrict government interference with them.

Trinidad and Tobago

Like South Africa and Malaysia to some extent, the underlying philosophy of the private sector as custodial of public assets for the citizens pending their ability to purchase their respective interests was an underlying influence of T&T's privatisation programme. Thus, the emphasis was one of improving the operating performance of PE through private-sector management in the interim. Apart from this characteristic, T&T privatisation programme was a mirror image of Jamaica's, that is, state-owned enterprises were classified into three broadly defined categories: The first category included those enterprises that were to be divested; the second category listed those that were not to be divested because of their strategic importance; whilst the third group were those where no decision had been made either because classification between the first two groups was not possible or because they needed to be readied before a final decision could be made.

The divestiture criteria were listed as:

- large asset base, providing a high purchase price;
- existence of a competitive market in the product;
- substantial reduction in the debt burden to result from the sale;
- minimum job losses;
- minimum government responsibility for debt; and
- minimum need for FDI.

Based on the above criteria, 12 enterprises were identified for divestiture. At the end of 1992, there were 5 completed sales. The three most important were National Commercial Bank, Trinidad Cement Limited and the telephone infrastructure. In the case of the National Commercial Bank, the process was a gradual release of shares to the citizens of T&T. By 1988, the government holding was halved. In 1989, an additional release of 10 percent was made to the public in a controlled fashion. Of the shares released, 20 percent were designated for employees of the bank, 10 percent to unit trusts and remainder to the general public. In the case of telecommunications, 49 percent in the reorganised 'TSTT' was sold to Cable and Wireless; the government continues to hold 51 percent controlling interest.

Privatisation in the Larger Developing Countries

In the larger, less economically-desperate developing countries, privatisation assumed different characteristics. For example, for most of the larger highly-indebted countries – Argentina, Brazil, Chile, Mexico and the Philippines to name a few – 'debt-equity swap' was a technique employed as a quick means to reducing the debt burden of many of them. Whilst the purpose of debt-equity swap was primarily debt reduction, because the identified or targeted investment was in some cases public enterprises, the process served to facilitate privatisation of those enterprises. However, with the exception of Chile and Mexico, most of the swaps were for new investment in the debtor country. For example, Argentina specifically prohibited the use of converted debt from acquiring an ownership interest in existing PEs. Beyond the initial spate of debt-equity swaps, more traditional techniques were the choice, as exemplified by the country experiences of Malaysia, Chile and Brazil.

Malaysia

As noted in Chapter 4, there are some concerns with respect to privatisation in Malaysia. To be sure, targeting special interest groups was never in doubt; indeed it was a stated policy of the government to utilise the process to redress for market failure. At the same time, wittingly or unwittingly, the process assumed the characteristics of patronage, as comprehensively discussed by Tai Wooi Syn (2004). For example, the divestiture of the container terminal at Kelang Port Authority (KPA) was not because the enterprise was making a loss. The port authority had never incurred a loss since it was established in 1963, and paid a 45 percent income and development tax like any other profitable private-sector business enterprise. The container terminal itself was established in 1973 and contributed about 60 percent to the authority's net profit. Moreover, earnings before taxes increased from M$204.3 million in 1983, to M$986.7 million in 1985 (see Nankani 1988, 84).

The concerns thus centre on the privatisation rationale. Despite what appears to be acceptable performance, it was decided to privatise the container terminal. Moreover, it was not for debt repayment that the privatisation was pursued. The reason for this privatisation perhaps lie in the transactions: The Kelang Container Terminal (KCT) was formed as a limited company and the assets of the container terminal were leased from KPA to KCT under a leasing arrangement. The function of container handling was also transferred to KCT under the arrangement. 51 percent of the shares in KCT were sold to Konas Terminal Kelang (KTK) a joint venture of Kontena Nasional and P&O Australia. The remaining 49 percent was held by KPA for eventual distribution to the public. The funds raised from the sale of movable assets to KCT were used to pay-off outstanding loans on the KPA project.

In terms of techniques, in general Malaysia employed the strategy of combining secondary offering of shares with the infusion of new equity capital. This method served to dilute the government's ownership percentage in Malaysian Airlines Systems Bhd (MAS), and was similar to the strategy employed in the privatisation of Singapore International Airlines. In the case of MAS, in 1985, a new issue of 70 million ordinary shares at M$1.80 per share were offered to the Malaysian public. At the same time, the government offered 35 million shares of its holding for public subscription. The offers were through the Kuala Lumpur Stock Exchange and were restricted to Malaysians. Both were over-subscribed six-fold. MAS was the first privatisation undertaken by the government to utilize the public offering of shares mechanism. Resulting from trading activities on the stock exchange, at the end of 1987 the Malaysian government's holding stood at 42 percent, from 90 percent prior to privatisation. As the single largest shareholder, the government maintained control of management of the enterprise. MAS was further divested to private hands, again with some concerns surrounding the transactions (see Tai Wooi Syn 2004).

A similar approach was taken with respect to the privatisation of the light rail transit: the expectation was for the private operators to infuse capital as needed. As with MAS, the light rail transit project proved too costly for the private operators and had to be renationalized.

Chile

The underlying goal of privatisation in Chile in the early stage of the programme was raising cash; but the method employed provided an interesting contrast to those employed by other countries discussed above.

As a first step, prior to the sale of the government's interests in many of the enterprises approximately 240 enterprises that were expropriated by the Allende regime were returned outright by the government to their previous owners; an unwritten requirement of the IMF and Bank. But, as a result of the financial crisis experienced in Chile in 1982–3, the Chilean government had to rescue most of the enterprises that were either returned or sold from bankruptcy. Many were abandoned by their owners and thus had to be re-privatised by way of a wider distribution of ownership.

In the re-privatisation of enterprises returned to the state, the process targeted employees and pension funds as potential owners. Shares in ENDESA,[9] the electric utility holding company, for example, were divested to pension funds and employees through the process of 'popular capitalism'. The process refers to the use of a sales force to sell shares directly to residents rather than through the stock exchange. Where the small investor was the targeted investor group, a deposit of 5 percent was all that was required. CORFO, the entrepreneurial arm of the Chilean government, provided a 15 year, no-interest loan for the remainder of the purchase price. In addition, a 30 percent discount was offered for early repayment and 20 percent of the total investment could be used as a tax credit against future income tax (Nankani 1988, 30). In this approach, Chile also sought to create broad-based ownership of the

---

[9]   In the late 1990s, the privatised Spanish utility holding company purchased a 55 percent interest in the Chile power group.

productive assets of the country and no doubt influenced the approach in the Czech Republic and Russia.

Whilst for the most part the targeted groups were a combination of employees, pension funds, domestic conglomerate investors, and foreign investors, outright employee buy-outs were other techniques utilised by the Chilean government. EMEL, an electricity generating enterprise, for example, was divested as an employee-buyout. Another successful employee buy-out was that of ECOM, a large computer firm. Here, *Sociedad Administradora de Empresas de Computacion* S.A (SAECOM) was formed by the employees to acquire the assets of ECOM. Assets were transferred at their liquidation price which totalled US$1.5 million. Of the purchase price, the state holding company – CORFO – provided 90 percent financing secured on the assets transferred from ECOM and on the shares of SAECOM. Other terms of the loan were: 10 year maturity with interest payment at a 5 percent real interest. While the two examples given above evidenced success, earlier employee-buyout arrangements failed and had to be sold as private sales.

The methodologies employed after the 1982–1983 financial crisis were mainly public secondary offerings and employees participation. The divestment of TELEX Chile, EMEC, *Pilmaiquen* and ENAEX, were by competitive bidding. The employee buy-outs were negotiated and employee participation was wide spread. As reported, 35 percent of the public sector work-force purchased shares either as individuals or as workers' groups. In all instances, individual or group holdings were limited to 20 percent of the issued share capital of the enterprise. Unlike Malaysia, there were no direct limitations on foreign share-ownership.

Brazil

Private capital flows to the more developed of the developing countries as noted in chapter 4 increased in the latter half of the 1990s. This prompted many Latin American countries to capitalise on this increased interest of Western investors and to step-up divestiture of their public enterprises, mainly infrastructure properties. Hence, as reported in the Financial Times,[10] Brazil's southern state, *Rio Grande do Sul,* opened two of its electricity distribution companies valued at US$1.0 billion to tender offers. Fifteen local and foreign banks and electricity companies, including one from Argentina and one from Venezuela, expressed an interest in the properties. The sale was completed later in 1997. The holding company CEEE was split into three separate units. The hydroelectric power station was retained by the state whilst the thermoelectric power station was transferred to the federal government in satisfaction of outstanding debts. The transmission infrastructure was retained by the state for future sale. In addition to the sale of its electric properties, in early 1997 *Rio Grande do Sul* sold a 35 percent interest in its telephone company to South Western Bell.

---

[10] Wheatley, J., 'Interest shown in Brazil's power sale', in *Financial Times*, 29 August, 1997.

Other privatisation in Brazil included the purchase in July 1997, of 65.6 percent of the shares in *Companhia de Electricidade da Bahia (Coleba)*, for US$1.6 billion by a consortium led by *Iberdrola*, a Spanish electricity company.[11] The premium was 77 percent above the minimum bid, and thus served to highlight foreign interest in Latin American infrastructural properties.

Earlier, *Copel*, another Brazilian electric utility from *Parana* state made a successful secondary offering of shares valued at US$500.0 million. An interesting phenomenon that emerged was the cross-border bidding for infrastructure properties by previously state-owned enterprises. In addition to the divestiture of the Brazilian utilities, the purchase of share-holdings in other sector and countries in the region assisted in directing the flow of private capital to Latin America. For example, Citicorp reportedly bought a 40 percent interest in Cable Vision in Argentina.[12] In April 1998 the Spanish electric utility *ENDESA* in consort with *ENERSIS* of Latin America purchased the Brazilian electric distributor *Coelec* for US$873.0 million. This new purchase brought *ENDESA's* interest – direct and indirect – of *Coelec* to 41 percent.[13] It should be noted that *ENDESA's* stock price had reached a high of 4000 pesos in a market that saw Spain's IBEX stock index increased by 40 percent in the first quarter of 1998; and evidenced the importance of market timing in the privatisation of state-owned enterprises.

Conclusion

The techniques of privatisation as a reform mechanism were examined from the perspective of countries at various stages of development. As shown, the more developed countries operating within the capitalist world-economy devised techniques that comport with their existing political and economic institutions so as to derive maximum benefit from the process. Success at the level of the developed countries largely informed IMF and Bank policy prescriptions to the developing countries, but with less than stellar results at the lower end of the development continuum. Moreover, as the evidence suggests, when the market is allowed to determine the flow of private capital, it is often to the country that offers the greatest prospect for capital accumulation. Indeed, whilst Brazil, for example, was attracting large scale foreign investments, a financial famine existed in Sub-Saharan Africa and other countries where the political and economic institutions were largely absent or weak. Moreover, in the more traditional societies, local customs dictated methodology and outcomes.

---

[11] Dyer, G., 'Brazil power sale nets $1.6bn', in *Financial Times*, 1 August 1997.

[12] Campbell, A., 'Citicorp in talks on CableVision stake', in *Financial Times*, 1 August 1997.

[13] *Reuters News Wire*, 3 April 1998.

Chapter 6

The Eastern European Countries and Russia

Introduction

Earlier chapters treated with the privatisation process in the developed and developing countries. As shown, with few exceptions the process in developing countries was mainly to raise cash to pay down external debts, provide opportunity for foreign investment and to reduce the budgetary burden on the state. However, since 1989 a new approach to privatisation evolved to accommodate the need to effect the quick transformation of the Eastern European Countries (EEC-3) countries and ironically Russia from the Soviet-type economic system to a market economic system.

The transformation of whole societies from one system to another was a major challenge to the privatisation process not previously encountered. Hence the extent to which this has been achieved in the EEC-3 countries – Czechoslovakia (now Czech Republic), Hungary and Poland – and Russia, and the challenges encountered in the process are the focus of this chapter; and offer yet another perspective on privatisation which challenges its original theoretical assumptions.

Historical perspective

The EEC-3 countries came under communist rule in 1948 in consequence of the Yalta Conference; and since that date followed a politically-coercive mode of production. Prior to World War II they had been largely market economies not unlike the UK. Indeed, as part of the Austro-Hungarian Empire, the region was a manifestation of East-European capitalism: Commercial code, business law and other laws supportive of a market economy were part of the institutional infrastructure of the region in consequence of having been part of the interstate system created by the Treaty of Westphalia. However, the liberation of Eastern Europe by the Soviet army at the end of the war and the subsequent agreements between the victorious Allies sealed the socioeconomic and political fate of the EEC-3 countries for decades thereafter. Collectivisation, nationalisation, central planning and redistribution replaced property rights, individualism and market-determined prices.

A common theme of the integration process into the Soviet system was the dismantling of market institutions and the de-emphasising of business and financial services and production of sophisticated consumer goods which characterise a market economy. This led to a general decline in trade with the West. However, as shown in Table 6.1, trade with the Western industrialised countries more than tripled in most cases after 1970, especially with West Germany in response to Bonn's *Ostpolitik* and the EEC-3 countries' discontent with Soviet repression.

Table 6.1   EEC-3 and Russia trade with the West

Country	Total Imports	Imports from West Germany		Total Exports	Exports to. West Germany	
		US$ m	%		US$ m	%
1970						
Czechoslovakia	725	289	39.8	664	199	29.9
Hungary	5734	143	24.9	497	134	26.9
Poland	803	180	22.4	946	203	21.4
East Germany	1,043	660	63.3	911	546	59.9
Russia	2,387	422	17.7	2,219	342	15.4
1975						
Czechoslovakia	1,848	679	36.7	1,595	469	29.4
Hungary	1,819	582	31.9	1,222	365	29.8
Poland	5,461	1,301	23.8	3,122	582	18.6
East Germany	2,695	1,594	59.1	2,346	1,359	57.9
Russia	12,395	2,824	22.8	8,675	1,313	15.1
1980						
Czechoslovakia	2,828	1,036	36.6	3,076	1,045	34.0
Hungary	3,178	1,207	38.0	2,698	999	37.0
Poland	6,335	1,459	23.0	5,535	1,376	24.8
East Germany	5,331	2,908	54.5	5,062	3,065	60.5
Russia	21,526	4,373	20.3	23,616	4,076	17.2

Source: Compiled from Lincoln Gordon, (1987: 334 and 336)

As conceived, Bonn's *Ostpolitik* was essentially aimed at reducing West Germany's dependency on the Allies for its security by engaging the East-European countries in trade, especially East Germany. The underlying philosophy was that 'there is less need to pay for insurance in the West if a reinsurance policy can be taken out in the East' (Joffe, 1989, 119). Thus as shown in Table 6.1, almost two-thirds of East Germany's trade with the West were with West Germany. Moreover, exports to West Germany from the EEC-3 countries and Russia increased both in absolute terms as well as a percentage of total exports.

Czechoslovakia (Czech Republic)

In the case of the Czech Republic, although the data suggest otherwise the transformation to a politically-coercive system was never quite completed. Its geographical contiguity to West Germany and Austria fostered the filtering of Western ideas and reminders of a market economy. Also, the steady stream of Western visitors served to further reinforce the process of keeping the memory of a capitalist heritage firmly in the minds of the people (see Joffe 1989).

Notwithstanding influences from the West, the Czech Republic was officially transformed to a centrally-planned economic system by 1959 when the process of nationalisation was completed. At the end of the official transformation, the contribution of the private sector to net national product (NNP) decreased from 33.4 percent in 1948 to 1.6 percent in 1960. During the same period the public sector's contribution to NNP increased from 65.6 percent to 93.4 percent. As NNP became a function of state-owned enterprises and agricultural collectives, the public sector's contribution assumed a larger proportion. Thus by 1980, it had reached a high of 97.4 percent whilst the private sector's share further declined to 0.5 percent as shown in Figure 6.1. The contribution from state-owned enterprises increased from 62.9 percent in 1948 to 87.5 percent in 1980, whilst the contribution from agricultural co-operatives tripled during the same period.

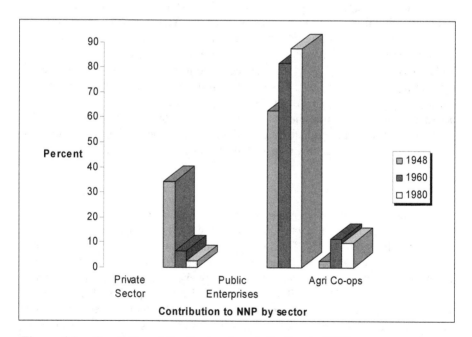

Figure 6.1   Czech Republic: Sectoral contribution to NNP

NNP = Net National Product
Source: Data extracted from Halavàcek and Mejstrik (1997, 5)

In addition to the change in ownership there was a change in production orientation, from exports to Western Europe to supporting the increasingly militaristic economy of the Soviet Union. This was reinforced by the Russian occupation in 1968 which brought to an end the economic reform of 'Prague Spring'. In consequence, many of the smaller enterprises were either eliminated or consolidated into larger units. According to Halavàcek and Mejstrik (1997, 6) state-owned enterprises with less than 500 workers declined from 13 percent in 1958 to 1.4 percent in 1980; they were replaced with heavy industries, with an emphasis on production of heavy chemicals, metallurgy, fuels, heavy machinery and military hardware, with an average labour force of 3,400 and accounting for almost one-half of the labour force. In this structure, the Czech Republic was second only to Russia.

From a PE management perspective, the central focus of the enterprise manager became one of convincing the central planning committee of the irreplaceable nature of its production and the necessity to increase allocations for its upkeep (Halavàcek and Mejstrik, 1997, 9). At the other end of this principal-agent information-asymmetry scenario were the bureaucrats at the centre whose main interests were to ensure that production targets were met and to increase their own power over the enterprise managers. In consequence, enterprise efficiency and quality control were not meaningful concepts to either the PE manager or to the centre (see Carson 1997).

The Soviet occupation after 1968 saw a further cooling of relations with the West: Political, cultural and economic relations with the West were kept to a minimum until mid-1985, when proposals for joint-venture legislation aimed at attracting Western capital were introduced. In spite of these controls, as Table 6.1 shows, trade with the industrial countries of the West began to increase from around 1975 when imports from and exports to the Western countries increased to US$1,848 million and US$1,595 million respectively. West Germany was its largest trading partner, accounting for US$679.0 million of imports and US$469 million of its exports. By 1980, there was an approximate 50 percent increase in trade activity with the West, especially with West Germany (see Rutland 1997).

Hungary

As with the Czech Republic, the communist party gained control of the production resources in Hungary in 1948, after which central planning techniques were introduced. Prior to the war, Hungary functioned as a market economy with one of the most developed capital markets in Europe. The imperial decree of 1860 which permitted the establishment of commodity exchanges throughout the Austro-Hungarian Empire derived the Budapest Commodity and Capital Exchange in 1864. The rules of the exchange had its roots in the concept of 'sworn brokers' established by the Budapest Chamber of Commerce some twenty years earlier. Sworn brokers were not allowed to trade for their own account until 1875, when the Hungarian Parliament abolished the concept. By 1905 there were '... 61 industrial companies, 51 financial institutions, and 38 other shareholding companies traded on the exchange'

(Fletcher 1995, 113). More importantly, the Budapest exchange had a role in the funnelling of European capital to the building of the American railroad and also benefited from the resultant demand for copper. The exchange ceased to exist in 1948 after the country came under communist rule.

In terms of output, Hungary's GDP was about two-thirds that of the Czech Republic's and with a private sector that was considerably larger. Whereas the public sector in the Czech Republic's accounted for 97.4 percent of output in 1980, Hungary's public sector's contribution to GDP was 65.2 percent in 1984. In addition, Hungary maintained contact with the West in spite of being under Soviet control. High-level visits by Western European leaders were regular occurrences, as were Mr. Kadar's visits to the West after 1968.

Although with only about two-thirds the output of the Czech Republic, Hungary's trade with the West was almost equal to the Czech Republic's. Indeed in 1980, as shown in Table 6.1, its imports from the West had surpassed the Czech Republic's. Also, the gap between it and Poland in terms of trade with the West had been significantly narrowed. Thus in terms of percentage GDP, Hungary's trade with the West accounted for about one-half of its total exports and 20 percent of GDP. This was in large measure due to the 'New Economic Mechanism' of the Kadar regime which began in 1968, and to the availability of cheap coal.

With respect to its agricultural sector, prior to 1968 the collectivisation of the agricultural sector resulted in 90 percent of farmland and 94 percent of its agricultural workers coming under central control. Moreover, Hungary had become dependent upon the CEMA countries, mainly Russia, for its agricultural exports (Berry 1997, 375). After 1968, the co-operative farms, which totalled 1,260 and accounted for about three-quarters of Hungary's agricultural output, were allowed to function with a high degree of autonomy. Approximately 120 state farms accounted for the balance in output.

Poland

Poland rounds off the EEC-3 countries. Its history is not dissimilar to that of the Czech Republic or Hungary's. Poland was part of the Austro-Hungarian Empire and like the Czech Republic was denied access to the Marshall Plan by the Soviets at the end of the war.

From a political perspective, Poland was second only to the Czech Republic in terms of organised pluralism and democratic socialism, both of which failed to take root in Hungary. However, Poland's pluralism historically benefited from having a strong Roman Catholic presence and equally strong ties to the West, as reinforced by Pope John Paul II. Hence arguably it was the invasion of Poland, not the occupation of the Sudetenland in September 1938 that led to Western military intervention against Nazi-Germany.

In terms of its public sector contribution to total output, Poland was between Hungary and the Czech Republic at 81.7 percent in 1985. And in terms of trade with the West, Poland's exports and imports in absolute terms were more than double that of Hungary's in 1975. It also exceeded Czech Republic's by half as much again. Thus of the EEC-3 countries, Poland had the highest level of trade and therefore contact with the West. Again, as with both Czech Republic and Hungary, West Germany was Poland's major trading partner, accounting for over one-fifth of its trade with the West and reflecting the West German government's commitment to its *Ostpolitik.*

Like the Hungarians and the Czechs before them, the Polish workers were also at odds with Moscow and its puppet regime, culminating with the Solidarity movement in 1980. This was the second time the Poles sought to break-away from the rigidity of the politically-coercive system. To the Poles, like to the Czechs and Hungarians, the historic promise of socialism to create economic wealth for all in addition to equality had failed to materialize. The declining standard of living and accompanied misery and repression of socialism were still capable of being contrasted and compared with the immediate past and indeed with progress in the West. As a consequence, the socialist ideological claim to popular legitimacy was being undermined by its failure to live up to its promises. However, unlike Hungary in 1956 and the Czech Republic in 1968, Poland's 1980–1981 revolution was derived from the masses – the workers – and thus was from below, thereby leading to the eventual replacement of the Jaruzelski regime with Lech Walesa and Solidarity. It was also aided by Mikhail Gorbachev's policies of *glasnost* and *perestroika* which were based on the realisation that the faltering Soviet economy could only be revitalised if it were relieved of the burden of a stagnating empire (see Gorbachev 1987). Thus instead of Russian tanks rumbling through the streets of Warsaw, Poland, like all other Soviet satellite-states of the time, was left to devise solutions to its own economic crisis and attendant social discontent. Uniformity and the concept of a single socialist model had given way to 'socialist pluralism' under *glasnost.*

Russia

Whereas a politically-coercive system supplanted a market economic system in the EEC-3 countries in 1948, it was implemented in Russia in 1917 and took hold in the late 1920s under Josef Stalin. Prior to Stalin's accession in 1928 some semblance of a market economy was restored under Lenin's 'New Economic Policy' (see Carson 1997). This was brought to an end by the Bolsheviks because of the perceived threat it posed to their power. As a result, central planning was vigorously pursued by Stalin and became well ingrained in the Russian psyche in comparison with the EEC-3 countries. This was more so since, at the time, Russia was essentially agrarian and collectivisation encompassed a larger proportion of the population and was easier to implement.

Another distinguishing characteristic between the EEC-3 countries and Russia was that Russia's industrialisation occurred under central planning, and after 1948 became heavily dependent upon the resources of EEC-3 countries. Indeed, it could be argued that CEMA was formed primarily to provide the Soviet economy with the necessary resources. But central planning was still an evolving technique, especially as it relates to state-capitalist industrialisation up to 1941 and after the war.

After the war, the industrial economic system benefited from the technology acquired through the war experience and by conquest. But the rigidity of central planning as an industrialisation strategy was found to be stifling from an enterprise efficiency and effectiveness perspective, and thus created the need for some decentralisation in the industrial administration. As a result, Nikita Khrushchev pursued some measure of decentralisation between 1955 and 1964 in an attempt to re-invigorate the post-war Soviet economy. After 1964, however, attempts to restore the classic Stalinist model were made by both Brezhnev and his successor Kosygin. As a result, the process of decentralisation was put on hold until the 1980s.

Amidst the political power struggle between the 'industrial administrative elite' which favoured central planning and the Soviet leadership, especially Khrushchev, the Soviet economy grew at a rapid rate. But in ex-post evaluations the growth was seen as being achieved at the expense of the environment, the natural resource base and human welfare (Clawson 1995, 17). Although not related to the Khrushchev era, it was only until after 1992 that the extent to which slave-labour was used between 1933 and 1953 in the mining of uranium in Siberia became known. Many of the prisoners were political dissidents and 3 million are estimated to have died in these camps.

The pressure to grow the economy was derived from the implicit promise of the political leadership to cushion the disadvantages of central planning by the provision of a social safety net – almost cradle-to-grave in dimension – for the people. But instead of adding to the range of products produced, the process resulted in increasing production of more of the same with little or no improvement in the quality or choice of consumer goods. As a consequence, the low-quality products of the Soviet factories were no match for Western-produced goods in world markets.

The political risks associated with improving enterprise efficiency by reducing the work force or the closing-down of whole plants were not risks any of the Russian leaders prior to Gorbachev was willing to take. However, Gorbachev, it should be noted, was drafted into the reform process by Andropov who began to question the ability of the Russian economy to respond to the challenge posed by the US military build-up under Reagan. It was Andropov who sought a more efficient Russian economy through changes in the production processes. And it was under Andropov, and later Chernenko, that Gorbachev experimented with ideas of overhauling the system prior to his assuming office in 1985 (Clawson 1995, 29).

With Gorbachev's accession to power in 1985, reforms to the system were introduced. In Gorbachev's view, the problems of Russia and the Soviet Union were derived from 'miscalculations by the ruling parties' (Gorbachev 1987, 163). Restructuring – *perestroika* – as an aspect of modernisation of the economic system was to be pursued by individual countries in the region, in an atmosphere of *glasnost* and *demokratizacya*. However, even before Gorbachev's accession to leadership in 1985 there was some evidence of market concepts at work in the EEC-3 countries. For example, in 1982, Hungarian enterprises were allowed to issue bonds to the public as a means of raising capital. Even in Russia there was evidence of attempts to reform the system through changes in the incentive system, for example, linking enterprise performance to bonus funds. Enterprises with revenues in excess of costs were allowed to utilize such excess income on improving the welfare of their workers instead of having to transfer it to the central authorities for reallocation. Hence, despite opposition from party die-hards the foundation for Russia's transformation to a market economy was unintentionally laid by Gorbachev's *perestroika* which sought reform within the context of a single political party system (Gorbachev 1987) and indeed, Marxism-Leninism.

As seen through the eyes of Margaret Thatcher (2002, 75), Gorbachev's notions of reform '... simply meant making the Marxist-Leninist system more efficient, not adopting a different system'. Her disappointment with Gorbachev as a reformist is unmistakable:

> For all his talk of the need for 'new thinking', in the end he just could not practice it. Faced in 1991 with a choice between continuing along the path of fundamental change on the one hand and a return to repressive communism on the other, he dithered (Thatcher 2002, 77).

It was thus left to Boris Yeltsin to lead the battle for Russian democracy in a Russia that had over 70 years become more oppressive of its people and in which, again, as seen by Baroness Thatcher (2002, 77), '... the only dominant principle was that of predatory egotism'. But it was under Vladimir Putin that Russia repaid its external debts – some US$22.0 billion – in advance of their due dates and have strengthened its foreign exchange reserves thereby limiting the leverage of the Western powers.

Prelude to transformation: Issues in common

The reform machinery set in motion by *glasnost* had gotten out of control from the perspective of the Kremlin, more precisely Gorbachev's, and although many of the Soviet satellites maintained their party loyalty the process was irreversible, culminating in the removal of Gorbachev and the accession of Boris Yeltsin in 1991 who promptly went about dismantling the Communist Party and the Soviet Union.

But even before Gorbachev, the East German economy having benefited from its unique trade relationship with West Germany had begun to indirectly exert pressure on the Kremlin by its relative strength. Indeed, by 1980 East Germany, the Czech Republic and Hungary enjoyed a higher GDP per capita than Russia. Other factors at play included debt ridden Hungary and Poland anxiously seeking debt relief from the West, including the IMF. And because their debts were to Western banks, both Hungary and Poland were included in the debt reduction programmes of the period. The Czech Republic, like East Germany, on the other hand, was essentially self-sufficient and showed no interest in Western financing at that point in time.

In addition to the above, there were certain shared characteristics of the EEC-3 countries and Russia that had been identified and are therefore analysed here in common.

Enterprises as social institutions

As noted above many of the smaller enterprises were consolidated into larger production units, mainly heavy manufacturing industries. The resulting large state-enterprises functioned as social institutions, serving the needs of their respective communities in accordance with the prevailing political, economic, social and cultural environment and, as noted in Chapter 3, served as the model for developing countries seeking to escape their history. A primary responsibility of these enterprises was the provision of employment to their respective communities. Other services included provision of schools and hospitals which are normally provided by state and local governments in market economies. As a result of their ascribed social-welfare responsibilities, many of these large scale enterprises remained to be privatised at the end of 1994, even though they were deemed inefficient, over-staffed and over-capitalised. Hence the challenges posed to the privatisation process in the EEC-3 countries and Russia were not dissimilar to those found in the developing countries.

Rehabilitation and restructuring

Arising from the structure described above, the central objective of the transformation process was improving the efficiency of the enterprises as a group while keeping the factors of production – mainly labour – fully employed. Thus, as regards privatisation of the large-scale enterprises, it was evident that rehabilitation and restructuring needed to be carried out prior to any privatisation; again, not dissimilar to the process in developing countries. Moreover, the military orientation of these enterprises in Russia and to a lesser extent in the Czech Republic operated as a constraint to their privatisation. Thus, in the interim many of the larger enterprises received relief from state banks in the form of grants and preferential loan terms and were allowed to be in arrears with their payments for customs duties, payroll and social security taxes. Plant-closings that would result in mass lay-off of the work force were not viable political options.

Relationship with the West

As depicted in Table 6.1, after 1970 trade with the Western industrialised countries increased three-fold – more so for Russia after 1975 – making these countries vulnerable to the ideas of the West and dependent on it for trade. In the specific case of the Czech Republic, firms that were previously dependent upon the Russian market have actively sought out markets for their products in the developing countries and in the EU, as 'low-cost manufacturers' (Rutland 1997, 301).

The combined effect of debt transfer to the state banks and the seeking out of export markets resulted in 80 percent of the large state enterprises, many privatised, becoming profitable at the end of 1994, compared with 60 percent in 1992. In 1995, Germany was the Czech Republic's leading trading partner, accounting for

25.8 percent of its imports and 31.8 percent of its exports. These results could in part be attributed to the 'associate member' status granted to the EEC-3 group by the EU in December 1992, and to the long-standing trading relationship developed under Bonn's *Ostpolitik*. However after 1994, the Czech Republic's imports were growing at a faster rate than its exports. This was mainly due to the lowering of tariff barriers in an effort to shorten the time to full membership of the EU, which it desperately sought, and to the lack of competitiveness of its outputs. The net results were a further delay to improving the efficiency of the larger enterprises and to their eventual privatisation (see Rutland 1997).

Hungary, like Czech Republic was also dependent upon foreign trade. However, unlike the Czech Republic, Hungary's industrial output depended upon imported raw materials. More importantly, Hungary's exports were essentially agricultural which accounted for about one-quarter of its hard currency earnings in the early 1990s. Agricultural supports were essential to protect the sector and amounted to 15 percent of the value of the sector's production. Moreover, agricultural exports to the EU were constrained by the heavy subsidies paid to EU's farmers and its extensive use of non-tariff barriers against other countries' agricultural exports as authorised by its CAP. The collapse of the CMEA, upon which Hungary depended for its exports, exacerbated Hungary's dependency on exports to the West.

Poland's dependency on the West was no less than that of the other two members of the EEC-3 group even though its trade with West Germany[1] as a percentage of total trade was considerably less than Czech Republic's and Hungary's. More importantly, Poland was heavily dependent upon debt rescheduling and no doubt had to be manifestly more outward oriented so as to secure debt forgiveness which it received und the Paris Club initiative.

Nucleus for a capital market

Despite their contact with the West, the EEC-3 countries had lost their ability to function in a competitive environment in consequence of the dismantling of their market institutions after 1948. In this regard, they were no better off than Russia which had to implement the necessary market-supporting institutions as a critical aspect of its transformation. But like the rebuilding of the Western European and Japanese economies following World War II, the EEC-3 countries had the unique opportunity to implement a more forward looking market economic structure instead of having existing and archaic systems foisted upon them by creditor institutions. Thus, for example, whilst the need for capital markets cannot be denied, the rules and procedures could be uniquely theirs in the same way that new ideas of privatisation were derived out of their specific needs.

As stated in Chapter 5, one of the advantages of broad-based ownership is to provide the nucleus for a capital market despite the absence of revenue flows to

---

[1]   In 1995, trade with a united Germany rose to 35.7 percent of exports to the west and 27.5 percent of imports, making Germany its largest trading partner.

the government in the short run and the concerns about corporate governance. The extent to which such new ideas could be independently pursued depends crucially upon the level of external debts and, like the developing countries before them, the level of their economic desperation.

Corporate governance

As noted above corporate governance has been a concern common to the EEC-3 countries and Russia. In addition to the discovery that 'privatisation does not automatically ensure internal efficiency [and that] ... natural monopolies need to be properly regulated' (Marial 1996, 142), the absence of private-sector managers further constrained the process. But as is well established in developed economies, the stock market serves as an oversight of management performance which is reflected in the price of the stock. Thus the establishment of capital markets in the EEC-3 countries and Russia was one of the means to effecting internal efficiency. Hence, despite the constraint of time on the effectiveness of capital markets, their establishment in both the Czech Republic and Russia served to encourage trading in both vouchers and shares and provided the nucleus of a capital market in both countries. As a result, there was some degree of consolidation of share-ownership into stronger and not exclusively Russian hands. Again too, the notion that enterprise efficiency is necessarily derived from a top-down approach to management has been long challenged by the Japanese idea of worker participation in the decision-making process. Nonetheless, the use of Western management under contract had been employed in both Hungary and Poland as an interim measure to make up for the absence of local private-sector managers and to appease the IMF and Bank, bearing in mind that the Washington Consensus narrative was extended to Hungary and Poland and to some extent to the Czech Republic and Russia and manifest in advice if not prescription to these countries.

Despite these measures to address the inadequacy in corporate governance, the involvement of the state in the decision making process especially with respect to maintaining inefficient enterprises is seen by advocates of a flash-cut approach in transition economies as a significant hindrance to the reform process. But as noted above, the larger albeit inefficient enterprises functioned more as social institutions rather than economic actors. Hence they remained under the control of the government until alternatives to them were developed and implemented.

Despite their differences, a common goal of the EEC-3 countries was to join the EU and to be under the security umbrella of NATO. In this regard, in December 1992 the EEC-3 countries signed an agreement with the EU whereby they were granted associate member status pending full integration. Under this agreement, the Czech Republic, Hungary, and Poland were expected to lower their tariffs against EU's exports. In exchange the EU's common external tariffs against imports from these countries were to be lowered over an eight year period, at the end of which full membership will be considered. Concurrent with their receiving associate member status in the EU, the EEC-3 countries signed the Central Europe Free Trade

Agreement (CEFTA), thereby creating a free-trade zone among them as a first step toward full integration into the EU. This move on the part of the EEC-3 countries clearly reiterated their commitment to the privatisation of their remaining public enterprises.

It is thus against this backdrop of the EEC-3 countries' and Russia's experience with central planning and *perestroika* that privatisation as the central strategy in the transformation to a market economy is further critiqued on an individual country basis.

The privatisation process

To the EEC-3 countries and Russia privatisation functioned as the dominant concept in the transformation process. The underlying goal of the EEC-3 countries as stated above was to be part of an enlarged and prosperous Europe which could only be achieved by reverting to a market economy. And since the experience with a politically-coercive system was nothing less than endured-repression, there was very little worth preserving. Nonetheless, ensuring a transition period that would permit adjustment by the people while at the same time obtain their full support for the programme were of concern. Thus in the complete absence of the required ideological and institutional infrastructure, the challenge was to arrive at an implementation programme that would serve both requirements. Consequently, the Czech Republic's privatisation programme was characterized by mass privatisation that had broad-based ownership as a goal as a first step, and restructuring for effective corporate governance after privatisation as the second. Hungary and Poland on the other hand preferred a more conventional approach to the process, if only to comply with creditors' requirements and reflected IMF/Bank prescriptions. But before analysing individual country experiences with the process, which differed in terms of emphasis and techniques, a description of the voucher-based system which was deferred in Chapter 5 is now offered.

The voucher system

In terms of the benefits of broad-based ownership discussed in Chapters 4 and 5, the mass privatisation programmes of the Czech Republic and Russia sought to capitalise upon those perceived benefits. Consequently, the voucher system was the primary privatisation technique utilised by these two countries.

Under this system, vouchers are distributed to eligible participants – considered to be all adults within the community – either free of charge or for a nominal price. The principal objective is to enlist popular support for the transformation to a market system by the creation of units of property rights and the subsequent distribution of such property rights to the population (see Gray 1996). These vouchers are either exchanged for shares in a particular state-owned enterprise or placed with a financial intermediary – mutual fund or investment fund. Where the vouchers are placed with a financial intermediary, bids for shares in the various enterprises are made utilising the vouchers of their members.

The use of vouchers allows shares to be fairly priced based on valuations of the enterprises. They could also be traded thereby creating a secondary market and providing participants with the experience of a capital market. More importantly, the existence of financial capital markets such as stock exchanges, for example, is not a prerequisite, although such markets could result as people begin to trade their shares.

Where the concern is about corporate governance, usually not a problem in market economies because of the existence of a core shareholder or shareholder group, financial incentives could be provided to the financial intermediaries to assume a leading role in the management of the enterprise. But even without such incentives, the accumulation of vouchers has the potential of creating a core group of investors by the trading of such voucher on the open market based on the perceived potential for profit maximisation (see Gray 1996). The drawback is the perceived difficulty and risk involved in accumulating numerous shareholdings by a strategic foreign investor if such is the desire of the government (see Megyery and Sader (1997, 15). Additionally, as employed in Russia, the voucher system did not generate any revenues to the government but this does not necessarily mean that there should not be a price attached to vouchers.

The Czech Republic

As shown in Figure 6.1 above, the Czech Republic's public sector accounted for 97.4 percent of NNP in 1980. By 1989, it was almost 100 percent. Thus of the EEC-3 countries, it had the most to convert from a percentage GDP standpoint. However, of the three, it was the strongest in terms of entrepreneurial traditions and political governance.

The Czech government had been consistent in its privatisation policies and followed a defined programme. As observed by Ernst *et al.* (1996, 52) 'the central objective was to divest the government of as many assets and responsibilities as quickly as possible'. In this, its programme was essentially one of restitution, small-scale privatisation, removal of restrictions on private enterprise formation and large-scale privatisation primarily but not exclusively through the voucher system.

Restitution

As was the case in Chile, restitution of property to former owners was an important aspect of the government's programme. However, former owners were given a defined time period to prove their claims. Under this programme according to Rutland (1997, 302), approximately 100,000 properties were restored to their former owners and included houses, shops and small factories. Included in the restitution process were about 800 Church properties expropriated by the communist regime in the early 1950s. According to Mladek (1997, 46) 74 properties were returned in 1991 to the Catholic Church under 'Czech Republic law No. 298/1990 – On Regulation of Property Relations of Religious Orders and Congregations and the *Olomouc* Archdiocese', with another 176 by law NO. 338/1991. The other 550 remained unclaimed because they were either in gross disrepair or were destroyed. Not settled were the Church's claim to land and forest nationalized in the early 1950s. In addition, 404,000 claims had been lodged by mid-1993 by farmers seeking restitution of their farms. In other cases of restitution, shares in the larger factories or government bonds were given in compensation. No cash payments were made (see Rutland 1997; Mladek 1997).

Small-scale privatisation

In February 1991, the small-scale privatisation programme was launched. Responsibility for the process was given to local authorities who sold about 22,300 shops, restaurants, and workshops to private bidders. According to Ernst, et al. (1996, 56), the government had no interest in lease as a method, and to facilitate quick sales provided bank loans at near market interest rates. It also assumed all debt obligations of the enterprises prior to their auction. The programme was regarded as successful – all enterprises were sold above their average starting prices – and added to the cash reserves of the National Property Fund (NPF). Thus the success of the restitution and small-scale privatisation programmes set the tone for the large-scale privatisation that followed.

Large-scale privatisation

The large-scale privatisation programme required that each of the enterprises prepares its own project proposal, indicating its preferred method: direct sale to local or foreign buyers, auction or sale by voucher. The programme was divided into two 'waves': The first wave which began in May 1992 included between one-quarter to one-half of all large state-owned enterprises within the Czech Republic and was completed by January 1993; the second wave started in October 1993 and ended in early 1995.

    Direct sales   As shown in Figure 6.2, direct sales were a mere fraction of total joint-stock shares offered in both first and second waves. In 1993, direct sales accounted for 7.0 percent of the shares offered in that year with about one-half taken-up by foreigners by way of competitive bidding (Ernst et al. 1996, 57). However, in 1994 direct sales accounted for 23 percent of the shares sold in that year; but this was only after 97.8 percent of total joint-stock shares were sold in 1993 as can be discerned from Figure 6.2. The majority of direct sales were of agricultural properties and professional practices: polyclinics, ambulatory health facilities, and the like. As earlier noted part of the restitution program included the issuing of shares as compensation. This amounted to 3 percent of the shares issued in 1993, and 4 percent in 1994. Foreigners were allowed to participate in the sale on the capital market and accounted for about one-half of the sale under that category. As shown in Figure 6.2 voucher privatisation accounted for 51 percent of the shares in 1993, and 49 percent in 1994; and accounted for 50.7 percent of total joint-stock shares sold on a combined basis (Ceska 1995, 113).

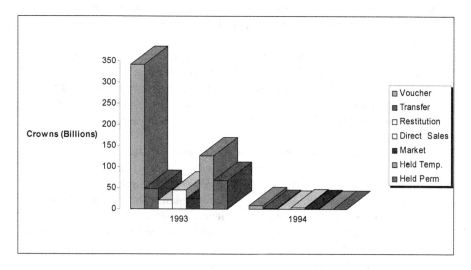

Figure 6.2   Czech Republic: Methods of privatisation 1993–1994

Source: Constructed from data in Ceska, R. (1995, 11)

Investment funds

Clearly, the preferred technique was voucher privatisation, with 50.7 percent for the two years. Approximately 80 percent of the population purchased vouchers of which 72 percent were invested with 220 investment funds for the purchase of shares on a pooled basis, on the promise of at least a ten-fold return on their investment within one year. After May 1993 when most of the shares were issued, trading began in the secondary market. This led to the 120 largest investment funds – mostly owned by banks – controlling over 60 percent of the total shares issued. The Czech savings banks controlled about 10 percent of all shares issued. Under Czech law, no one fund can own more than 20 percent in any given company (see Ernst et al. 1996; Rutland 1997).

Investment fund scandals   The decline in share prices resulted in a liquidity shortage, and all but one, the Czech Saving Bank, honoured its promise of a ten-fold return on investment return within a year. According to Rutland (1997, 303), the largest privately-owned investment fund, the Harvard Fund with 820,000 shareholders acquired assets at a 45 to 1 ratio but lacked the liquidity to honour its obligation to its shareholders. In consequence, it sought to defer payment by advancing the argument that payment was due one year after acquisition of shares in the companies and not, as was the general interpretation, one year after acquisition of the vouchers.

Other Scandals   In 1997, other issues relating to private investment funds in the EEC-3 countries and Russia surfaced. For example, two officials of AID in Moscow were accused of abusing the trust of the US government by using personal relations for private gains. As reported the two officials allegedly used US financed resources to support the private investment fund controlled by the spouse of one of the officials.[2]

At the end of 1995, about 71 percent of the large scale privatisation had been completed. In addition to the 7.2 percent of shares representing properties transferred to the municipalities – fire-fighting services and hospitals, for example – 9.8 percent of the total transferred represented properties to be held permanently by the state. The temporary holding represented the state's control in those enterprises that were not quite ready for full privatisation.

Cross-ownership   A significant characteristic of the Czech Republic's privatisation programme was the extent to which cross-ownership existed. Many of the investment funds were owned by banks which were also either in the process of being privatised or not at all. As a result, these investment funds acquired shares in their parents as the process was evolving. Hence, the state's holdings in privatised enterprises are believed to have been understated because of this indirect ownership. Indeed, although the restructuring in the banking sector reduced the number of state banks to one, the NPF at the end of 1996 still controlled between 40 percent and 50 percent of the shares in the privatised banks (see Ernst *et al.* 1996).

Absence of incentives for foreign participation   Another distinguishing characteristic of the Czech programme was the initial lack of incentives to attract foreign investors, preferring instead to establish Czech business interests during this period.[3]

Hungary

Hungary's privatisation program was almost the reverse of the Czech Republic's. Its primary objective was to attract FDI and therefore avoided the voucher system which, as explained above, targeted the population for broad-based ownership. What is more, based on a relatively larger private sector – representing about one-quarter of GDP, compared with Czech Republic's 1.0 percent – Hungary by 1990 was much further along in rebuilding its market institutions: A commercial code was in place, foreign investment was legalised and private enterprises were accorded the same legal rights as public enterprises. Recall also that Hungary was a bastion of Eastern European capitalism before it was co-opted into the Soviet system.

---

[2]   Robbins, C. and Liesman, S., 'How an Aid Program Vital to New Economy of Russia Collapsed', in *The Wall Street Journal*, 13 August 1997.

[3]   Frank, R., 'Czechs Join Rivalry in Eastern Europe to Lure Foreign Firms with Incentives', in *The Wall Street Journal*, 22 September 22, 1997, A18.

With market-oriented institutions in place, Hungary patterned its privatisation programme along the lines of the UK's programme. As a result, public sale of shares and competitive bidding were the primary techniques employed by the Hungarian government after a flurry of questionable sales to insiders under what had been referred to as 'spontaneous privatization' (see Csepi and Lukacs, 1994).

The abuse of power by the old regime in the early stages of privatisation led to the centralisation of the process in March 1990 under the State Property Agency (SPA). Sale by competitive bidding was a legal requirement and targeted foreigners. All preparation of the enterprise to be privatised and negotiations were conducted by the SPA. By October 1994, sale to foreigners amounted to US$2.9 billion for 385 companies out of a total of 871 companies that had been prepared for privatisation by the SPA (Csepi and Lukacs 1995, 189–90). Nonetheless, there were accounts of bureaucratic delays encountered by foreign companies in negotiations with the SPA in the early years of its functioning as the central privatisation authority.

Foreign investor participation versus local ownership

Corruption and delays notwithstanding, by 1992 Hungary reportedly had sold the most financially attractive enterprises. Since these sales were mainly to foreigners, many Hungarians regarded the process as selling 'the crown jewels' of Hungary. According to Fletcher (1995, 56), 20 of the best enterprises with a total asset value of US$1,123 million and aggregate sales of US$1,431 million were chosen for the initial programme in 1990. As a result, at the end of 1994 the private sector accounted for 65 percent of GDP; and with it the expansion of the capitalist world-economy had been assured a foothold in Eastern Europe in short order.

With the best sold, foreign demand for Hungarian enterprises began to wane by the end of 1992. As a further consolidation step in the process, the Hungarian State Holding Company (HSHC) was formed in 1992 to manage those enterprises remaining under direct state control. At the end of 1994 these totalled 158 firms. The SPA became bogged-down in controversy and in-fighting, resulting in slowing the process still further.

In an effort to boost its privatisation programme and to appease its critics, the government changed its strategy in 1993 and began targeting enterprise managers and workers. Employee-assisted buy-outs and instalment sales at below market interest rates were introduced, as were leases to managers.

However a new government was elected inn 1995. This was followed by the passing of the Privatisation Law in May 1995. Under this law, the SPA and HSHC were merged and became the Hungarian State Property and Holding Company (APV Rt.). The 1995 law also reinstated the preference for cash sales mainly because of budgetary and balance of payments needs and a still substantial external debt overhang. It was also occasioned by the perceived need to de-emphasize employee assisted buy-outs and instalment sales at below market interest rates in the light of criticism of the previous government and of speculation in vouchers.

Because Hungary's privatisation programme was directed at foreign investors and not at Hungarians, it did not receive the same popular support as did the Czech Republic's. The expressed concerns were over equity of the process, especially as regards privatisation of the larger PE, and for jobs (Ernst *et al.* 1996, 49). In addition, the perceived aggressive behaviour of Western companies in obtaining domestic market share was intimidating to Hungarians not accustomed to the workings of the invisible hand.

Despite these concerns, at the end of 1994 ownership of Hungarian production structure showed that employee-ownership had doubled to 4.39 percent, and that domestic investor holdings had increased to 30.04 percent from 17.32 percent in 1993. Foreign ownership stood at 12.09 percent whilst SPA holding was 53.48 percent. In addition, private sector development benefited from the private capital flows that accompanied the removal of restrictions on the private sector. This was especially noticeable in the banking sector where foreigners controlled '... just under 50% of the assets in the country's banking system, and the buying [was] continuing'.[4] Nonetheless, in terms of its earlier comparative advantage in the transformation process derived from its 'business environment' and 'foreign business perception', Hungary at the end of 1995 was a distant second to the Czech Republic in terms of attracting FDI.

Restitution

Hungary, like the Czech Republic, had adopted a programme of restitution to political dissidents. Vouchers were issued to those who were able to establish claims to land and other properties expropriated under communism. These vouchers were for specific enterprises. But the failure to assign enterprises to vouchers as a way of ascribing value to them resulted in a decline in the value of the vouchers which had been freely traded. Also, vouchers for land could be exchanged only for land, and then only prior owners were allowed to exercise claims to land.

Poland

Like Hungary, Poland adopted the more established techniques of privatisation on the concern that mass-privatisation would result in a lack of effective governance and does not raise cash. Recall also that the goal of Poland was to join the EU and to have its huge debts forgiven. Hence, unlike the Czech Republic, Poland's privatisation programme was linked to the IMF structural adjustment program (SAP) and to the Paris-Club arrangement under which Poland sought to have its debts with Western countries rescheduled and reduced. Hungary also was a client of the IMF during this period and also sought rescheduling of its US$20.0 billion debt under

---

[4]   Reed, J., 'Foreigners Transform Hungary's Banks' in *The Wall Street Journal*, 24 September 1997, A18.

similar arrangements. With the IMF in common, the similarities in their approaches to privatisation were not unexpected.

Privatisation framework

As was the case with the Czech Republic and Hungary, Poland's 'informal privatization' in 1988–9 operated to the benefit of existing enterprise managers and party officials who structured the early programme to their benefit. As a result of this abuse and the added need to formalise the programme, the 'Law on the Privatization of State-owned Enterprises' was passed in July 1990. This law governed the conversion of PE to corporations and the selling of their shares. It also addressed procedures with respect to privatisation through liquidation (see Krzysztof 1995).

In addition to new laws specific to the privatisation process, the old 'Bankruptcy Law' and the 'Polish Commercial Code', both enacted in 1934, were revived with amendments. In this regard, Poland merely updated commercial practices that were dormant during the period of communism. The institution responsible for the privatisation process was the Ministry of Privatisation which came into being in July, 1990.

The general procedure was that the process would be initiated by the enterprise which was responsible for bringing itself to the point of conversion to a joint-stock company. Feasibility studies were then conducted and a decision made based on the results of the studies. The next stage was the documentation process which included receiving reports from various other government agencies on matters affecting the enterprise, for example, environmental impact and impact on employment. Hence, in terms of procedure, Poland was the model given that one of its underlying objectives was to secure debt forgiveness under Paris-Club and London-Club arrangements. But as a consequence of following prescribed privatisation procedures, the process was deemed excessively lengthy, extending to as much as 18 months after initiation.

Debt-reduction Notwithstanding the tedious nature of Poland's privatisation procedures, from the perspective of the country as a whole, they served the general needs of the country. Thus, while foreign investors found the process tedious, the Polish government was able to secure substantial reductions to its approximately US$49.0 billion external debts outstanding in 1991 simply by complying with the requirements of the IMF. Additionally, in 1994 Poland reached agreement with the Western commercial banks affiliated with the London Club to further reduce its existing external debt of about US$13.0 billion by 45.2 percent and to repay the balance over a 30 year period (Krzysztof 1995, 302). At the same time there were allegations of under-pricing shares, especially in connection with the privatisation of the Bank *Slaski* in December 1993, which resulted in the resignation of the Minister of Finance (Sword 1997, 547–8).

The process

As regards the actual programme, 2,862 state enterprises out of a possible 8,441 registered in 1990 were transferred to the privatisation programme by the end of the third quarter of 1994. Of these, 1004 were placed under the law governing privatisation through liquidation and were sold to managers and workers: Unlike Hungary, Poland had to be more accommodating to insiders – mainly workers – because of their political influence. To facilitate the process, workers or operators were offered lease-buy arrangements or options to buy. As a result, the majority of the enterprises identified for liquidation were sold to existing operators and workers by early 1991. In addition to restaurants, retail outlets and consumer service units, the smaller units from the break-up of larger enterprises were included in the sale to employees and operators.

Restitution   With respect to restitution to former owners as a method, Poland did not adopt a programme of direct restitution like the Czech Republic and to some extent Hungary. Instead, it opted to set aside a proportion of the privatisation revenues for future compensation in lieu of restitution through the legal process.

Mass privatisation   Despite earlier reluctance to pursue mass privatisation, the voucher system was eventually implemented in November 1995. The results of the voucher system in the Czech Republic and Russia were now common knowledge. Indeed, even the Bank had begun to endorse and recommend the use of vouchers as an acceptable technique to its other clients. Under this scheme, all citizens were allowed to buy vouchers for a nominal price. These vouchers could then be exchanged for shares in the 15 National Investment Funds in which some 400 state enterprises were transferred. Workers in the companies transferred to the National Investment funds were guaranteed 19 percent of the shares in their respective companies and representation on the supervisory boards. The funds were managed by Western managers under management contracts.

Relative outcomes

Despite these successes, when measured in terms of private-sector share of GDP at the end of 1994 Poland has been the least successful of the three EEC-3 countries in the transformation process. At the end of 1994, the private-sector's contribution to total GDP was less than one-half. In the case of Hungary's it was 55 percent and for the Czech Republic, it was 70 percent who, it may be remembered did not pursue an IMF-led strategy. In terms of unemployment, again Poland had the highest rate at 16 percent compared with Hungary's 10 percent and the Czech Republic's 3 percent (Ernst *et al.* 1996, 168).

Similar disparities existed in the case of inflation. Poland had an inflation rate of 32 percent compared with Hungary's 19 percent and the Czech Republic's 10 percent. Also, both Hungary and Czech Republic had higher inflows of FDI – in value as well as percentage – resulting from their privatisation programmes. Since then, data published by the European Bank for Reconstruction and Development showed FDI to the Czech Republic at US$1.2 billion in 1996, down from US$ 2.6 billion in 1995. A more significant drop occurred in the case of Hungary where the comparable figures were US$1.9 billion and US$4.5 billion respectively. Poland, on the other hand experienced an increase in FDI flows, from US$ 1.1 billion in 1995 to US$2.3 billion in 1996.

In terms of per capita income, as shown in Table 2.3 at the end of 1994 Poland trailed both Hungary and Czech Republic. And this was so despite the latter's emphasis on mass privatisation which was generally regarded as a constraint to internal efficiency and problematic in the exercise of corporate governance (Borish and Noël, 1996, 9). But even in Poland, which did not engage in mass privatisation and employee participation to the same extent as the Czech Republic, corporate governance was no less a challenge. This said, Table 2.3 also shows Poland's per capita income increasing by 34 percent in contrast to a decrease of 7.3 percent for the Czech Republic.

Privatisation in Russia

By far the more significant of the four countries' privatisation programmes was the Russian programme, not only because of its size but also because it represented a transformation from an entrenched politically-coercive mode of production to a market economy within a very short time. As marvelled by Martin Feldstein, it was '...one of the 20th century's most remarkable achievements ...'[5] The necessary market institutional infrastructure – legal framework to enforce a system of property rights, markets of all descriptions and a regulatory framework for privatised monopolies – arguably dormant in the EEC-3 countries and only to be revived during the transition, were all embryonic in the case of Russia with no recent historical support; Russia had for too long been a communist state. So also was the notion of corporate governance which had given way to central planning and was not part of the Russian vocabulary. The infancy or shallowness of these institutions would operate to constrain the privatisation effectiveness (see Desai and Goldberg 2000).

Mass privatisation a priority

Adding to the quality of uniqueness of the Russian programme was the decision of the Russian government to go a step further than that established by the Czech Republic and make mass privatisation a priority in preference to corporate governance (Starodubrovskya 1996, 57; see also Gray 1996). The logic quite simply was to establish property rights and to transfer them to the Russian people through a distribution system that was all-encompassing. In this way, the support of the people which was deemed essential to the transformation process would be more forthcoming.

---

[5]   Feldstein, M., 'Russia's Rebirth', in *The Wall Street Journal*, 8 September 1997, A22.

In contrast, the established process of the Bank (1996, 45) categorically required that 'the first step in transition is to move from the centrally planned regime of transfers and subsidies to one that allows for risk, ensures financial discipline, and creates strong profit-oriented incentives'. The rationale for this dictum stemmed from the belief that firms irrespective of ownership will 'make efforts to restructure if their avenues for rescue close and competition increases' (Bank 1996, 45). However, in context of the Russian experience this belief took no cognizance of the social-welfare functions ascribed to public enterprises in a society that was largely defined by its redistributive mode of production as discussed in Chapter 2 nor, indeed, of the reluctance of 'insiders' to part with control which was facilitated by their access to approximately 65 percent of vouchers (see Blasi and Shleifer 1996). It also evidenced the mechanistic approach to reform for which the Bank had been severely criticised in the 1980s. Moreover, to Russian policy-makers the earlier privatisation experiences of Hungary and Poland as examples of economic orthodoxy stood in stark contrast with that of the Czech Republic which privatised primarily on the basis of the voucher system. It is thus against this backdrop of contrasting approaches that the Russian privatisation is critiqued.

Institutional framework

With the collapse of the Soviet Union in 1991, state property was reclassified into four categories: exclusive federal property; municipal property; transferable federal property; and private property already owned by citizens. This classification preceded the privatisation process which began in 1992. The exercise of rights over these properties was also defined by the Supreme Soviet of Russia, with the State Property Committee (GKI) assuming a controlling role over all state-owned property or interests. Thus the GKI role was to oversee the transfer of property to other entities, enter into leases or other agreements as to utilisation of state property; and represents the state in partially-owned enterprises in which the state is majority owner.

In addition to the GKI there were two other state agencies which were considered significant actors in the transformation process. These were the Federal Property Fund and the Federal Agency of Bankruptcy. The Federal Property Fund's role was to represent the government's minority interests in partially-privatised enterprises pending their full privatisation. It was also responsible for the sale of state properties in accordance with the privatisation plan endorsed by the GKI. The Federal Agency of Bankruptcy assumed responsibility for those enterprises that were considered insolvent as defined by the governmental resolution no. 498 of 20 May 1994.

The process

With the privatisation over-arching institutional framework in place, including the passage of laws and decrees which authorised the disposal of state property and the subsequent protection of rights thereto, the government embarked on its privatisation programme in 1992. Its primary objective was two-fold: First, to privatise the greater part of state and municipal properties as quickly as possible within the framework of the free distribution by way of vouchers to employees and citizens of the enterprises to be privatised and second, to defer restructuring of enterprises until after their privatisation.

The programme was essentially in stages: The first stage was the 'small privatisation' by which small enterprises – catering, retail shops, consumer services and the like – were sold; the second stage dealt with the 'corporatization' of large and medium-sized enterprises; and the third stage was the large-scale privatisation through the distribution of vouchers.

Small privatisation

The privatisation of small enterprises which began in April 1992 was left to the municipalities to administer under whose authority they were transferred by the 1991 privatisation law. The 1991 privatisation law also stipulated that these enterprises were not to be transformed into corporations but were to be sold for cash through either auction or tender.

The GKI estimated 270,000 small enterprises existing at the beginning of 1992 of which 94,300 were in the mandatory privatisation category. The others remained under the control of the municipalities and as such were viewed by the Bank as a negative aspect of the programme. Thus, according to Lieberman and Rahuja (1995, 25), by March 1994 only 75 percent of the mandatory small privatisation units were sold.

Method of disposal   The techniques employed were commercial tender (50 percent), auctions (20 percent) and lease with right-to-buy (30 percent). In addition, contrary to the International Finance Corporation's (IFC) expectations, more than 90 percent of the combined sales by tender and auction was 'as going concerns, rather than liquidation prior to sale' and then, mainly to worker-collectives which accounted for two-thirds of the transactions. Given the IFC's perceived preference to invest only in large well established enterprises,[6] this programme presented it with little opportunity for investment. Nonetheless the transnational capitalist class was not denied, especially in St. Petersburg and Nizhniy Novgorod where about 90 percent of the sale to the workers was believed to be funded by outsiders (Vassilyev 1995, 355).

Corruption   Responding to the negative account by the IFC on the process in Russia, Dmitry V. Vassilyev, Deputy Chairman, State Committee for State Property Management, Russian Federation, observed that 'privatization has improved the services provided by many small business, and it has also raised their effectiveness' (Vassilyev 1995, 355). Others, such as Ernst *et al.* (1996, 224), while acknowledging the inevitable corruption, irregularities, favouritism and the like that attend such a large-scale undertaking, preferred to focus on the official framework and the basic outcomes. However, to be sure, the process had been attended by corruption: Auctions

---

[6]   Millman, J. and Friedland, J., 'World Bank Finance Arm Tends To Aid Least Needy', in *The Wall Street Journal*, 23 September 1997, A16.

of the telephone company *Svyazinvent* and the metals giant *Norilsk Nikel*, were questioned by losing bidders;[7] six top bankers were ordered to comply with the rules of transparency; and Mr Chubias' life was threatened.[8] Moreover, the earlier noted problems surrounding a member of the US advisor team to the Russian government served to extend the charge of corruption and irregularities to non-Russians.

Corporatisation and employee distribution

The conversion of enterprises to joint-stock companies of medium and large enterprises began in July 1992 as a first step to their privatisation. An important feature of the process was the compulsory conversion to companies of all large and medium-sized enterprises and the involvement of the management and workers in the process. In addition, up to 1994, shares of enterprises to be privatised were valued at book-value. Whilst some enterprise managers delayed the conversion process, the majority complied within the required time frame mainly because their choice of privatisation options was conditioned on the enterprises becoming joint-stock companies (see Lieberman and Rahuja 1995; Vassilyev 1995).

Offer to managers and employee

Managers and workers were given three options from which to choose. The first option gave 25 percent of the shares to the workers free of charge but carried no right to vote. Workers had the right to purchase an additional 10 percent at a 30 percent discount on face value. Managers also had the right to purchase an additional 5 percent at face value. Thus combined, management and workers could acquire up to 40 percent of the company under option one. Option one was the default option. Under option two, employees were allowed to purchase up to 51 percent of the common shares by prior subscription to the public offer. They were also allowed to acquire an additional 5 percent under an employee stock option plan after privatisation. Option two required the agreement of two-thirds of the employees of the enterprise. Option three was essentially an instalment arrangement between the employees of an enterprise and the GKI, and was conditioned upon achieving a required level of performance by the enterprise within a specified time period. If the required level of performance was achieved, the employees were allowed to purchase 20 percent of the shares at face value. They also had the option to purchase an additional 20 percent at a 30 percent discount to face value and to pay for them over three years. Of the three choices, 75 percent of the enterprises preferred option two whilst the remaining 25 percent chose option one (see Boycko *et al.* 1995).

It is with this method that Desai and Goldberg (2000, 5) took issue; as seemingly constraining to 'institutional concentration of ownership through financial

---

    7   Staff Reporter, *The Wall Street Journal*, 16 September 1997, A16.

    8   McKay, B., 'Yeltsin Implores Bankers to Stop Attacking Reforms', in *The Wall Street Journal*, 16 September 1997, A16.

intermediaries such as investment funds ... [which the designers believed] ... would occur spontaneously as the [foreign] investment funds, acquiring vouchers from employees, would use them to gain sufficient blocs in privatised enterprises'. Recall, however, that foreign investment funds were not above questionable practices in the grab for vouchers.

Disposal of remainder

The shares remaining after employee distribution were transferred to the GKI or other designated regional committee for sale to the public as recommended by the managers and workers of the enterprise. Of these shares a pre-determined percentage had to be sold by way of voucher auction based on unused vouchers, that is, the percentage of shares to be sold by voucher was required to be reduced by the vouchers given to employees on the assumption that these would be used in the employee distribution. However, because employees did not utilised all of their vouchers on the purchase of discounted shares, their vouchers were included as part of the allocation.

Because 75 percent of the enterprises chose option two, managers and workers retained a controlling interest in these enterprises prior to any sale in the secondary market. At the end of September 1994, there were 31,700 registered corporations of which 24,000 were classified as 'open joint-stock companies' that is, where their share can be traded in the secondary market (see Vassilyev 1995).

The voucher programme

The Russian voucher programme benefited from the Czech Republic's experience before it. However, whereas the Czech Republic charged a nominal price for vouchers, in the case of Russia vouchers were distributed among the Russian people free of charge. This stage of the programme was designed to accomplish the participation of the remaining population not affiliated with the enterprises privatised as part of the overall transformation policy of the government. Vouchers began to be issued in August 1992 and by the end of January 1993 about 144 million vouchers were picked up by the people (see Boycko et al. 1995).

The issue of vouchers catapulted the Russian people into the world of transnational capitalism; they had become members of the capitalist class. A market for vouchers emerged almost overnight. Those that were not used in closed subscription for shares in the employee distributions described above were either traded for cash or were invested in one of the over 600 investment funds that were formed. Whilst some of these investment funds were formed by managers of the larger enterprises to purchase additional shares in their own companies, the majority were private investment funds, all with the objective of profiting from the privatisation process.

As a result of the free trade in vouchers, many Russians were deprived of the opportunity to own shares in the more than 14,000 enterprises sold by voucher auction between December 1992 and June 1994 (Boycko *et al.* 1995, 106–107).

Many lost their vouchers to scams that attended the process. Also arising from the free flow of vouchers nationally, and the uneven distribution of the enterprises around the country, vouchers were largely concentrated in the more affluent cities and regions: the existence of the six powerful oligarchs speaks to this.

In terms of ownership control, it is estimated that 30 percent of the vouchers were used by employees to purchase shares under the closed subscription programme. Of the remaining 70 percent, approximately 45 million were concentrated in the 630 investment funds representing about 25 million people as shareholders. Although these funds were limited to no more that 20 percent of the shares in any one company, they were able to effectively invest in the more attractive enterprises by reason of their relative strength at the auctions. The majority of investment funds are located in the three main cities: Moscow, St. Petersburg and Sverdlovsk.

To the established Russian capitalists and foreign investors excluded by the process of mass privatisation, however, the voucher programme was an inefficient method of privatisation and was seen as a major source of problems in corporate governance. According to Desai and Goldberg (2000, 2), the mass privatisation programme was characterized by: 'ineffective corporate governance, little new investment, and the distortions of continuing government intervention ...'. Ex-post evaluation notwithstanding, despite the inevitable problems associated with such a large-scale project, the voucher programme achieved what it was set out to do, and that was to bring Russia into the capitalist world-economy and to involve ordinary Russians in the transformation process. While to be sure control stopped at the level of managers, President Boris Yeltsin continued to stress the need for the benefits of the Russian transformation to a market economy to 'trickle-down' to the masses[9]. This he had hoped to achieve by introducing regulation for privatised monopolies, a new land code that would permit the open purchase and sale of land, a lower budget and a tax code that reduces the burden on businesses.

Conclusion

This chapter dealt in more specific terms with the privatisation process of the EEC-3 countries and Russia as an aspect of their transformation to market economies and provides a contrast with earlier privatisation programmes in the developed and developing countries. As shown, the techniques were largely dictated by the goals of the process which were markedly different from those found in the OECD and developing countries. Where debt repayment was a significant concern, as was the case in Hungary and Poland, IMF/Bank prescriptions prevailed; in other cases the concern centred on maintaining national cohesion through mass privatisation and offered lessons from which to draw.

---

[9]   Brzezinski, M., 'Yeltsin Calls For Reforms In Economy', in *The Wall Street Journal*, 25 September 1997, A16.

PART IV
The Guyana Experience:
A Country Study

Chapter 7

Guyana: From Recovery to 'At a Tipping Point'

O what a tangled web we weave, when first we practice to deceive! (W. Scott)

In its Draft 2003 Development Policy Review (DPR) on Guyana issued on 23 June 2003, the Bank characterised Guyana as being 'at a tipping point' of becoming 'a failed state' which was later changed to '[going] backwards' in the final DPR issued in December 2003 to appease the government of Guyana.

Terminology notwithstanding, the considerable slow down in economic growth and 'the crisis of governance' were cited as concerns in both draft and final versions of the DPR. The government's response was immediate and unequivocal. It accused the Bank of being biased in favour of the opposition political party, dubbing the DPR 'political, filled with allegations and complaints and lacking in quantitative or qualitative analysis'.[1] It further cited the several achievements of the PPP/C since it took office in 1992 as evidence of good governance.

Under the PPP/C watch, to be sure, the external debt declined from over US$2.1 billion in 1992 – arising mainly from accumulated debt service cost and interest thereon[2] – to less than US$1.0 billion in 2003, albeit mainly through international debt-relief initiatives; poverty reduced to under 35 percent of the population; inflation to single-digit numbers, with GNP per-capita income increasing from US$350 in 1988 to US$783 in 2003, allowing it to be classified as a middle-income developing country by the British government in March 2004.[3] Moreover, Guyana reached the completion point of the 'Enhanced Heavily Indebted Poor Countries Initiative' (EHIPC) and in consequence became eligible for debt relief of US$334 million over the next twenty years; now fully written off as a result of the Gleneagles decision of the Group of eight (G-8). No small feat to be sure since the government had to satisfy stringent requirements in terms of both macroeconomic performance and submit a Poverty Reduction Strategy Programme (PSRP) acceptable to the donor community. So why in the light of these achievements did the Bank seemingly puts itself out on a limb with such a critical DPR on Guyana?

---

[1]   Singh, G., 'World Bank says Guyana suffering a "crisis of governance" – government takes umbrage', *Stabroek News,* 14 September 2003.

[2]   Lowe, S., 'The 1992 US$2.1 billion debt consisted largely of interest on arrears', *Stabroek News,* 8 July 2005.

[3]   'UK cuts Guyana funding – in favour of "low-income" countries', *Stabroek News,* 31 March, 2004.

The evidence

Despite the rhetoric of the government of Guyana, since 1998 rather than maintain the momentum established in the early-to-mid-1990s, the economy has stumbled rather badly with the government seemingly not in full control. In other words, the slippage in governance and economic growth since 1998 if allowed to go unchecked is great enough to negate much of the progress that has been made between 1992 and 1998. Of significance are the several anomalies which are manifest in the management of the economy and in governance.

First, the private-sector which has been officially billed as the engine of growth is in reality controlled by the President creating a credibility gap between rhetoric and reality: Access to capital is restricted by the operation of Guideline Five of the Financial Institutions Act, 1995 which constructively forces the commercial banks to hold surplus liquidity and to invest in Treasury bills to effectively finance the government's growing domestic debt as depicted in Figure 7.1 which is a concern of the Bank.[4]

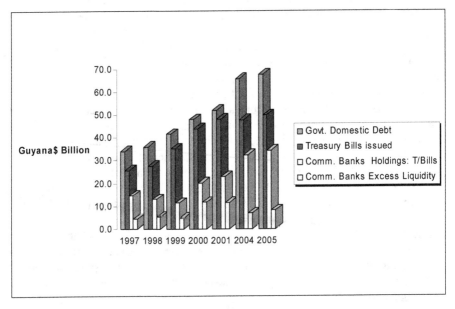

Figure 7.1   Government domestic debt and treasury bills issued; Commercial banks T/Bills holdings and excess liquidity

Source: Bank of Guyana, Statistical Bulletin (2005, 49–50); Statistical Abstract (2005, 25)

---

[4]   'Domestic debt could be a source of vulnerability – World Bank', *Stabroek Business,* November 2003.

At the same time the granting of investment incentives and privileges are handed down on the basis of 'personal likes and dislikes'.[5] In consequence, 21 companies many of which were well-established private enterprises declared bankruptcy in less than two years.[6]

Second, Growth in real GDP slipped from an annual average of 7.1 percent for 1991–1998 to negative 1.4 percent in 2000, declining still further to -3.0 percent in 2005 as shown in Figure 7.2. Nonetheless, the government persists in pursuing the public sector as the main economic driver.[7]

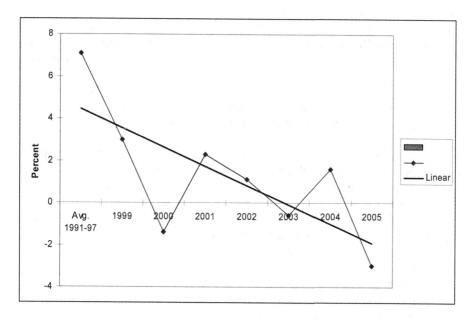

Figure7.2   Guyana: GDP growth rates

Source: Government of Guyana, Budget 2000; Budget 2004; Budget 2006

Third, corruption not only is deemed endemic but according to the US State Department International Narcotics Control Strategy Report (INCSR) for 2003, 'allegations of corruption are widespread, and reach to high levels of government,

---

[5]   Narain, D., 'In answer to query by former CEO, Go-Invest says it recommends projects on Government's Ge', *Stabroek News*, 15 November 2003.

[6]   Ming, S., 'PPP has brought private sector to its knees – PNCR charges, cites 21 bankruptcies in last 21 months', *Stabroek News*, 12 November 2003.

[7]   'Poverty Report: Low growth key problem – negative growth seen this year: 2006', *Stabroek News*, 27 June 2005.

but continue to go un-investigated'. Moreover, crime has increased dramatically during the 1998–2002 period and is partly traceable to drug-trafficking; the INCSR for 2003 describes Guyana 'as a transhipment point for South American cocaine destined for North America and Europe'. In 2006 the US State Department INSCR was no less indicting: It identified government projects in which local drug lords are involved and cited the acquisition of substantial landholdings and timber concessions as evidence. So blatant is the connection between the drug lords and the government that the Minister of Home Affairs has openly expressed concerns.

Fourth, the alleged state-sponsored 'death squad' with alleged extra-judicial killings that implicated the former Minister of Home Affairs is a concern of civil society and the international community. With respect to police killings, according to the Guyana Human Rights Association (GHRA), 'public investigations rarely were conducted into such killings; in general, police abuses were committed with impunity'.

Last but not least, persistent conflict, state failure and political collapse increasingly are being perceived as alternatives to political power-sharing manifesting in an 'ethnically polarised political system' that 'constrains governance reform in three key dimensions' (Bank, 2003).

In summary   The above has been summed up by the Bank as 'a government weak and unable to deal with ingrained crime and corruption'; 'ineffective use of donor resources'; 'increasing budget deficits'; and 'circumvention of existing rules on expenditures, and the lack of oversight and ineffectiveness of existing mechanisms'. Moreover, the Bank further found Guyana's political institutions and civil-society groups to be perceived as lacking 'cross-ethnic legitimacy' which '... serves to disempower and inhibit their involvement in social action'; requiring 'policies of social cohesiveness and political inclusiveness'.

The Inter-American Development Bank   In similar fashion, the Inter-American Development Bank (IDB) found 'the difficulty of obtaining broad stakeholder participation and consensus on major policy issues and the recent increase of criminal activity, represent major obstacles to national development'.

Parliament Reform Report

The MFI are not alone in their criticisms of Guyana. The Parliament Reform Report prepared by Sir Michael Davies as part of the Governance and Institutional Development Division project funded by the Commonwealth Fund for Technical Co-operation was issued in early March 2005. The report found that the role of the Guyana parliament in the governance of the country as envisaged in the constitution was constrained due in part to the lack of independence from the control of the executive. According to the report, the executive decides when the legislature meets and the issues that it will deal with but that:

It should not be left to the whim of the government when to hold a sitting ....

The government's response was to reject the report as 'one-sided'.

The government's response

Evidence and findings notwithstanding, the leader of the PPP – who is not the President – continues to steadfastly hold to the notion that 'power-sharing' in any form is not an option in a winner-take-all political system, reiterating thereby her party's – and therefore the government's – bent on maintaining control over the level of participation by the excluded in the social, economic and political life at the community and national levels. These views were reiterated in June 2005 by the Minister of Foreign Trade and International Co-operation, who is member of the Executive/Central Committee of the ruling party.[8]

How Guyana reached this state of affairs is the subject of the remainder of the chapter.

Historical Background

Guyana is made up of 83,000 square miles located in the north eastern quadrant of South America. Its population mainly of East Indian (Indo-Guyanese) and African decent (Afro-Guyanese) was an estimated 754,400 in 1990 – it has remained at this level in 2000 in consequence of immigration – and is concentrated mainly along the coastal belt. Of the Caribbean Community (CARICOM) member-states, Guyana is the most diversified and endowed in terms of natural resources, with a virgin forest accounting for over 75 percent of its area. In terms of per-capita income however, as shown in Table 7.1, it ranks a very distant last in 1990, having lost its growth momentum in the 1980s.

Post-independence economic system

Informed partly by 'reactive nationalism' and partly by notions of utopian socialism that characterized emerging nations in the 1960s, a policy of state-ownership was pursued by the Peoples National Congress (PNC) government upon gaining political independence from Britain in May 1966. Pursuant this policy, all business enterprises owned by the British conglomerates – Booker Bros. McConnell and Jessel Holdings – who controlled the economy during the colonial era, were nationalized in the mid-1970s, as was the Canadian-owned and operated Alcan subsidiary, The Demerara Bauxite Company Limited. Also nationalized, were the subsidiaries of the Royal Bank of Canada and Barclays Bank Limited which together controlled the financial sector in Guyana; and the Canadian-owned and operated electric utility. Thus, at the end of 1989 the state controlled all public infrastructures, the sugar and bauxite industries, the banking sector and the various marketing boards. In addition, the Public Corporation Secretariat was created as a central controlling agency and

---

[8]   Rohee, C., 'The PNC has a great deal to apologise for', *Stabroek News*, 2 June 2005.

supervised 32 enterprises that were involved in a wide range of business activities. Remaining in private hands were small business enterprises that posed no threat to the economic agenda of the PNC. These were mainly Indo-Guyanese merchants.

Table 7.1   CARICOM member states: Selected statistics: 1990

Country	GDP per capita	Est. Population ('000)
Antigua & Barbuda	4,985	84.0
Bahamas	11,096	253.3
Barbados	6,645	257.4
Belize	1,973	184.9
Dominica	2,050	83.5
Guyana	340	754.4
Jamaica	1,662	2,403.5
Montserrat	6,133	12.0
St. Kitts & Nevis	3,560	42.9
St. Lucia	2,415	151.3
St. Vincent etc	1,620	118.0
Trinidad & Tobago	4,060	1227.4

Source: Extracted from Statistical Profile of the Caribbean Community (CARICOM), The West Indian Commission, 1992, p. 1

Concurrent with nationalisation, Guyana pursued an import-substitution policy as part of its economic strategy. Support came mainly from the increase in sugar revenues derived from the ACP Sugar Protocol that granted preferential access – and a substantial price increase – to the EC market in 1975 on Britain's membership to that body in 1974. Indeed, as noted by the EU's Mariann Fischer Boel, 'Britain brought with it a strong tradition of buying farm goods from its former empire – including large volumes of sugar. Instead of cutting this link, in 1975 the EU signed the Sugar Protocol with 19 African, Caribbean and Pacific countries'.[9] As an integral aspect of the import-substitution programme, the importation of many items – wheat-flour, apples, alcohol, soft-drinks and foreign cigarettes, for example – were banned and high excise taxes imposed on others. This policy hit at the middle class and was viewed in the same light as similar policies pursued in many newly independent Africa countries and certain South American countries such as Chile, for example, in the 1960s to early 1980s.

---

[9]   Boel, M., 'Sugar's Role in Development Policy', *German Marshall Fund*, Brussels, Hotel Dorint Novotel, 30 May 2005, Speech 05/341 (10 July 2005).

Economic collapse

Because Guyana like many other small developing countries imports its fuel supply, the two oil shocks of 1973–1974 and 1979–1980 had a devastating impact upon its fragile, over-extended and over-leveraged economy. This was exacerbated by the high external interest rates emanating from the US in the early 1980s. It was also plagued by political and social unrest led by the PPP and the Guyana Agricultural Workers Union (GAWU) – the membership backbone of the PPP – which adversely impacted sugar production in the 1980s, and arguably led to the near-destruction of the industry.

By 1985 then, Guyana like many of its contemporaries in Africa found itself in a balance of payments crisis, unable to service its external sovereign debts which by this time had grown out of control by any standard, as shown in Figure 7.3. Indeed, with a GDP calculated at US$340.2 million at the end of 1994 it was one of the few countries with an external debt burden greater than five times its annual GDP.

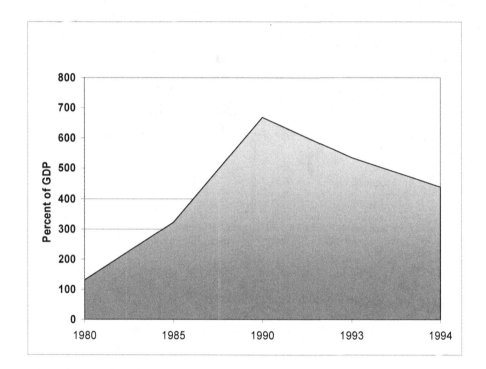

Figure 7.3　Guyana external public debt: 1980–1994

Source: The West Indian Commission Secretariat (1992, 2); Guyana Budget (1995, 37, 59); Guyana Budget (1997, 3)

With a decayed economic infrastructure and an unsustainable debt-service cost of 61.1 percent of exports, Guyana's economy was in a state of collapse by 1989. In addition to its inability to service its external debts it suffered from a susceptible foreign exchange rate (the local currency was devalued by 1700 percent between 1980 and 1990); high unemployment; an inflation rate of over 50 percent in 1990; and sub-poverty per-capita income. As published by The West Indian Commission (WIC 1992, 2), Guyana's reported GDP of US$256.3 million in 1990 was mainly derived from agriculture (27.6 percent); mining and quarrying (16.4 percent); manufacturing (11.5 percent); construction (6.5 percent); government (14.6 percent); and services (23.4 percent).

As shown in Figure 7.4, since 1980 the government continuously operated with a fiscal budget deficit which fluctuated between a high of US$313.3 million in 1982 and a low of US$25.0 million in 1989. In 1990 it went back up to US$90.7m (46.8 percent of revenues and grants) or 35.8 percent of GDP.

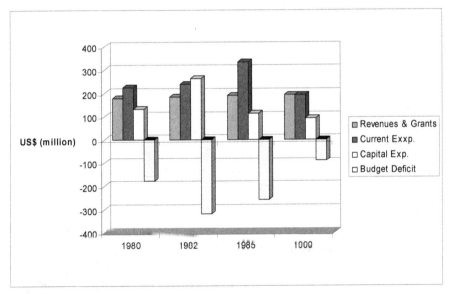

Figure 7.4   Guyana fiscal budget: 1980–1990

Source: Constructed form The West Commission Secretariat (1992, 10)

External debt service

Servicing the external debt became a major challenge for Guyana in the 1980s and early 1990s mainly in consequence of the debt to GDP ratio which was at over 6:1 in 1990 (see Figure 7.3) exacerbated by increasing budget deficits as shown in Figure 7.4 and high external interest rates. While therefore the actual external debt increased by 88.1 percent in 1985 over 1980 and by 15.5 percent in 1990 over 1985, the increases when measured in terms of the percentage of debt to GDP for the same periods were 140.8 percent and 108.4 percent respectively. Indeed, the positive correlation between external debt and fiscal budget deficits is unmistakable. Thus as early as 1982 the indications were that of an economy challenged by an unsustainable debt burden even as it seeks to reduce its capital expenditure as shown in Figure 7.4. By almost all economic indicators then, Guyana had reached it lowest point in 1989–1990.

Survival mode

During the 1980s, economic survival took the form of an informal economy fuelled by smuggling and what had become known as the 'barrel trade'.[10] As disclosed by Guyana's Chief Statistician in interview, the barrel trade accounted for about one-third of non-oil imports for most of the second half of the 1980s and supported the informal economy which became woven into the fabric of Guyanese society of the time.

Like Peru's informal economy (De Soto, 1989), street-vending began to invade the thoroughfare, often on the side-walks in front of state-owned enterprises whose shelves were sparsely stocked. Whole sections of streets in the centre of the business district were taken over by street-vendors as indeed were private properties not fenced – a phenomenon that continued into the 2000s, albeit not at the same level. Most of the street vendors operated without licenses, paid no taxes, and were susceptible to extortion by municipal police who were predominantly Afro-Guyanese. As witnessed first hand, open threats and acts of violence against the vendors – even in state-established and controlled markets – were commonplace and were perceived in racial terms.

In addition to street-vending which served to alleviate the economic distress, and in an effort to divert attention from the severity of the economic woes of the time, squatting on private and public property was condoned by the PNC government. As a result, many unsecured properties were taken over by the poor for gardening and housing. Public lands were also squatted on by some of the politically-connected elite. Thus a generation of disaffected Guyanese grew up in the belief of squatters' rights and openly resisted eviction by legal owners, including the government.

---

[10]   Barrel trade refers to goods sent to Guyana by relatives living abroad. Since goods sent by relatives for private consumption were generally exempted from taxes, the process became an important means of tax evasion.

Economic repression and tax evasion

With an absent middle class,[11] Guyana's fiscal budget revenue base in terms of
traditional tax regulations and collection procedures was almost in a state of collapse.
The inability of the government to impose and collect income taxes led to the imposition
of a consumption tax on imports and on local manufactures; an increase in the sugar
levy – as evidenced by the increase over the years despite the drastic decline in sugar
output particularly in 1989 arising primarily from politically-motivated industrial action
– and increasing excise tax. Because of the established points of collection, excise tax
and consumption tax became significant sources of revenues for the government and
by 1990 they accounted for approximately 15.3 percent and 27.2 percent respectively
of the government's current revenues as shown in Figure 7.5.

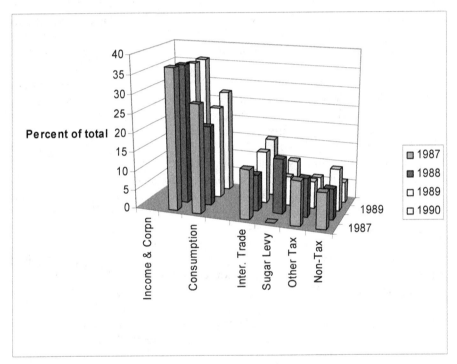

Figure 7.5   Guyana government revenue sources: 1987–1990

Source: Constructed from World Bank Guyana Public Sector Review, (1993, 292)

---

[11]   The mass migration (estimated by the Bank at 500,000) that took place in the early
1970s was mainly the essential middle-class and included almost all of the Europeans.
Thereafter, Guyana's population was divided almost equally between Indo-Guyanese and
Afro-Guyanese.

Indo-Guyanese who in the main represented the private sector as it were after nationalisation interpreted the imposition of the consumption and excise taxes as the PNC government's attempt to limit wealth creation and to transfer the tax burden onto them.[12] Based on this perception and because of the high incidence of taxes upon the private-sector and the cascading effect of the consumption tax, under-invoicing and under-reporting of sales revenues was resorted to by most merchants. This was facilitated by wide-spread corruption in the customs and excise department as the economic system disintegrated in consequence of a collapsed economy. At the same time, '… decades of wholesale arson in the cane-fields, sabotage of the aqueducts on the sugar cane estates, and explosions in the sugar factories',[13] obliquely attributed to the PPP which was the majority opposition party in Parliament contributed to the economic and social instability of the period, and thus exacerbated Guyana's economic decline. Sugar production declined from a high of 340,815 tonnes in 1974 to 164,800 tonnes in 1989 and exports from 292,555 tonnes in 1978 to 160,979 tonnes in 1989.[14] Tonnes sugar per acre (TS/A) declined from 2.36 in 1978 to 1.91 in 1989.[15] Lost man-days increased from 84,637 in 1980 to 737,713 in 1989.[16] Under private-sector management, sugar production rebounded to 230,808 tonnes in 1995; and TS/A to 2.41 in the same year.

Capital flight attendant on hyper-inflation and foreign exchange control was also prevalent. In addition to the smuggling-out of hard currencies bought on the 'curb-market', ingenious ways were devised to legally transfer capital out of the country. For example, from the survey of businesses conducted for the World Bank-funded Consumption Tax Study in 1991,[17] several privately-owned companies were making interest payments to external lenders – primarily family members who had immigrated during the 1970s. Other techniques included the setting-up of off-shore intermediaries or dummy corporations through which all purchasing, shipping and servicing of the local business enterprise were conducted. By this latter means, profits were remitted abroad in foreign currency as an externally-derived cost. Hence, whilst the off-set was an increase in consumption tax payable on the imported goods – absent under-invoicing – income tax was almost negligible because of the substantial reduction in taxable profits; there were also no with-holding taxes on interest payments or dividends.

---

[12] The Consumption Tax was assessed on distribution of locally produced goods and imports, not on retail sales and was payable irrespective of sale to consumers. This is still the practice in 2005.

[13] Wallerson, W., 'Burnham had a vision and a plan', *Stabroek News*, 13 September 2005.

[14] See GUYSUCO's Report and Accounts, 1978–1989 issues.

[15] Ibid.

[16] GUYSUCO's Annual Report and Accounts, 1980 and 1990.

[17] The author was a member of the UNDP team on this project.

Social consequences

Guyana was a society traumatised by the upending of norms and rules – established by its former colonial masters – in the name of nationalism and egalitarianism conceptualised on the perceived availability of external funding at negative real interest rates and growth premised on an inward-oriented economic strategy. Smuggling of flour, gasoline, cigarettes and other banned consumer goods reached down to the level of the individual. Social degradation attendant on hyper-inflation[18] and pervasive abject poverty[19] exacerbated by high unemployment in the mid-1980s were especially evident in urban areas. Unprecedented crime in terms of both form and frequency traumatised the society: Criminals, mainly Afro-Guyanese, ran rampant in the streets of the capital city robbing and pillaging at will until stopped by the late President Hoyte who expanded the death penalty to such crimes. These issues overshadowed the earlier progress made in the areas of education, housing for the poor and transport infrastructure and became the basis for a change in government in 1991.

State-induced corruption

Within the political framework of a socialist economic system, managers in state-owned enterprises were encouraged to pursue small business enterprises as a means to supplementing subsistence-level wages and to foster the notion of self-help. At one of the government-controlled banks, it was found that some senior officials interpreted this to mean voting themselves business loans and to defer payment for as long as it takes for their businesses to be profitable or the loan forgiven or lost in obscure record-keeping. Junior employees were left to devise their own secondary source of income. Corruption became common place within the bank. No detailed creditors or debtors ledgers existed; and details of what existed were obscured or lost in the migration to a computerised system that was plagued with data-related challenges. The bank's lending criteria were often perfunctorily applied. Hence unserviceable and unrecoverable loans were a substantial percentage of the bank's portfolio of loans. Consequently, many of the loans were written-off or substantial legal expenses incurred in later attempts at recovery as part of rehabilitation of the bank prior to privatisation under the PPP/C government. Indeed, as required by the Co-operative Financial Institutions Act 1976 – applicable only to state-owned financial institutions – the central bank was obliged to refinance about G\$7.0 billion of bad debts in 1995 – it received interest bearing debenture issued by the government in exchange – only to find itself with an additional G\$9.0 billion of bad loans, mainly to rice farmers, which had to be written off to facilitate privatisation.

---

[18] Estimated at 61.1 percent in 1989 (CARICOM Statistical Profile, 1992).

[19] 70 percent of the population was estimated to be below the poverty line in 1994. (1994 Budget, p. 27). However, this number is closer to 46 percent.

Corruption at GUYSUCO Evidence of system manipulation arising from system degradation by attrition was also found in other public entities. At the largest state-owned enterprise, GUYSUCO, corruption was found to be less overt but nonetheless present, even with external management with extensive private-sector business and financial management experience. What at first observation could be attributed to a lack of internal efficiency was in reality system-manipulation to accommodate large transactions – including transfer pricing – on the one hand and petty schemes devised by junior employees on the other. GUYSUCO's accounting for debtors and creditors were found to be equally deficient. No detailed and separate ledgers were maintained. Staff debtors were co-mingled with non-staff debtors and creditors, often with untraceable balances because of poor record keeping and misplaced source documents. Creditors were paid on statements rather than on invoices. Where invoices were used these were almost always photocopies. In addition, prior to mid-1994 no details of payment were included on the remittance advice attached to the cheque which had to be reviewed and signed by a senior finance executive and the finance director. Payments were often misapplied, deliberately in some cases. As a result many suppliers were paid more than once as part of the elaborate scheme devised by insiders. Cheques were never mailed and had to be collected by suppliers. This process allowed some members of the finance staff to with-hold cheques until a suitable personal financial arrangement was arrived at with the supplier anxious to receive payment. The evidence further suggests that corruption was not limited to the junior and poorly compensated staff members[20] whose survival depended on their ability to manipulate the system at a basic level. Personnel rules and regulations were inconsistently applied to accommodate the politically connected with compliance by lower level employees secured through intimidation.

Economic recovery

It is against this backdrop of economic and social collapse that Guyana embarked upon structural reform under the IMF's Enhanced Structural Adjustment Facility (ESAF) in July 1990. Under this programme the government of Guyana filed the required Policy Framework Paper (PFP) and agreed to among other fundamental reforms the privatisation of all state-owned enterprises and to have its progress evaluated every six months.

ESAF programme

The ESAF programme was one of the most stringent of policy-based lending devised to effect restoration of macro-economic balance in countries with protracted balance

---

[20] At the end of 1995, after the more than doubling of salaries in 1991 and 1992, the average monthly salary for an accounting supervisor was under US$200.00, of which over one-half (before income tax) went for shelter.

of payments problems. As defined by the Bank, structural adjustment loans are 'non-project lending to support programs of policy and institutional change necessary to modify the structure of an economy so that it can maintain both its growth rate and the viability of its balance of payments in the medium term' (Michalopoulos 1987, 57).

Implicit in the above definition is that imbalances however derived must necessarily be corrected internally and within the framework of economic orthodoxy. As such, improving the allocative efficiency of resources by rationalising public-sector investment was an automatic Bank policy prescription for Guyana. As with other poor IMF and Bank clients, the expectation was for immediate and swift implementation of the programme irrespective of prevailing unstable country conditions and increasing evidence of the constraining influence of demography, geography and institutions.

Privatisation under ESAF

The IMF's unrelenting approach to economic reform now firmly embedded in its policy prescriptions was no less evident in Guyana. As a result, Guyana found itself faced with complying with policy prescriptions that had as their main objectives the servicing of external debt through the dismantling of its public enterprises and the consequential reduction in the state's sphere of influence. In addition, the budgetary burden of subsidies to PEs was to be reduced. The take it or leave it attitude of IMF missions to which Killick (1995, 29) referred appeared to be especially evident in Guyana where several state-owned enterprise were generally regarded as having been expropriated from foreign transnational corporations. Hence, in the short-term the pressure to privatise exacerbated economic and social misery, increased the external debt-burden and subordinated the state to external influences. To counter some of the social consequence of adjustment, the externally-funded 'Social Impact Amelioration Program' (SIMAP) provided substantial funding to enable affected groups to carry out projects – rehabilitation of schools, day care and health centres, roads, drainage systems, potable water supply systems and food support to vulnerable groups – on a self-help basis and could be looked upon as the forerunner to the HIPC programmes in the late 1990s.

Subordination of the State

The subordination of the state – implicit in the reform process under the ESAF – was evidenced by the tone of the IMF's communication with the government of Guyana. In an *aide-memoir* dated 11 November 1993, to the newly-elected PPP/C government, the IMF demanded that '... the government agree with the World Bank by end-January 1994 on a detailed time-table for the privatization plan, including dates for bringing an initial list of enterprises to the point of sale'.[21] And this was notwithstanding an earlier report by the Bank which observed that the privatisation

---

[21]   'Guyana Aide Memoir', *International Monetary Fund*, 11 November 1993, Para. 11.

programme initiated by the former PNC Government '... was flawed by lack of transparency, diffusion of management responsibilities and questionable procedures' (Bank 1993a: x).

Prior to the *aide-memoir* subordination was less direct but nonetheless clearly intended: The 1990 management-service contract between the government and Booker Tate Limited (B-T) for the provision of management and technical services to GUYSUCO speaks to this observation. A specific requirement of the contract was that GUYSUCO will be invoiced for salaries and related staff expenses from B-T without a detailed rendering of the charges. Any questions as to 'mathematical accuracy' – not derivation – of the billing were to be reviewed by an independent UK auditor. Neither the government nor its local auditors had access to any details. This contract had the benefit of review and approval by the IMF and was held out as the absolute authority to B-T to manage the industry.

Early Privatisation Programme

As with the privatisation programmes of Poland and Hungary – indeed others in Africa – which were IMF and Bank supported, the explicit expectations for the Guyana programme were for the liquidation and sale of assets free of encumbrances. The process was simply one of either the Public Corporations Secretariat identifying the enterprise to be sold or interested parties approaching the government. As such, enterprises were either broken up and their assets sold or sold as going concern in 'open cry auction'. Utilities – telephone, electric and water – were to be divested by the government so as to reduce the budgetary burden upon the state; it matters not whether or not they were profit making. No ownership interests were to be retained by the government or conditions as to employment levels attached to any of the sales (Bank 1993a, 49).

Implicitly, restitution of expropriated properties was expected to be made or the outstanding debts from their nationalisation paid out of the proceeds realised from their sale – an expectation with respect to the Guyana sugar industry. Thus in keeping with the agreement with the IMF and Bank, the PNC government quickly amassed the technical support of foreign consultants and began the dismantling of the public sector.

Given the stated objectives of privatisation in Guyana, consideration for state-firm, state-labour or state-welfare recipient relationships was notably absent from evaluations in the early privatisation programme. Instead, early privatisation analyses were more financial rather than social. Indeed, privatisation effectiveness was measured in terms of the number of enterprises sold or liquidated. Thus privatisation was mainly effected through a process of asset sales to foreigners, and by foreign contract management in the bauxite and sugar industries pending their expected speedy divestment: ideally returned to their previous owners.

By October 1992 an estimated 15 of the 32 enterprises under the Public Corporations Secretariat were either sold or in the process of being sold (Bank

1993a, 6).[22] In evaluation, the Bank observed: 'in the early stages of the programme, an important goal was generating foreign exchange, and executing transactions was critical to realizing of targets set under the IMF program' (Bank 1993a, 8).

Of the entities sold, the two largest were Demerara Woods limited, a forest product company, and Guyana Telephone Corporation renamed Guyana Telephone & Telegraph Co. Limited (GT&T). But as noted by the Bank, (Bank 1993a, 7) both enterprises were sold in private negotiations outside the privatisation framework. In consequence, charges of irregularities were levelled against the government by the political opposition party, the PPP and others interested in the process. The more controversial of the two was the sale of 80 percent interest in GT&T for US$16.0 million to Atlantic Tele-Network (ATN) of the US Virgin Islands. At issue was the lack of transparency and alleged corruption, despite monitoring by both the IMF and the Bank and the available advice of a cadre of foreign experts. A review by the Bank on the privatisation programme in November 1992 concluded that:

> There was no clear-cut process, and the procedures to publicize invitations for bids and their subsequent evaluation were not always consistent. Valuation of companies [was] also inconsistent and in certain cases negotiations were held with only a single buyer (Bank 1993a, 8).

In consequence of the perceived irregularities in the privatisation of the telephone utility, the privatisation programme was suspended in November 1992 by the newly-elected PPP/C government.

The PPP/C government and the IMF

The election of a new government in October 1992, under the leadership of Dr. Cheddi Jagan, brought with it new challenges not heretofore addressed by either the IMF or the Bank. Although the outcome of what was billed as the first democratic election in 25 years was not entirely unexpected, the international community was not prepared for radical changes. Expectation for a continuation of the reform programme was premised on the uptrend in the social and economic indicators: GDP growth of 6.1 percent and 7.7 percent were experienced in 1991 and 1992 respectively, in contrast to the negative growth rates of the previous 3 years; current account balances had improved substantially from its 1990 negative balance; and consumer prices declined from a high of 90.0 percent in 1989 to 26.3 percent in 1992 (Bank 1993a, 103). However, militating against these improvements were the Marxist-Leninist ideology of the incoming PPP[23] and despite assurances from Dr. Cheddi Jagan during the political campaign, the spectre of retribution based on claims of atrocities committed by the PNC government and its supporters against Indo-Guyanese during the 1970s and 1980s.

---

[22] See also Co-operative Republic of Guyana, *Privatisation Policy Framework Paper*, June 1993, Appendix iv.

[23] 'PPP rolls out new Guyana programme – says it remain true to socialism', *Stabroek News*, 3 August 2005.

From a reform-implementation perspective, close working relationships had been established with the PNC administration and no one at the IMF or Bank had any prior interaction with any of the new heads of government. Ordinarily, this should not have been a problem. The process had been started by the PNC government and a privatisation infrastructure acceptable to both the IMF and Bank was in place; the PPP as the main opposition party in Parliament had ample opportunity to debate the ESAF programme in the Guyana Parliament. Thus, within six months of signing the agreement with the IMF, the PNC government had contracted for private-sector management for the sugar and bauxite industries, and as noted above several small enterprises were sold; the leadership of the PNC had fully embraced the notion of the private-sector as the engine of growth. As a result, there was no disputing the need for privatisation of the many enterprises that could be more efficiently managed and financed by the private-sector.

Economic recovery programme suspended

Rather than engage in constructive relationship with the IMF and Bank, the PPP/C government to the dismay of the international community discarded the economic recovery programme established by its predecessor PNC government: To the new government privatisation was asset-stripping.[24] The sale of public enterprises was perceived by the new leaders as being conducted at a pace that did not consider the social ramifications of the dismantling process. Moreover, as acknowledged by the Bank the process indeed had the appearance of favouring foreigners (Bank 1993a, 9). The Economic Recovery Programme Monitoring Unit which was set up to monitor the progress of the reform programmes was disbanded, so also was the PCS which had responsibility for the privatisation programme.

From a political perspective, many in the PPP saw the rush to privatise as, among other less wholesome purposes, a political manoeuvre by the PNC government designed to convey to the IMF and donor community Guyana's willingness to become part of the capitalist world-economy and to return nationalized assets back to their original owners, as was done in Chile in its privatisation programme. Indeed, with the collapse of the Soviet Union to which Guyana's economic fortunes had been aligned, Guyana needed Western support which it had kept to a minimum for twenty five years. But privatisation of the sugar industry as envisaged by the IMF and Bank would fundamentally disturb the political support base of the PPP. Hence the PPP/C government did little more than pay lip service to the notion of privatisation in the first twelve months of being elected, thereby fostering a growing frustration with it as evidenced by the *aide-memoir* quoted above. Moreover, in addition to requiring the privatisation programme to be reinstated, the *aide-memoir* went on to state: 'In addition, the government would send an important message regarding

---

[24] See Co-operative Republic of Guyana, *Privatisation Policy Framework Paper*, June 1993, 4.

its commitment to the privatization process by implementing during the same time frame the sale of its remaining shareholdings in several private sector companies'.[25]

From earlier privatisation, the PNC government retained equity interests in about seven enterprises, three of which had been well managed by international standards and became profitable since their divestiture. Indeed, the Guyana Pegasus Hotel in which the government retained an interest had been mooted as one of Forte Crest's – the British hospitality firm – most profitable investment. GT&T was the second foreign-controlled enterprise in which the government retained a 20 percent interest. Since its privatisation, the company has been managed from a profit-maximisation perspective and has provided reliable albeit highly-monopolised telecommunication services to the community. Demerara Distillers Limited (DDL), a domestically-owned and managed enterprise is yet another privatisation that has served the community well. Indeed, in 1996 DDL became the first manufacturer in Guyana to receive ISO 9000 certification.

Back in compliance

Given the profitability and the potential for growth of the enterprises noted above, by explicitly requiring the government to divest its holdings in them the IMF had clearly signalled its agenda of asset-stripping on behalf of creditor-nations and the subordination of weak nation-states in the eyes of the PPP/C government. Nonetheless, unable to resist the pressure from the IMF the Guyana government re-established the privatisation process by setting up a Privatisation Unit under the Ministry of Finance.

In further compliance, the president formally announced his government's policy on privatisation at the Caribbean Group for Cooperation and Economic Development Conference held in Guyana on 26 January 1994. As required by the IMF four state-owned enterprises were identified for divestment, one by the deadline of end-March 1994 set by the IMF. In an effort to portray some semblance of independence and control over its affairs, as part of the announcement it was clearly stated that the privatisation unit '... will continue its work in selecting and preparing other enterprises for privatisation while continuing to explore the use of other instruments of Private Sector involvement'.[26]

In addition to the president's announcement in January 1994, and as a further justification for the government's deliberate approach to the process the Senior Minister of Finance in his 1994 Budget Speech read into the legislative records:

> As a matter of national policy, this Government has adopted a Privatization strategy which is being implemented in a streamlined and transparent manner. This framework is in contrast to the practice of the past government on the 'divestment' of State-Owned Enterprises (SOEs) about which the Guyanese people and the international community,

---

[25]   'Guyana Aide Memoir', *International Monetary Fund*, 11 November 1993, para. 11.

[26]   Government of Guyana, Address to 'Caribbean Group for Cooperation and Economic Development Conference held in Guyana on 26 January 1994', 1994, 15.

including the World Bank, have expressed grave concern with respect to transparency and accountability.[27]

To its supporters, the PPP/C government had by these pronouncements stood up to the IMF and was more in control of its destiny. Nonetheless, the window of opportunity for adjustment arising from the change in government had been considerably narrowed: Rhetoric gave way to policy implementation and as shown in Figure 7.6 proceeds from divestment increased dramatically in 1994 and 1995; but only to return to 1993 levels in 1996.

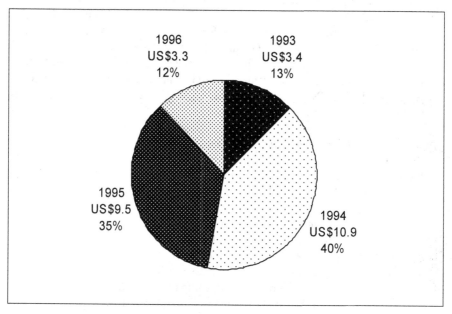

Figure 7.6   Guyana: Proceeds from privatisation 1993–1996

Source: Guyana budget (1995, 58); Budget (1997, 8)

In a question and answer booklet on 'Privatization in Guyana'[28] the government strategy for privatisation is described as: '... a case-by-case and gradualist approach to privatizing eligible state-owned entities listed in the Policy Framework Paper' [which] ... allows for flexibility in adopting the best option of privatization'. Moreover, as if to reiterate the government's option, the booklet further states: 'public enterprise reform is also actively being pursued by Government through the

---

[27]   Government of Guyana, *Guyana 1994 Budget Speech*, 7 March 1994, 38.

[28]   Government of Guyana, Privatization Unit, *Privatization in Guyana*, 1994.

reorganization of state entities along private sector lines to achieve similar economic and social objectives'.

Privatisation since 1994

It was thus in an atmosphere of muscle-flexing by the IMF and local resentment that Guyana reluctantly reinstated its privatisation programme. Indeed, with an external debt of over five-times GDP and the need to have such debt forgiven and rescheduled under Paris-Club arrangements, Guyana had no option but to demonstrate its commitment to a privatisation programme. As revealed by its 'Fiscal Profile'[29] by the end of 1992 debt-service cost accounted for 71.4 percent of revenues – including capital revenues – and 80.9 percent of the fiscal budget deficit. Moreover, since its low of US$256.2 million in 1990, Guyana's GDP has been steadily rising. In 1992, GDP was reported at US$323.1 million and in 1993 it further increased to US$390 million.[30] Economic growth had returned to Guyana whose creditworthiness was re-established by the PNC government in July 1990, as evidenced by the return of investors.

Enterprises and holdings identified to be privatised

At the beginning of 1993, the government held shares in several entities partially privatised between 1990 and 1992. The more significant of these were in:

1. Demerara Distillers Limited (DDL)
2. Guyana Telephone & Telegraph Co. Limited (GT&T)
3. Guyana Bank for Trade and Industry (GBTI)
4. National Bank for Industry and Commerce (NBIC)
5. Guyana National Co-operative Trust Company Limited
6. Guyana Seals and Packaging Company Limited (SAPIL)
7. Guyana Pegasus Limited

In addition to its partial holdings there were 25 fully-owned enterprises.[31] These were:

1. Berbice Mining Enterprise (BME)
2. Guyana Airways Corporation (GAC)
3. Guyana Broadcasting Corporation (GBC)
4. Guyana Co-operative Mortgage Finance Bank*
5. Guyana Electricity Corporation (GEC)
6. Guyana Fisheries Limited (GFL)

---

[29]   Government of Guyana, *Guyana 1994 Budget*, 7 March 1994, 47.
[30]   *Guyana 1995 Budget*, 1995, 59.
[31]   Government of Guyana, *1994 Budget*, 7 March 1994, 74. *Not included in Budget.

7. Guyana Glassworks Limited (GGL)*
8. Guyana National Co-operative Bank (GNCB)*
9. Guyana Co-operative Insurance Service*
10. Guyana National Engineering Corporation (GNEC)
11. Guyana National Newspapers Limited
12. Guyana National Printers Limited
13. Guyana National Shipping Limited
14. Guyana Oil Company Limited (Guyoil)
15. Guyana Pharmaceutical Corporation (GPC)
16. Guyana Post Office Corporation
17. Guyana Rice Export Board
18. Guyana Rice Milling and Marketing Authority
19. Guyana Stockfeeds Limited
20. Guyana Stores Limited (GSL)
21. Guyana Sugar Corporation (GUYSUCO)
22. Linden Mining Enterprise
23. National Edible Oil Company
24. National Padi and Rice Grading Centre
25. Sanata Textiles Limited

Since the establishment of the privatisation unit in early 1994, several entities were identified to be brought to point of sale. Five of these were scheduled to be privatised in 1994. These were the Dairy complex operated by GUYSUCO; GNEC; GSL and Guyana Glassworks Limited. Shares in GBTI were also scheduled to be sold in 1994. In addition, Design and Graphics Limited was liquidated and the assets sold to its employees at book value.[32]

Privatisation in 1994 and 1995

As reported to the Guyana Legislature in 1995 the privatisation unit became operational in early 1994.[33] The government's holdings in GBTI were sold in June 1994, albeit amidst controversy. Because of the method of sale employed, a majority interest in the enterprise was acquired by a single domestic private holding company. The absence of an organised capital market and a lack of financial intermediation in Guyana resulted in the shares of GBTI being sold to the highest bidder on a subscription basis as recommended by the Bank (Bank 1993a, 49). The assets of GGL were sold at book value. However, the GUYSUCO Dairy Complex remained unsold as at the end of 1996. It should be noted that whilst the sale of GBTI shares to the Beharry Group – a local holding company – was criticised by the PNC, the acquisition of fifty-one percent of the shares in NBIC by the Republic Bank of Trinidad & Tobago did not attract any such criticism. The transaction was seen

---

[32] See Government of Guyana, *1994 Budget*, page 39.
[33] Government of Guyana, *1995 Budget*, 6 February 1995, 24

as bringing-in foreign exchange despite the fact that control had been passed to a foreign entity, albeit within the CARICOM. The government continues to hold 49 percent of the shares in NBIC.

In 1995, two subsidiaries of GNEC were divested to local investors and the remaining assets sold to a local company in 1996. Also, GSL was converted to a public limited company and shares were offered to the public on a subscription basis with some restrictions as to number of shares to be allocated to any one individual. The issue was under-subscribed; less than one-half was subscribed primarily because of the perception of inefficient incumbent management and an overburdened payroll. Indeed, the management of GSL, a former subsidiary of Bookers, continued to view GUYSUCO as its primary customer despite GUYSUCO's shift away from sole-sourcing to purchase by tender after 1991. GSL was privatised in 2001 by way of negotiated sale under the strangest of circumstances: the initial payment of the purchase price was paid by way of a suitcase of US currency brought over from New York by the purchaser; the balance has not since been paid.

In contrast to the failed attempt at the public offer of shares in GSL, the public offer of a part of the government's holdings in DDL was over-subscribed because of the perceived efficient management of that company. In addition to the divestment activity, the GPC, Guyana Stockfeeds, National Oil, National Printers, the Mortgage Finance Bank and the Insurance Services enterprises were to be brought to point of sale in 1995.[34] All have since been privatised, including Sanata Textiles.

Privatisation held back

Given the Marxist-Leninist inclinations of the PPP, divestiture of GUYSUCO, GNCB, the Guyana Water Authority (GUYWA), and the GEC was fiercely resisted by the government. With respect to GUYSUCO, the government has openly stated that it has no intention of selling the entity and, indeed, has sought to expand sugar production through extensive and costly rehabilitation[35] of the industry against the advice of the Bank and in defiance of the EU's proposal to reform the ACP Sugar Protocol. The GNCB was eventually sold to the GBTI on the basis of the break-up value of its assets, having been plagued by mismanagement and un-recovered loans; GUYWA was made a public corporation and is currently being managed by Severn Trent Water International of the UK – under a management service contract with the government in 2003 – albeit under difficult and humiliating circumstances, with Board interference a major concern to the management team.[36] The GEC as fully

[34]   See 1995 Budget Speech, 6 February 1995, 24.

[35]   The government of India has provided US$100.0 million soft loan for this project, at the consternation of the Bank.

[36]   Williams, N. 'Water utility chafes under board control – says projects delayed due to indecision', *Stabroek News*, 19 September 2003; Williams, N. 'Baksh blasts management of water utility' *Stabroek News*, 28 June 2003.

discussed in Chapter 8 was privatised but was returned to the government in April 2003, again, under humiliating circumstances.

Attempts at privatising the bauxite industry

Successive attempts by the government to get ALCAN of Canada to take over the operations at the Linden Mining Enterprise have failed. ALCAN's refusal was based on the amount of capital required to return the industry to its former state which it was clearly not prepared to advance. The Berbice Mining Enterprise (BME) on the other hand had been operating as a joint venture between Aroima and Alcoa/Reynolds Metals; the latter from whom it was nationalized. However, on 17 January 1998 the government announced the privatisation of the Linmine power plant by way of a lease-sale agreement with Texas Ohio Energy Inc. (TOE). Under the terms of the agreement, TOE will pay a lease rental of US$250,000 per annum for 15 years and invest about US$8.0 in rehabilitation of the plant so that it produces 20 megawatts at the end of two years. For its part, Linmine will purchase its energy requirements from the Linmine Power Plant. During the signing of the agreement, TOE also announced its intention to enter a bid for Linmine Enterprises Limited which is scheduled for privatisation at the end of June 1998. In 2001, Alcoa/Reynolds withdrew from the joint venture in Aroima.

Use of proceeds from privatisation

Proceeds from the sale of state-owned enterprises are included in the government's fiscal budget as 'Capital Revenues'. Figure 7.6 gives an indication of the proceeds from divestment; these were less than one-quarter of the country's external debt service cost for the period. Moreover, the government retains a privatisation account from which extra-budgetary transactions are made. This account is under the direct control of the President and administered by the Head of the Privatisation Unit.

Dual political system – of the verandha and of the air conditioner[37]

'Patrimonialism' as a form of governance, according to Turner and Hulme (1997, 51) 'seemed not only to have survived in the Third World but has prospered in the context of development'. In the case of Guyana, whereas the basis of corruption prior to 1992 could be traced to a collapsed economy and resultant poverty – supporting Minogue's (2004) contention that corruption, at least some aspects of it, is a form of behaviour – patrimonialism and with it corruption morphed into bureaucratic and political corruption under the PPP/C government as a result of the flow of foreign aid and the control of the banking system as discussed above. Indeed, in regard to the latter, having had its claim that Treasury bills are issued merely to 'mop

---

[37]   Terray 1996, quoted in Turner and Hulme (1997, 51).

up excess liquidity'[38] debunked, the government has sought to tap into protected funds of agencies in which there is an arms-length relationship and a clear fiduciary responsibility to their members by changing the laws.[39]

Public works projects

Large-scale public works projects provide opportunities to award major government contracts to cronies, and to grant tax remissions and concessions despite expressed concerns of the MFIs. The announced write-off of the external debts to the IMF and Bank – and presumably the IDB – has served to vindicate the PPP's approach to economic management and to further embolden those who regard the developed countries as a 'cash cow'. Moreover, as noted above they have become havens for drug traffickers and for money laundering.

The verandha effect

Bureaucratic and political corruption to be sure became mutually reinforcing by the appointment to high office on the basis of patronage, the verandha effect. As a result, the increased flows in foreign aid in the 1990s became a target for leakages – especially after the death of Dr Cheddi Jagan, co-founder and leader of the PPP, in 1997 – and have been exploited to the fullest in the form of political corruption – transactions between the public and private sectors – to the benefit of corrupt politicians and crony public officials who function as 'party cashiers'.

Keeping key political elites loyal The blatant display of wealth in the form of luxury houses (by Guyana standards) constructed on previously state-owned lands with Toyota (Prado) SUVs by key ministers and public officials speak to the verandha effect of the dual political system: To paraphrase one of the leaders of the Working People's Alliance (WPA) political party, what the PNC never achieved in 28 years was achieved by the PPP in 8 years. Never had so many become so rich is so short a time, and all on a minister's salary in an EHIPC, to be sure. A recent survey conducted by Transparency International ranks Guyana as among the most corrupt countries in the Americas, placing it at 117th of 159 countries surveyed in 2004 (see page Chapter 3).

---

[38]   Kowlessar, S., 'This government was able to return Guyana to creditworthiness', *Stabroek News*, 7 July 2005.

[39]   'Scepticism persists over NBS investment in Berbice River Bridge project', *Stabroek New*, 17 February 2006; see also 'Some interest in US$30m GPL re-privatisation', *Stabroek News*, 5 January 2005; see also Nandram, B. 'Some directors are seeking to amend the New Building Society Act to give powers to invest depositors' savings in other projects', *Stabroek News*, 15 June 2005.

The air conditioner effect

The ability to attract foreign aid in the form of debt-relief, grants and loans on concessional terms to be sure is the sine qua non of the air-conditioner effect. Evidence, for example, the Minister of Finance proudly pronouncing that having 43 percent of the government's fiscal budget financed by debt-relief, grants and soft loans as 'a testimony to the government's efforts to return Guyana to creditworthiness and eligibility for new grants and loans to finance much-needed developmental public investments';[40] the Minister of Foreign Trade and International Relations in the matter of the EU's proposed reform of its sugar regime reportedly declared: 'We will need at least 300 million euros every year in order for us to adjust' (see Chapter 3) notwithstanding the Chief Executive Officer of GUYSUCO and head of the Booker-Tate management team's dispassionate observation: 'The local sugar industry will survive changes in the world trading system – even a loss of its preferential access to Europe' (see Chapter 3).

Furthermore, such grants and other assistance are looked upon as a right by the government and its supporters: The PRSP unabashedly accuses the donor community of not being timely with promised aid[41] while the Head of the Caribbean Sugar Association – a proponent of industry expansion in Guyana – gratuitously greets the EU's representative's promise of financial assistance to the government to help restructure the economy with Virgil's *Timeo Danaos et dona ferentes* [I fear the Greeks even when bearing gifts].[42] The 'Trojan horse' if ever there was one arguably was in the form of the ACP Sugar Protocol in 1975 – to the extent that it served as a perverse incentive to most of the 19 ACP countries for over thirty years – which as an executive of GUYSUCO in 1975 he welcomed and for almost three decades defended as 'enshrined', 'sacrosanct [with] ... a life of its own'; all the while disparaging dispassionate economic analyses and professional advice with which he found disagreement.[43] Meanwhile Mauritius and others, including St. Kitts whose economy derived from sugar for over three hundred years, have either diversified out of sugar or have accepted the EU's offer of assistance with restructuring.

Conclusion

The above together with the several references to Guyana throughout this book provide the background against which the issues discussed in Chapter 8 are analysed.

---

[40] Kowlessar, S., 'This government was able to return Guyana to creditworthiness', *Stabroek News*, 7 July 2005.

[41] Government of Guyana, *Guyana Poverty Reduction Strategy Progress Report 2004*, p. 1.

[42] McDonald, I. 'Europe gives but will Europe also take away?', in *Stabroek News*, 15 July 2005.

[43] McDonald, I. *Letter to the Permanent Secretary, Ministry of Agriculture*, 18 July 1994.

Meanwhile, the saga of the dual political system continues: donor-countries compete for projects to be paid for by their respective heavily-taxed citizens while staff rotation in the international missions and the absence of a coordinated external monitoring system provide on-going opportunities to the incumbent government to perfect the dual political system to its advantage.

Chapter 8

The GEC: Anatomy of a Failed Privatisation

On 1 April 2003 Americas and Caribbean Power Limited (AC Power), a consortium of the Commonwealth Development Corporation (CDC)[1] and Electricity Service Board of Ireland (ESBI), offered to sell its interest in Guyana Power and Light (GPL) to the government of Guyana for $1.00, and to end all agreements relating to its involvement in GPL by 30 April 2003.[2] This action came a little over three years since AC Power acquired a fifty percent interest in the electric utility, formerly the Guyana Electricity Corporation (GEC), and invested US$20.0 million in rehabilitating and upgrading the system pursuant the 'Shareholders' Agreement Respecting Guyana Power & Light Inc'. and an 'Operating and Agency Agreement' (Agreements) executed by the parties on 1 October 1999.

In announcing its intention to withdraw from the joint venture, CDC, the senior partner of AC Power, observed: 'The risks associated with investing in GPL make it less attractive for CDC to invest further funds than walking away'.[3] The offer was accepted by the government and the investor relinquished control of GPL on 30 April 2003 as offered and with dignity.

Prior to the decision to walk away from its investment, AC Power had proposed the withdrawal of ESBI from the joint venture in January 2003 in response to criticisms of its performance as managers by consumers, the government and the PUC. CDC further proposed renegotiation of the investment agreement between AC Power and the government to include:

- The recovery of US$1.2 million representing management service fees due to ESBI, a requirement for its withdrawal from the contract.
- Changes to the management of GPL, from contract management to salaried managers.
- Reduction in the power of the PUC to impose any penalty on GPL for non-compliance with its targets.

---

[1]   Through its subsidiary, CDC Globeleq.

[2]   Singh, G., 'Gov't buys back GPL for $1 – seeking local investors', *Stabroek News*, 1 April 2003.

[3]   Singh, G., 'Gov't buys back GPL for $1 – seeking local investors', *Stabroek News*, 1 April 2003. Singh, G., 'CDC ready to sell GPL for $1 – investing in Guyana is not for the faint of heart says official', *Stabroek News*, 13 March 2003, *Stabroek News*, April 1, 2003.

- The reduction of those targets in the light of current experience and the revocation of the June 2002 G$1.3 Billion Refund Order of the PUC.
- Capping of any future penalties at G$20million or 10 percent of dividends paid.
- Implementation of a 21.8 percent increase in rates on the heels of a 14.0 percent increase in 2002. The proposed rate increase is premised on the company's reported loss of G$475.0 million for 2002 which included bad-debt write off of G$1.1 billion, more than double that of 2001. Payment of the final tranche of US$3.45 million and additional investment of US$ 4.5 million on guarantee that there would be no interference in the revenue flows to GPL.[4]

The government and the Head of the Privatisation Unit responded to the proposal with charging the ESBI management team with 'incompetence', concurrently stating that it was '... not bent on keeping AC Power as a joint-venture partner'.[5] AC Power reiterated its position that the utility was run 'as efficiently as it could have been run in the last three years [and that there was] ... no future for the company if rates do not go up'.[6]

The issues

What makes a well-respected foreign investor and highly experienced electric utility manager walk away from its US$20.0 million investment without seeking recompense or a public acknowledgement of its contribution? What are the risks to further investment in the electric utility mentioned by CDC and by extension the implications for future FDI in Guyana? What are the implications for development and poverty reduction in consequence? What lessons can be drawn from this privatisation experience?

While answers to the many questions are discernible in Chapter 7, this case study seeks to articulate a reasoned contemplation of the issues. In addition, it approaches the subject from the perspective of the privatisation effectiveness evaluated in terms of development rather than from the nomothetic pretensions of privatisation. Hence the substantive agreements between the parties and the operating practices of the utility are critiqued not only in terms of the privatisation policy framework articulated by the government (see Chapter 7), the general principles and practices of privatisation and good regulation but also in terms of privatisation as a contributing asset to development as broadly defined in Chapter 3.

---

[4]   Singh, G., 'Gov't calls for GPL managers to go – says rate hike unjustified', *Stabroek News,* 31 January 2003.

[5]   Singh, G., 'Fuel shortages loom at GPL – Hinds says all options on table', *Stabroek News*, 15 February 2003.

[6]   Singh, G., 'Power Crisis, GPL plans shutdown of buffer generation', *Stabroek News*, 19 February 2003.

The theoretical basis for privatisation

The theoretical basis for privatisation has been fully discussed in the preceding chapters. However, for purpose of this analysis three concepts are recalled as having direct bearing on the issues:

- transparency and public accountability;
- the political will to honour legally-binding agreements; and
- a regulatory framework that is capable of being perceived by investors as representing credible commitments to the notion of private-sector development and upon which they can make investment decisions (Juskow 1998, 69; Kirkpatrick 2001).

In regard to the latter, where the enterprise to be privatised is a monopoly service provider, an oft-stated essential requirement is for the regulatory framework to be in place prior to privatisation; it limits confusion and rent seeking, as evidenced by the Argentine experience (see Marial 1996) and the privatisation of the telephone company in *Cote d'Ivoire* (Stiglitz 2002, 56). Furthermore, from a development perspective the regulatory framework must take cognisance of the impact of cost-recovery that attend on privatisation of essential basic services previously provided by the sate on the poor and other vulnerable groups. To this end, there should be a clearly stated policy on rate of return guarantee to the investor on the one hand and cost-covering tariffs the investor is allowed to set on the other. Subsidised services to the poor and other vulnerable groups should be unambiguous in both intent and application.

Privatisation Policy Framework Paper (PPFP)

Even before the entity was advertised for privatisation in October 1996, it was directly or indirectly mired in controversy. The cancellation of the privatisation programme that underpinned the country's Economic Recovery Programme pursuant structural reform under the IMF's ESAF by the newly-elected PPP/CIVIC government in October 1992, cast a pall over the liberalisation momentum and to FDI in Guyana. To the essentially neophyte government, the privatisation of public enterprises by its predecessor PNC-government was contrary to the ideological underpinnings of the PPP whose support derives from the sugar industry and whose notion of economic governance is rooted in Marxist-Leninist ideology, as recently revealed by the General Secretary of the PPP[7]. Hence, as discussed in the preceding chapter the PPP/C government's approach was to do little more than pay lip service to the privatisation programme in the first twelve months of being elected.

---

[7]   'PPP rolls out new Guyana programme – says its true to socialism', *Stabroek News*, 3 August 2005.

In general, the Privatisation Policy Framework Paper (PPFP) mirrored the recommended privatisation model for developing countries. It outlined the government's criteria for privatisation and required authorisation; procedures with respect to advertising for bids; dissemination of prospectus; inspection of the enterprise; pre-qualification of bidders; and receipt and evaluation of bids. An added feature of the PPFP was the rejection of bids if they do not comply with the prescribed legal, technical and financial requirements as indicated in the bidding rules, or where bid prices received were lower than the floor price fixed by the Government. A Cabinet level Privatisation Board with responsibility for ensuring that procedures, safeguards, and transparency are strictly adhered to was established as a distinguishing characteristic of the process and was incorporated in the PPFP[8].

It is against this backdrop of an articulated privatisation policy of the government and established regulation on the one hand and the reality of the process in a country that has been deemed politically and socially unstable on the other that the privatisation of the GEC is now examined.

Privatisation of GEC

The PPP/C government regarded the GEC as essential to its control of the economy; but its reluctance to have one of the 'commanding heights' of the economy privatised gave way to the need for debt forgiveness and rescheduling under multilateral terms and conditions, the debtor's dilemma if you will. Furthermore, its failure to deliver on its promise to bring the entity to an acceptable level of performance as a public corporation since it assumed office in 1992 and its failure to reverse the operating losses of the enterprise and to secure long-term financing for rehabilitation were equally compelling.

Bidding and selection

The privatisation of the GEC was announced in 1996 in keeping with the PPFP. However, given the poor operating condition of the entity – notwithstanding earlier attempts at rehabilitation financed by the Inter-American Development Bank (IDB) – and prevailing political and social instability they were few bidders. As a consequence, the government entered into negotiation with Sask Power Commercial of Canada (SASK), the bidder who was closest to meeting the government's selection criteria as provided for in the PPFP.

By Letter of Intent dated 2 May 1997 SASK proposed acquiring 50 percent of the shares in the GEC for US$22.65 million and for its management under a management service contract. SASK further proposed a guaranteed 18 percent after-tax annual return on investment and the exclusion of the entity from the jurisdiction of the PUC in the rate-making process as added measures of protection of its investment.

---

[8]   Co-operative Republic of Guyana, *Privatisation Policy Framework Paper*, June 1993.

However, in the light of increasing concerns over the economic and political instability of Guyana, and poor record-keeping at the GEC, the Saskatchewan Provincial government decided not to approve the SASK's proposal, even though the government of Guyana had agreed to all conditions.

On failing to complete the agreement with SASK, a new invitation to bid was posted by the Privatisation Unit with an expected completion date of 30 June 1998. In addition to the offer of 50 percent of the shares in the entity and a contract for management services, 20 percent of the share-holdings of both government and investor were required to be offered to the private sector within 5 years. The proceeds from the sale of the initial 50 percent by the government were to remain with the utility for rehabilitation purposes. As an incentive to the investor, based on these financial arrangements no new capital infusion would be required in the first three years after privatisation.

Three bids were received by the government in response to its proposal. These were from AC Power, Leucadia National Corporation and Eldorado Energy & Industrial Development Corporation.

Selection of AC Power

Although a higher price and a lower acceptable rate of return were proposed by one of the two other bidders, the government selected AC Power as the 'preferred bidder' with which to negotiate an agreement. According to the government's Press Release,[9] price and rate of return made up only 25 percent of the weighting, with 'Response to Government's conceptual framework and objectives' and 'Management and governance' accounting for 15 percent and 25 percent respectively. 'Business plan' and 'financial model' accounted for another 20 percent of the weighting. In deciding in favour of AC Power, 'ability to pay' and 'consistency of price and rate of return with the bidder's proposed business plan and financial model' were deemed overriding attributes.

For its part, AC Power proposed:

- the acquisition of 50 percent interest in the new GEC for US$23.45 million (which as noted above, the government agreed to plough back as part of the capital expansion programme as payments are received in tranches);
- a pre-tax rate of return of 23 percent;
- world class management personnel (annual cost of US$3.6million);
- a proposed capital expansion programme of US$104.0 million over 7 years;
- a strong commitment to Guyanisation, and to decreasing management fees progressively over the first 10 years.[10]

---

[9] Office of the Prime Minister, *Government of Guyana Announces Preferred Bidder for a 50% interest in the Guyana Electricity Corporation*, 22 June 1998.

[10] Office of the Prime Minister, *Government of Guyana Announces Preferred Bidder for a 50% interest in the Guyana Electricity Corporation*, 22 June 1998, 2.

Concern over transparency and accountability

The final terms of the agreement raised concerns over the process. In the first place, with the government agreeing to plough back the proceeds from the sale the privatisation did nothing to alleviate the debt or budgetary burden on the government. Furthermore, to the PNC, labour unions and the Consumer Advisory Bureau alike, the secret negotiations between the government and the preferred bidder were seen as being contrary to the expressed policy of the government as articulated in the PPFP. The Bid Review Committee which comprised only office-holders within the government with the Head of the Privatisation Unit as Chairman was also a concern.

In addition, the government's explanation for rejecting the bidder with a higher price and a lower acceptable rate of return and its refusal to identify that bidder served to exacerbate public concern. To be sure, the weighting attributed to price and rate of return appears not to reflect the stated policy of the government with respect to '... ensuring that the Government obtains the best price, which should not be lower than the highest bid submitted at the failed bidding'[11] Indeed, the process appeared skewed in favour of management, business plan and financial model, abstractions in comparison, to be sure. Furthermore, regulations '...designed to ensure that consumers' interests are protected especially in terms of price, quality and availability of essential goods and services'[12] were markedly absent, and to the extent embodied in existing legislation were negotiated away in the absence of the public-comment process.

Management service contract

Also of concern was a management service contract which, in addition to imposing a US$3.6 million burden upon the rate-payers annually, had the potential to accommodate hidden charges. In this connection, recall that the purchase consideration was to be paid in tranches and retained in the enterprise for capital improvement and addition.

Regulatory oversight subject to the Agreement

To accommodate the agreement with CDC/ESBI (used interchangeably with AC Power), the authority of the PUC was made subject to the Agreement. Hence in addition to the requirement that the PUC 'shall be bound by and shall give effect to the Agreement', Section 33 (b) of the Public Utilities Commission Act 1999, states that either the Agreement or Licence shall prevail in the event of a conflict between

---

[11] Co-operative Republic of Guyana, *Privatisation Policy Framework Paper*, June 1993, 21.

[12] Co-operative Republic of Guyana, *Privatisation Policy Framework Paper*, June 1993, 14.

the law and the Agreement or Licence. As a result, the Guyana Power and Light Inc. (GPL) – successor to the GEC – was clearly placed outside the regulatory scope of the PUC ex-post the bid-selection process which arguably goes to the integrity of the bidding process.

Indefensible rate of return

Further exacerbating criticisms of the process, the government having previously criticised the privatisation of the telephone utility in 1991 appeared to have been insensitive to the need to protect low-income and vulnerable groups and to be wary of the perception of 'briberization' which as observed by Stiglitz (2002, 58) is attached to privatisation in many countries. In this connection, the granting of a rate of return of 23 percent could be regarded as reflecting an inordinately high country-risk premium in the light of the progress claimed to have been made by the country in terms of economic growth and political governance since 1991, and the available body of evidence which suggests a changing approach to monopoly service providers in general. It further serves to constrain the sharing of the benefits of privatisation with other stakeholders by imposing an additional financial burden upon an already financially-strapped enterprise. Moreover, the rate of return could be regarded as inappropriately timed in the absence of any actual investment by AC Power other than the purchase consideration paid in tranches and utilized by the management for rehabilitation work.

Electricity Sector Reform Act 1999

To further accommodate the transaction with CDC/ESBI, the Electricity Sector Reform Act, 1999 (ESRA) was passed on 13 September 1999 without the benefit of public comment. The government relied on the 'Quadripartite Agreement' with the 'social partners' – trade unions and Consumer Advisory Bureau – executed in December 1998 as evidencing public participation. However, from the perspective of the social partners the 'Quadripartite Agreement' signifies consensus only on the proposed rate increases announced in 1998, to the staggering of such rate increases over a two-year period commencing 1 January 1999 and to the government's funding of any shortfall in the revenues between the required 'headline rates' and the actual rates in effect for the period identified. It does not evidence consensus on the resolution of a 'new set of issues'[13] which arose subsequently: These arose out of negotiations in secret and in consequence served to compromise defensibility, transparency and public accountability of subsequent agreements.

In addition to repealing prior Acts governing the old GEC, Part II of the ESRA specified the broad principles governing the rates that can be charged to consumers by public suppliers. The First and Second Schedules to the ESRA in conjunction

---

[13] Brassington, W., *Brief Comments – GEC Capitalisation Transaction*, Press Conference held by the Head of the Privatisation Unit on 24 June 1999.

with GPL's Licence 'set forth the specialised procedures, principles and formulae for determination of the rates that Guyana Power & Light Inc. will be permitted to charge consumers'.[14] Also, Part IV of the ESRA clearly endows the Minister (the Prime Minister) responsible with regulatory powers and limits those powers to 'areas appropriate for governmental regulation, e.g. public safety, the definition of technical standards and the procedure for licensing the supply of electricity ...'[15] with a first order requirement of balancing the interests of both consumer and investor. From the perspective of the investor, the ESRA guaranteed the agreed rate of return of 23 percent and placed the utility outside the scope of the regulatory authority of the PUC with respect to the setting of rates.

Questionable appointments

Public opinion was also on the side for greater transparency in the light of the revelation that the Head of the Privatisation Unit, the government's chief negotiator and signatory to the Agreements, and the accounting advisor to the government who was also Chairman of the GEC were to be appointed non-executive Board members of GPL – as indeed they were – at an unprecedented fee of US$1,000.00 per meeting in addition to US$1,000.00 per day for travel in addition to reimbursement for travel expenses. Of significance, these benefits were to apply only to the two government appointed board members.[16] Such fees to the two local board members according to the CEO of GPL amounted to over G$20 million (over US$100,000) in 2002.[17] In contrast, the average salary of a Permanent Secretary in the government at that time was around US$1,800 per month and Director Fees in public corporations and agencies averaged US$50.00 per meeting, with the latter fiercely defended as appropriate by the president.

In addition to passing ESRA and the PUC Act, 1999, the government granted GPL an exclusive Licence for 25 years effective October 1, 1999 to perform all or any of the activities associated with transmission and distribution of electricity service throughout the 'Authorised Area'. GPL was further granted a non-exclusive Licence for 25 years for the generation of electricity other than by hydropower.

Notwithstanding that Section 3 of the Licence states that the Licence is subject to ESRA, the PUC Act 1999, the Guyana Energy Agency, Act, No. 31 of 1997, the Environmental Protection Act, 1996, No.11 of 1996 and 'any other applicable law or regulation of Guyana', the Shareholders' Agreement and indeed Section 33 (b)

---

[14] Hinds, S., Prime Minister, *Explanatory Memorandum attached to the ESRA*, tabled in the Guyana General Assembly and passed into Law as Act No. 11 of 1999 on 13 September 1999, 94.

[15] Hinds, S., Prime Minister, *Explanatory Memorandum attached to the ESRA*, tabled in the Guyana General Assembly and passed into Law as Act No. 11 of 1999 on 13 September 1999, 95.

[16] Article 4.5, *Shareholders Agreement Respecting Guyana Power & Light*, p. 12.

[17] Singh, G. 'Power Crisis, GPL plans shutdown of buffer generator', *Stabroek News*, 19 February 2003.

of the PUC Act, 1999 place GPL outside the jurisdiction of any and all regulatory processes, unless specifically provided for in either the Licence or the Agreement. Moreover, as regards operating standards and performance targets, to the extent that the Licensee used its best efforts to implement, achieve and maintain them in accordance with the Second Schedule of the Licence, it '... shall be deemed to satisfy all such requirements under the Act ... and there shall be no requirement for approval by the Commission of the Operating Standards and Performance Targets ...'.[18] Once again, neither ESRA nor the Licence was open to public comment.

Further compounding the issue of transparency, neither the 'Shareholders' Agreement Respecting Guyana Power & Light Inc' nor the 'Operating and Agency Agreement' executed by the parties on 1 October 1999 was made open to public comment. Protestations by the leader of the opposition political party were largely ignored by the government.

Outcomes

The GEC was privatised on the basis of guarantees by the government with respect to rate of return and a management contract in exchange for capital infusion that would address badly-needed service improvement, reduce high system losses, and expand service at the national level. According to the Prime Minister, Guyana's electricity woes were at an end. Indeed, according to the Head of the Privatisation Unit[19] the 'deal' provides for:

- The management team '... to reduce the significant inefficiencies that currently exist'.
- '... capital for the rehabilitation of the New GEC through new equity and access to additional debt based on a recognized manager ...' and '... for the IDB to disburse the balance of US$30m on a US$40m credit provided for GEC capitalisation in 1996'.
- 'Reversing the trend of Government subsidies/loans ...' with expectations of '... dividends, taxes and other revenue from the New GEC'.
- '... the best package to maintain rates at its lowest sustainable level ...'.

However, the report card for the three years since privatisation tells a different tale when analysed in terms of:

- the investment and performance obligations of the investor;
- the objectives of good regulations; and
- economic and social consequences.

---

[18]   Co-operative Republic of Guyana, *Licence to Supply Electricity for Public Purposes Granted to the Guyana Power & Light, Inc.*, 1 October 1999, 11.

[19]   Brassington, W., *Brief Comments – GEC Capitalisation Transaction*, Press Conference held by the Head of the Privatisation Unit on 24 June 1999.

Investor obligations

Despite a highly lauded resume of achievements by the investor in other parts of the world, GPL failed to '... provide a supply of electricity to every person who requests such supply ...'[20] in keeping with Section 10 of its Licence which clearly places a duty on it, subject to Section 24 of ESRA. The results were increasing complaints and mass protests by residential customers, with several business consumers pursuing self-generation as a viable alternative, many having been accused with 'stealing electricity' by the company, however. To be sure, many meters were found to be defective. Even after the departure of AC Power, the accounting firm of Jack A. Ali Sons and Co of which the chairman of GPL is a partner was found to have been under-billed for electricity services.[21] It is perhaps coincidental that the contract for the preparation of GUYSUCO's tax returns was abruptly transferred from Deloitte and Touche to Jack A. Ali and Sons in 1995 at a time when the present chairman of GPL was at that time a board member of GUYSUCO and chairman of its audit committee.[22]

In its defence, GPL relied on the provisions of Section 24 of ESRA, which states: 'Nothing in this Act shall require the public supplier to supply electricity to any premises if and to the extent that the public supplier is prevented from doing so by circumstances not within its control'.[23] The circumstances in this case, according to GPL, were:

- Tariff charges form the basis of its capital expenditure as a result of its inability to secure the required funding externally and, therefore, must be increased; and
- Debt-financing is '... dependent on the revenue stream provided by the tariff setting mechanism enshrined in GPL's licence'.[24]

But, as stated by the PUC in its 19 April 2002 letter to GPL, having been brought into the regulatory loop by the President ex-post privatisation and in contradiction if not in violation to the several agreements, '... the company was attempting to use these criteria as a means of excusing its inadequacy to undertake agreed improvements in the power sector [and that] in consideration of the company receiving the stipulated

---

[20]   See *Licence* granted to GPL, 1 October 1999, 6.

[21]   'WPA wants GPL Chairman to step aside for impartial billing, meter probe', *Stabroek News*, 22 November 2003.

[22]   Deloitte and Touche had expressed concerns about the high inventory levels maintained by the corporation despite write-offs in earlier years and evidence to suggest that most of the materials and supplies purchased in the intervening years were not related to end use.

[23]   See Guyana Act No. 11 of 1999, *Electricity Sector Reform Act 1999*, 13 September 1999, 26.

[24]   Statement by GPL's CEO at PUC public Hearing 16 April 2002; See also Singh, G., 'Power company slammed on deplorable billing, increased losses', *Stabroek News*, 22 April 2002.

rate of return it must make good on its undertaking'.[25] It is perhaps appropriate to recall that, by the several agreements the GPL was placed outside the jurisdiction of the PUC on matters of rate-setting; that the Head of the Privatisation Unit and the former Chairman of GEC were the government-appointed Board members of the utility; and that the Cabinet headed by the President approved the several Agreements. Moreover, access to the IDB loan was clearly stated as part of the package announced by the Head of the Privatisation Unit. Hence the president's action signalled a willingness to condone disinformation as part of negotiation and to unilaterally go outside the framework of legally-binding agreements as and when it suits him.[26] It is for this latter reason that the Prime Minister had been rumoured to have resigned.[27]

Loss reduction not met

The company has also failed to achieve the targeted loss reductions. At the end of 2002, system losses stood at 44 percent, an increase of 8 percentage points since privatisation, instead of the reduction by 20 percentage points ESBI agreed to in its Management Agreement. System losses in the Caribbean in contrast are: 8.6 percent in Antigua, 3.9 percent in Barbados, and 0.7 percent in Trinidad & Tobago, with St Lucia and Dominica, both owned and managed by CDC's Globeleq, at 10.7 percent and 19.0 percent respectively. As a result of this high level of system losses, GPL had to generate an additional 160,000 megawatts at a cost of G$1.9billion (US$10.0million) to meet the demand for electricity in 2002. The company's position was that it was 'over-optimistic' with respect to its ability to reduce system losses; that the business plan developed by it in its bid documents was based on 'flimsy' information; and that the level of losses now is an accurate reflection of the state of the company, despite improvements made by management.[28]

External financing not forthcoming

ESBI attributed its failure to achieve the targeted loss reductions to a lack of cooperation from consumers and the inadequacy of capital to finance transmission and distribution plant replacement. To be sure, attempts to raise debt-financing from the European Investment Bank (EIB) were met with a requirement for matching funds which the company claimed it was unable to generate internally. GPL was also unable to access the earlier-approved IDB (US$30.0 million) facility in consequence

---

[25]   Singh, G., 'Power company slammed on deplorable billing, increased losses', *Stabroek News*, 22 April 2002.

[26]   'PUC to review power company's performance – At Cabinet's request', *Stabroek News*, 2 August 2001.

[27]   'Cabinet stance on power tariff hike unified – Luncheon', *Stabroek News*, 14 February 2002.

[28]   Singh, G. 'Power Crisis, GPL plans shutdown of buffer generator', *Stabroek News*, 19 February 2003.

of multilateral loan restrictions imposed on the government. However, given the experience base of the strategic investor the possibility of this occurring should have been known if not disclosed to it. Moreover, the government knew that it was not allowed to borrow externally without authorisation from the IMF, and being a 50 percent partner puts it in the position of borrower.

Collection of accounts receivables

Compounding the problem of financing, on the basis of the evidence the investor appears to have placed a great deal of reliance on collecting the substantial – on paper at any rate – accounts receivable of the old GEC – for which it had negotiated an agency agreement – as a means to reinvesting in plant and equipment under the agreements. But given the poor record-keeping at the entity, the true value of the receivables had been overstated and the enormity of the task of collection seriously misjudged by the investor. Also, the payment of the management fee (US$3.6 million) annually left very little of the privatisation proceeds – paid in tranches, as agreed – for reinvestment. Indeed, as disclosed by the CEO of GPL, the utility was experiencing US$600,000 negative cash flow per month.[29]

The absence of effective regulation

Relying upon the terms of the several agreements between the strategic investor and the government, the Licence, and on Section 33(b) of the PUC Act, 1999, GPL regarded the PUC actions in the rate-making process as intrusive. Indeed, the Licence specified that 'headline rates' and the actual rates, to be charged by the Licensee '... shall be those determined in accordance with the Second Schedule of the Act'.[30] Moreover, the Licence was specific as to the regulatory authority of the Minister. Thus from the very beginning, the PUC was caught in the dilemma of having no authority over the entity while public expectation was one for intervention. On the other hand the Prime Minister clearly relatively ill-equipped to perform the duties of regulator in keeping with the principles of good regulations necessarily articulated the terms of the agreements much to the publicly-articulated made displeasure of the President.[31]

To be sure, the Prime Minister approached regulation of GPL from the perspective of the agreement in contrast to the prevailing public perception that '... the best protection for the consumer would have been an independent PUC not the shell of a body emasculated by the government'.[32] The terms of the various agreements

29 Singh, G., 'GPL tariffs up sharply – to pay for 2.6 billion shortfall', *Stabroek News*, 29 January 2003.

30 GPL Licence, 12 (a), 1 October 1999, 6.

31 'Cabinet to review power company performance', *Stabroek News*, 18 July 2001.

32 Clarke, O., 'Prime Minister seems to be spokesman for GPL', *Stabroek News*, 13 February 2002.

notwithstanding, the President also publicly expressed dismay at the Prime Minister's unequivocal support of the company's position in authorizing further rate increases despite the barrage of public criticisms. This public rebuke by the President resulted in the government requesting the PUC to critically review the technical performance of GPL as noted above.

The legal status of the several Agreements, GPL's Licence, and ESRA notwithstanding, the PUC found itself obliged to find ways of holding GPL accountable for service deficiencies and billing discrepancies. In its hearing on April 16, 2002 the PUC advised the company that '... it is engendering consumer dissatisfaction with its deplorable billing system ...' and that it should discontinue such irregularity.[33] The PUC further ordered the GPL to refund G\$1.3 billion representing over-billing to consumers. The matter was referred to the Courts for judicial determination and was made one of the issues for renegotiation with the government.

Implications for development

In terms of pro-poor growth and development, of significant concern both at the level of the individual consumer and for its implications for development is the practice of billing on the basis of estimated consumption. In this case, GPL is allowed to bill '... on estimates for those billing periods when the meter is not read, such periods to be kept to a reasonable minimum. Estimates will be based on the previous and expected usage patterns for the customer'.[34] However, a review of utility bills and complaints filed with the PUC up to the end of 2001 revealed a significant number of consumers were billed on estimated consumption in three out of four months. Moreover, such estimates were consistently higher than actual usage (often, more than doubled), and in the light of the difficulties experienced in obtaining external financing arguably suggests that GPL saw the provisions of Section 7.2 of the 'Standard Terms and Conditions' as a mechanism to raise needed cash flow while at the same time engaged in constructive load-shedding through the disconnection process.

This practice of estimated billing and disconnection for non-payment after 21 days from date of billing when such billing does not reasonably represent usage, apart from being ruled irregular by the PUC, raises two significant social and economic concerns. The first centres on the impact on the consumer both in terms of access to a basic service, and as a person; the second centres on the economic consequences of over billing, which estimated billing as practised by the GPL clearly represents.

---

33 'Power bills should reflect rate at time of consumption – PUC', *Stabroek News,* 21 February 2002.

34 Section 7.2 *Guyana Power & Light Inc., Standard Terms and Conditions for Electric Services*, 1 April 2000, 19.

Social impact of over-billing

With respect to the first issue, during the period of investigation, the reconnection fee was G$3,200.00, the magnitude of which becomes apparent when related to the minimum wage of G$19,000.00 per month for public servants or the national minimum wage of G$500.00 per day. Moreover, the average electricity bill has been rising rapidly and can represent as much as 30 percent of income at the lower-income level. Given this electricity cost-income relationship, the following are implications for pro-poor growth arising from this practice:

- Pro-poor growth is adversely impacted by the higher than actual estimate and by the high reconnection fee, both of which clearly represent misappropriation of resources. Indeed, given the electricity cost-income relationship at the level of the poor and the relatively high cost of reconnection, the poor can be regarded as being deprived the ability to undertake economic transactions proportionately greater than the more affluent segment of society.
- In terms of development, estimated billing as practised by GPL operates to disturb in a fundamental way instrumental as well as substantive freedoms that should be part of the privatisation effectiveness. Since the poor is the group most frequently disconnected and given the correlation between low-income and social degradation, the perceived but yet unmeasured economic and social cost at the level of the poor is likely exacerbated by the reduction in available income resulting from the relatively high cost of reconnection.
- The consequential impact of the reduction in access to electricity service resulting from disconnection for non-payment of estimated billing further operate against notions of environmental protection. The poor is forced to seek alternative sources of energy which, in addition to being time-consuming often leads to destruction of the environment.
- The concern for environmental degradation thus remains at the awareness level; wood fire remains a source of energy and, in the case of the coastal population, destruction of the mangrove continues to adversely impact on sea defence, requiring transference of scarce resources from other productive activities.

Macro-economic impact of over-billing

The second concern centres on the implications for the economy and for development arising from allocation of resources away from other economic activities. Clearly, by over-estimating consumer usage the GPL engages in misappropriation of resources, thereby depriving other sectors of the economy from accessing such resources. The effect can be likened to that of a tax by the government with all its ramifications for individual choice and, in this case, for the national-income stream if the funds generated from such over-billing were used to meet external management service fees which are repatriated.

Furthermore, in this particular case the economic costs are not restricted to the reconnection fee that the consumer is required to pay. Time spent at GPL's central location, often up to 4 hours to obtain reconnection of service, indeed even to request change-service (a requirement of the company and a hold-over from the past) serves to exacerbate inefficiency at all levels of production.

Subsidies

Adding to the misallocation of resources by way of over-billing is the payment of subsidies to the GPL of almost G$2.5 billion at the end of 2001 as required by Section 3.4 of the *Shareholders Agreement* – a fact kept hidden from the public as well as from the IMF and Bank review missions. The rationale was that such subsidies would allow the investor to earn the agreed 23 percent rate of return in the first two years of operations by which time the savings from loss-reductions, implementation of an efficient billing system and service expansion would materialize to keep rate-increases at a minimum.

Rate increases

Instead of keeping rates low, residential and commercial rates have increased by 99.0 percent and 76 percent respectively since 1 October 1999 with no end in sight as technical and commercial losses are even greater than were represented to the investor, and the desperately-needed improvement in the billing system still an objective. Such rate increases and the prospects for more are particularly daunting to a society plagued by high unemployment, low wages and the absence of a social safety-net, consideration of which are conspicuously absent in the agreements and in the government fiscal budgets. In contrast, industry practice suggests that in a regulated monopoly utility service environment safeguard for the vulnerable is a shared responsibility of the service-provider, consumer and government by way of effective regulation and income redistribution mechanisms. In such an environment, subsidisation of rates is usually tied to providing service to the poor and other vulnerable groups and not merely as a means to making up revenue short-falls. Thus, to the extent that the payment of subsidies to GPL does not conform to industry practice, it further deprives low-income earners of both instrumental and substantive freedoms when viewed from the perspective of the incidence of consumption and excise taxes in an inefficient tax collection system. Moreover, the subsidies paid to GPL were not included in the fiscal budget as financing items; indeed, they were represented to the IMF and Bank review missions in June 2000 as loans from the 'privatisation account', an extra-budgetary fund of the government under the control of the President.

Beginning of the end

In the light of the operating constraints encountered by ESBI – a 20 percent partner in the AC Power and the management service provider – and the barrage of criticism from all quarters, including the call for its removal by the Office of the President, the joint venture began to unravel and as detailed in the opening paragraphs was brought to an end.

Conclusion

From the very beginning, despite an established privatisation policy that exalts transparency as articulated by the late President Cheddi Jagan and the public chastisement of the PNC over its privatisation of the telephone utility in 1991 by the Senior Minister of Finance in his 1994 Budget Speech, the privatisation of the GEC was clouded if not shrouded by what must be regarded as rent-seeking, misinformation if not disinformation, and miscalculation. More importantly, the decision to privatise was not only based on archaic reasoning and failed to consider the fiscal and macro-economic implications of a change in net worth of the government and the revenue/expenditure flows but also failed to consider the attendant social disruption and its implications for pro-poor growth and for future FDI; indeed, the privatisation effectiveness was arguably completely ignored.

Also, of particular concern on a going-forward basis is that the Head of the Privatisation Unit not only was allowed to benefit himself and the former Chairman – reinstated as chair of GPL on the departure of AC Power – at the expense of electric rate-payers whose interest they were appointed to represent but also remains a director of the utility. Moreover, it is a contradiction to the notion of good governance that the Head of the Privatisation Unit continues to function in this Bank-funded position in the face of the revelation of irregularity. The failure of the government to act to correct this anomaly must be seen in context of the relationship of the Privatisation Unit to the Office of the President in regard to the utilization of the proceeds from privatisation which are kept as extra-budgetary funds and administered by the Head of the Privatisation Unit and away from parliamentary oversight, despite attempts by the Auditor General and the author as former Secretary to the Treasury to have all extra-budgetary transactions treated as financing items in the fiscal budget.

With respect to the agreements, as discussed integrity arguably was compromised not only by *legerdemain* in the negotiations but also by the disregard for the public-comment process at a stage when it mattered most. It was thus a curiosity that the investor with its vast experience in privatisation around the world should have overlooked the value of this all-important mechanism and arguably opted for some form of perceived asymmetric advantage that empirical evidence suggests can only be short-lived in an unstable political and economic environment.

Also, the investor arguably had over-estimated its ability to perform in an unstable economic, social and political environment that is Guyana's. Moreover, as played out the investor was not only ill-informed on the condition of the utility's generation, transmission and distribution plant and equipment but also was clearly deceived by the prospect of collecting the purported substantial accounts receivable of the 'Old GEC'. Indeed, it was to their dismay that the author as Secretary to the Treasury refused to accede to demands to consolidate and authorise payment of a list of government accounts purported to be outstanding to the 'Old GEC' without proof of obligation.

The inability of the management team to substantially collect from other consumers also exacerbated their frustrations. Indeed, with the agreement that the government's share from these 'outstanding accounts' was to remain in GPL for reinvestment, the calculation that any new equity capital infusion by the investor could be timed to increases in the revenue-stream derived from the attendant service improvements and loss-reductions was at risk. Also, the Managers stood to benefit handsomely from the collection of the old accounts receivable under the Agency Agreement if only they were capable of authentication and indeed collection. Moreover, that the investor arranged for an instalment payment-plan for its equity investment in GPL and sought to fund its capital expansion programme almost entirely from these sources suggest a cautious approach to investment in Guyana, a predictable reaction to investment in an uncertain economic and political environment and the absence of clearly stated regulatory rules within a well defined regulatory framework.

From a technical perspective, the lessons from this privatisation are clear:

- The principles of defensibility, transparency and public accountability were not strictly adhered to throughout the privatisation process. Their importance were rationalised to foster personal or political interests without consideration for consequences in a democracy.
- The privatisation did not alleviate the budgetary burden of the government; rather it added to it by the subsidies that were paid in 2000 and 2001.
- The investor was risk averse going into the privatisation despite assurances and became disillusioned by its inability to move forward as envisaged. In this regard, it underestimated the challenges associated with working with a government with a tendency to micro-manage. It also failed to verify the veracity of representations made to it in negotiations. In this regard, evidence the investor's parting observation: 'We do not feel welcome in Guyana. Investing in Guyana is not for the faint of heart'.
- From the perspective of good regulation, ex-post regulation has been proven once again to be a bad policy-option. Moreover, the commitment to sound regulatory practices had clearly given way to political expediency; the rules of the game were also not applied equitably and consistently.
- From the perspective of good governance, the agreements reveal a decided tendency to corruption in the absence of transparency.
- While there were consultations with the social partners, these were cut short at crucial points in the negotiations with the strategic investor. As a consequence, customer dissatisfaction and activism became overwhelming, leading to policy reversal.

Finally, as important as the economic consequences arising from lapses in the implementation process are to a developing country, the resultant loss of the several freedoms which could be had from privatisation properly conceived and implemented have been lost on this government. In this regard, the government has failed to recognise that the articulation of concerns by community and political opposition is also a tenet of democracy and will necessarily resonate with the socially excluded and that public participation in the political-decision and social-choice processes are desirable ends in a democracy.

PART V
Concluding Policy Perspective

Chapter 9

In Praise of a Holistic Approach

Privatisation has been a contentious issue for more than two decades: It was framed in the vocabulary of Cold-War politics – the East-West dichotomy if you will – in the first instance and later found description in the vocabulary of market fundamentalism in consequence of the failure of Keynesian economics in the 1970s and the economic deterministic pursuits of President Reagan and Prime Minister Thatcher in consort. But as shown, privatisation effectiveness cannot be measured merely in terms of efficiency of the enterprise or in the use of resources or in regime change, as some proponents are wont to believe.

Inconclusive evidence

Whilst there is empirical evidence to support the contention that privatisation contributes to enterprise efficiency in countries in which demography, geography and institutions are facilitating, there still remains no conclusive evidence that privatisation in the poorer developing countries has significantly improved enterprise performance or contributed to development. The Bank, in offering the results of an analysis of sixty-one companies privatised in eighteen countries as evidencing improvements in four measurements – profitability, sales, operating efficiency and capital investment; all financial measurements to be sure – omitted to identify the countries in which such improvements occurred. However, analysing the results further it is evident the improvements were found in two-thirds of the enterprises privatised and that developed countries made up two-thirds of the sample countries. It is thus instructive that the Bank should observe that, 'in established market economies and middle- to high-income developing countries there is little doubt that private ownership is a significant determinant of economic performance' (Bank 1996, 49).

The poverty of privatisation

Following on from the Bank's analysis quoted above, the poverty of privatisation as an economic theory is very much in evidence when examined from the perspective of non-industrial low-income countries. In these low-income countries in which reciprocity and redistribution continue to determine integration, privatisation having been automatically prescribed without much consideration to readiness in terms of institutions and to the inevitable social disruption arising there from was anything but successful. It is not surprising therefore that there should be no mention of any success at the level of low-income countries.

Multidimensional, multi-disciplinary

Clearly, as demonstrated privatisation is multidimensional and multi-disciplinary. As documented in the preceding chapters, the outcomes of privatisation varied considerably between regions and countries within regions with demography, geography and institutions determining outcomes in all measurements. Where the right environmental conditions and institutions existed, privatisation outcomes supported its theoretical economic constructs; where privatisation was pursued in economic deterministic terms – with effecting a change in the mode of production and providing opportunities for foreign investment as objectives – it was with few exceptions met with resistance not unlike that encountered in nineteenth-century England during the Industrial Revolution (see Polanyi 1944, 77), especially at the level of the poorer more traditional societies.

Moreover, where the economy is an embedded aspect of society – as opposed to being the determinant of society as in the developed countries – privatisation imposed from the outside disturbs in a fundamental way the workings of that society. In this regard, the rush to privatise on the basis of its nomothetic pretensions calls to mind Myrdal's (1969, 57) observation: 'It is a tragedy of economic inquiry that the further we have advanced in our attempts to observe and explain social phenomena, the further away we have moved from our aim of defining the conditions for the maximization of social utility.' Not surprisingly, developing countries are perceived as having paid too much for the notion of a universal ideology and for the learning experience of the IMF and Bank in national cohesion, dignity and economic welfare.

Maintaining national cohesion

Where privatisation was used as a means to ensuring national acceptance of the transformation from certainty to uncertainty, as was the case in the Czech Republic and Russia, the process gave birth to new ideas in terms of techniques and implementation: Privatisation effectiveness was measured not in terms of enterprise efficiency, debt repayment or opportunities for foreign investment but rather in terms of maintaining social cohesion through inclusivity; paradoxically a tenet of democracy which seemingly had escaped the consciousness of the IMF and Bank in their bid to conform to the Washington Consensus. Even with the inevitable political influence of communist hardliners, corruption and the lack of sophisticated corporate governance in the early years of privatisation especially in Russia – criticisms levelled by the MFIs – when measured in terms of societal transformation both the Czech Republic and Russia had established the nucleus of a modern market economy comparable to that of Hungary and Poland's within an unprecedented time span. Moreover, the transformation was as much instructive to the IMF and Bank as it was enormously impressive and contributed to the vocabulary of privatisation.

Privatisation as zero-sum game

Equally supportive of the belief in economic determinism was the language of the Bank that speaks to a strip-and-sell policy and pursued as a zero sum game by a cadre of automatons. Countries – Chile for example – that recognized and complied with the implicit requirement to redress for expropriation of transnational corporations' assets found the multilateral agencies and Western investors more willing to support their economic reform programmes. Indeed, as shown by the Hungarian and Polish experiences, substantial debt forgiveness was the *quid pro quo* for compliance and conformance. Governments that did not get the message were humbled, humiliated and even had their assets covertly and systematically confiscated as recompense within the IMF and Bank supported privatisation framework. Hence, Sklair's (1995, 1) observation that transnational corporations have been known to recover the value of their seized-assets through a combination of transfer-pricing and control over processing or marketing of the product is supported by the evidence, with Guyana as a case in point.

Even when the political will was present, the absence of appropriate mechanisms to adequately facilitate the process and to address issues of development and contradictions arising there from have had an overriding influence on outcome, as has been shown to be the case in several of the countries referenced. Indeed, the ex-post observation of the former Chief Economist of the Bank speaks powerfully to this point:

> Perhaps of all the IMF's blunders, it is the mistakes in sequencing and pacing, and the failure to be sensitive to the broader social context, ... forcing liberalization before safety nets have been put in place, ... forcing policies that led to job destruction before the essentials for job creation were in place ... (Stiglitz 2002, 73).

With privatisation arguably pursued in developing countries as a zero-sum game by the multilateral institutions, the cost of the learning curve can be measured in terms of the widening income gap between the developed and the poorer developing countries and indeed in terms of the mountain of external official debt of the latter. It is thus no accident that despite two decades of restructuring and billions of dollars of foreign aid, write-off of almost US$40.0 billion of official multilateral debts of these countries – arguably made poorer by privatisation – became a moral imperative of the twenty-first century.

A holistic approach

As shown, privatisation is neither entirely economics nor is it scientific but rather an amalgam of ideas drawn from economics, sociology and politics expressed in financial techniques. As such, its underpinnings in economic orthodoxy notwithstanding, prevailing societal values, customs and mores have proven to be as much determinants of outcomes and cannot be ignored at the policy-making level nor indeed in any evaluative framework that seeks to measure privatisation effectiveness; indeed the state of the political and legal frameworks so essential to privatisation effectiveness reflect these intrinsic values and debunk the notion of economic determinism in the short to medium term.

While to be sure the very nature of a market economy requires that there be freedom of choice by participants – the *raison d'être* of U.S. privatisation – such freedom cannot operate to promote substantive development if other complementary forms of freedom – the freedoms to work, to be educated, to be healthy, and to political expression and civic involvement as identified by Sen (1999) – that seek to reduce social inequality are absent. Hence, while selective emphasis on freedom is inevitable in policy-making and evaluation, it becomes dangerous for evil when other forms of choice are concealed, disguised or denied. In other words, for privatisation to be a contributing asset to development it must necessarily incorporate mechanisms to empower the poor and disadvantaged. But it can only do so if in addition to traditional economic results the framework were to take cognisance of the impact – direct and indirect – of privatisation on:

- the extent to which the distribution of resources benefits the disadvantaged;
- the accumulation of assets by the poor;
- the fiscal budget as the source of financing poverty reduction (Bank 2001, 81); and
- on political expression and civic involvement, all of which must be transparent and sustainable.

The framework must further define mechanisms for the monitoring and evaluation of the process on a consistent and regular basis not merely by bureaucrats but by the citizens as stakeholders.

Moreover, a conscionable approach to privatisation would take into consideration Fukuyama's (1999, 15) observation that:

> [a] society dedicated to constant upending of norms and rules in the name of increasing individual freedom of choice will find itself increasingly disorganised, atomized, isolated, and incapable of carrying out common goals and tasks.

One-off compensation for termination should not be looked upon as the end of responsibility to workers displaced by privatisation. Often, such workers are ill-equipped to pursue alternative employment opportunities and eventually end up as destitute, adding to the unemployment if not the poverty statistics. On the other hand, workers displaced through privatisation present an opportunity to governments and the donor community to developing and fostering entrepreneurship at the grassroots.

Impact on the fiscal budget

Privatisation has a decided impact on the government's fiscal budget. As a prerequisite, based on the linkages between privatisation and development, the role of the enterprise in the economic and social make-up of the society and its contribution to or drain on the financial resources of the government as a state-owned and operated enterprise should be measured against the estimated impact on the fiscal budget as a private-sector owned and operated entity. In other words, the government's approach to privatisation as far as possible should seek to mirror the approach to divesture by a private-sector corporation, that is, increasing stakeholder value.

The standard argument for increasing private participation is that government revenues will be increased because of the expected increase in the tax base and efficiency gains, especially in the longer-term. Hoverer, while some countries have experienced increases in government net revenues after privatisation – many, because of being relieved of loss-making public enterprises – others, such as Tanzania, have found the granting of tax exemptions, tax holidays and other investment incentives to foreign investors pursuant privatisation fiscally debilitating. Also, in the case of the privatisation of the telecommunications enterprise in Guyana not only did the government give up US$9.0 million in annual revenue contribution from the entity, but also it did not receive any dividend for almost 10 years since the entity was privatised in 1991. When a dividend was declared in 2001, it was because the investor wanted to reduce the cash reserves of the entity in response to the government's challenge to its monopoly power. The investor meanwhile was able to extract and repatriate tax-exempted 'advisory fees' of six percent of gross revenues annually. Moreover, the government's attempts to tax certain revenue streams which fell outside of the privatisation agreement were challenged in the courts by the investor (see Chang 2004). Clearly, these and other impact on the fiscal budget should be factored into the privatisation decision and can be measured in net present value terms as suggested by Davis *et al.* (2000).

In terms of assessing the social cost, every financial transaction – income as well as expenditure – directly and indirectly connected with the enterprise both before and after privatisation should as far as possible be evaluated for their net impact on the fiscal budget. This must necessarily include any social cost or savings associated with the proposed privatisation as measured by an increase or decrease in the fiscal budget income/expenditure stream and the knock-on effects on programmes designed to reduce social inequality and poverty: often, the reduction in or elimination of one expenditure item might require increasing expenditure elsewhere, such as in healthcare or education. In this connection, it should be noted that many state-owned enterprises are not necessarily organized as commercial entities per se, but as means to achieving social goals, including the provision of employment opportunities and the fostering of social integration (see Katz 1992), reflecting the mode of production espoused by Polanyi as discussed in Chapter 2, or redress (see Henry 1990, 251).

The Guyana sugar industry, woven into the fabric of Guyanese society as it is exemplifies just such an enterprise in which divestiture on the basis of orthodox economics would have untold social consequences; a realisation that has been seized upon by the government and has been utilised as a means to extracting foreign aid. In this latter connection, evidence the claim by the Minister of Foreign Trade and International Cooperation that it costs US$0.40 to produce one pound of sugar in Guyana, requiring a subsidy of 300 million Euros a year for the country to adjust to the proposed reform to the EU's sugar regime,[1] when in reality, the average cost is about USS$0.18 per pound.

Derivation and use of proceeds from privatisation

It follows also how proceeds from privatisation are derived and used would have a direct impact on the objectives of reducing social inequality and poverty. Procedurally, as noted above, proceeds from privatisation should not be sheltered from public oversight and should be accounted for in the fiscal budget. Absent such oversight and accountability, proceeds from privatisation become a source of discretionary spending by the government. For example, one of the several extra-budgetary transactions by the Guyana government was the funding of the revenue deficiency of the privatised electric utility – which it was obliged to fund under the privatisation agreement – by accessing funds from prior privatisations kept in a 'Privatisation account' under the control of the President.

From a policy perspective, the government should be clear on the impact from a sudden increase in capital inflows and on the use of privatisation proceeds on the local exchange rate – if the sale is to a foreign investor – and on the fiscal budget if the proceeds are used to pay-down interest-bearing external debts (see Davis et al. 2000). The pay-down of external debts with foreign proceeds or the sterilisation thereof could result in an over-valued local currency, making local products uncompetitive vis-à-vis imports and thereby keep unemployment high. Where a sterilisation policy is pursued, funding the social disruption attendant on privatisation with higher-priced domestic debt – rather than from the proceeds from privatisation – places an added burden on resources and makes the government a competitor for funds in the domestic financial market as is the case in Guyana: While Guyana's external debt declined from US$2.1 billion in 1991 to US$1.2 billion in June 2003 mainly through debt-forgiveness and rescheduling, domestic debt increased from G$10.4 billion in 1990 to over G$67.0 billion in 2005 as depicted in Figure 7.1 – with the commercial banks holding almost 50.9 percent of the debt – and has become 'important source of vulnerability' (Bank, 2003).[2]

Governments must also be clear on addressing the direct and immediate consequences of privatisation. Often severance pay and employee retraining are properly treated as cost of privatisation and are funded from the proceeds from privatisation. However, as noted above one-off transfers in the form of severance

---

[1]   'Guyana needs huge aid to survive EU reforms – Rehee', *Stabroek News*, 26 September 2005.

[2]   World Bank draft: *Development Policy Review on Guyana*, 23 June 2003.

pay and retraining should not be looked upon as discharging social responsibility, especially when unemployment opportunities are limited. In this regard, it should be borne in mind that unemployment is an aspect of social exclusion and that the unemployed becomes more vulnerable to diseases and other health problems. Furthermore, disturbing the community structure, a consequence of high unemployment which privatisation tends to create, also contributes to social exclusion, anomie and crime, with tangible costs which must be reflected in the fiscal budget as a cost of privatisation to the extent identifiable. Ideally, these estimated costs should be matched by set-asides from the privatisation proceeds and not left to the generosity of aid-donors as so many countries are inclined to do. Moreover these costs should be factored into the privatisation decision-making matrix.

Political expression and civic involvement

Beyond the direct economic costs and benefits of privatisation is its impact on society-building, that is, its contribution to social capital. Privatisation effectiveness in countries where participation in civil society is controlled by the government either by suppressing freedom of expression, with-holding or restricting access to information or by limiting the public-comment process – aspects of social exclusion – must necessarily be less that optimal. In Guyana, for example, the Inter-American Development Bank (IDB) found obtaining broad stakeholder participation and consensus on major policy issues difficult which represent major obstacles to national development. In this connection, the South African experience stands as a model in terms of seeking national unity on the basis of reconciliation of disparate entities through a policy of inclusion.

The public consultation imperative

Looking beyond standard features, the privatisation framework must in the first instance provide for public participation in the decision to privatise which must be undertaken within an established regulatory and legal framework (See Parker and Kirkpatrick 2004; Kirkpatrick 2002; Juskow 1998). As is well recognised in a growing number of developing countries, public consultation not only promotes inclusiveness, an important attribute of social capital, but also provides the investor with the opportunity to assess the accuracy of representations made by the government and the expectations of consumers and their readiness for cost-covering tariffs in the case of utility services.

Additionally, the public-comment process provides the investor with a level of comfort when a transparent policy rooted in national consensus is forthcoming and could reflect in a lower country risk-premium and added foreign direct investment, features that defined the privatisation programmes of, for example, Malaysia, Botswana, South Africa and Mauritius. It also reduces the opportunity for investors to extract special privileges that detract from privatisation effectiveness and therefore development. Opportunities for rent-seeking by public officials – all too prevalent in privatisation negotiations conducted in secrecy (Stiglitz 2002, 58) and evident in the privatisation of the GEC (see Chapter 8) – are likewise reduced.

Determining the nature and level of private participation

Unlike privatisation in the developed countries, privatisation on the basis of domestic capital mobilisation in low-income countries was highly problematic and presented a challenge to policymakers (see Kumar *et al.* 1997; Ferreira and Khatami 1996). Clearly, with the weighted average GNP per capita of low income countries in 1994 well below the weighted average for the next category (see Table 2.3 page 68), low GNP per-capita served as a constraint to any significant local participation in privatisation in these countries. Moreover, given that sixteen of the 38 low income countries in Sub-Saharan Africa (see Figure 3.1, page 80) have an average GNP per-capita of less than US$250 (Bank 1997, 214), it is highly unlikely that indigenous private resources could have been mobilised to support privatisation requiring large investment over the longer term.

   Where foreign private participation is necessary, the level of such participation in the privatisation process should be determined by the government in consultation with other stakeholders as a first-order requirement. Seeking national political and public support signals the government's commitment to the process and more importantly to a transparent and publicly-accountable approach; it also reduces the risk of cancellation through a change in government. In this regard, the South African approach to the restructuring of state assets is one of the better examples of openness.[3]

   Equally important, the outcome of such an approach would necessarily reflect local concerns with respect to foreign-ownership and the sharing of the opportunities of privatisation through broad-based ownership with local investors, employee or other groups, either in tandem with the strategic investor or at some future date. It should also reflect the government's position with respect to redressing social inequalities, especially in low-income and previously economic and politically repressed societies, as evidenced by the Malaysian (Nankani 1988) and South African[4] approaches.

   In the case of South Africa, private participation in privatisation was approached from the unique perspective of encouraging economic growth through private-sector investment within a social-policy framework that speaks to redressing prior wrongs committed against a large segment of the population: Safeguards for employee and other forms of local investor participation at a determined future date, and

---

[3]   See Government of South Africa, *Review of Development Since 1994*, http://www. southafrica.net/economy/finance/app1.html; see also *Restructuring State Assets*, http://www. southafrica.net/economy/transport/restruct.html.

[4]   See Government of South Africa, *Privatisation*, http://www.southafrica.net/economy/ profile/private.html; see also *Opening Address 1997 Budget,* http://www.southafrica.net/ government/speeches/speech9.html.

employment guarantees were made conditions to foreign private participation in the privatisation of the country's infrastructure (see AFDB, 1999).

Where guarantees with respect to local participation at some future date and to employment reflective of an acceptable period of adjustment are not forthcoming, privatisation likely will be rejected. For example, whilst privatisation of state-owned enterprises was adopted and actively pursued by the Tanzanian government, many in Tanzania considered the process to have gone awry, with sale of profitable enterprises to foreigners being the main criticism and the process as a whole being regarded as looting public resources. In Lesotho, the government's privatisation programme was unanimously rejected by the unions out of concern that their members will not be able to participate in the process and likely will be treated no better than workers in Zambia and Malawi who reportedly had to wait six years to receive their settlement pay. Thus, data provided by the Bank shows that of the 1,161 projects completed between 1984 and 1994, only 80 (about 7 percent) of such projects were ascribed to Sub-Saharan Africa (Kerf and Smith 1996, 6). Clearly, irrespective of the derived benefits envisaged by policy-makers, privatisation under these conditions is unlikely to succeed if only out of protest by the disaffected. Evidence the protest of employees and customers of the Belize telephone against the privatisation of the local telephone company in 2005. At issue were job-security and the absence of consultation and national consensus.

Where the stated objective of the government is for broad-based local participation, a system of financial incentives was employed as was done in Chile (see Nankani 1988, 30). But even when broad-based local private participation is a government objective, macro-economic policy prescriptions attached to debt-forgiveness or soft loans often operate to frustrate facilitating such an objective. To overcome hard-budget and other constraints, several developing countries – *Coté d'Ivoire*, Tanzania, Malaysia and Zimbabwe for example – adopted a policy of warehousing shares for future employee participation, or alternatively the establishment of unit trusts or mutual funds for participation by the general public. Others – Morocco with Bank support, for example – encouraged local pension fund participation with appropriate safeguards lest the fund should become overly exposed to any one particular enterprise.

Constraints notwithstanding, there has to be savings within the host country for indigenous investment to take hold and form a base for further economic growth and development. To this end, the development effectiveness of privatisation is better served when there is reinvestment of income generated from foreign or domestic investment in the host country. In this regard, the repatriation of income generated is a double-edged sword for the host country and requires that the investor be provided with a sense of security for the future. Clearly, there has to be national consensus for a credible and transparent approach to the process on the one hand and investor-integrity on the other; challenges that must be met if privatisation were to contribute to development substantively. At the same time, difficult as it may be, developing country governments should be able to walk away from privatisations that do not adequately address the long-term needs of the country; yet another challenge for donor-countries and the HIPCs who are faced with balancing the management of poverty reduction by way of debt-forgiveness and grants, against poverty eradication by way of long-term economic growth and development.

Where privatisation by way of divestiture is not a viable option, performance contract management not unlike China's 'contract responsibility system' may be an effective interim measure (see Tenev *et al.* 2002). Not only will it import a performance-based incentive system in the management of the enterprise but also allow the government time to transition to a market-economic system – not just a market economy embedded in society – without the level of social disruption attendant on a flash-cut approach. In this regard, the precursory restructuring approach of many African countries – in particular Botswana, Mauritius, and South Africa – were seen as providing the basis for full divestiture in the telecommunications and energy sectors.

Last but not least, the opportunity for political corruption is increased with contracting out. There are numerous examples of politicians receiving political contributions for favours rendered, often in the awarding of government contracts. With corruption endemic in many developing countries, contracting out offers yet another means to be exploited by corrupt politicians and bureaucrats in environments where access to foreign grants and soft loans is seemingly perceived as a right of passage.

Towards a new theory of privatisation

From the perspective of development, then, the dynamic of privatisation as a change-agent in developing countries should be analysed not only in terms of its ideological rationale and features but also in terms of its distributive effectiveness In this regard, the extent to which the disadvantaged is benefited both in terms of access to services and the accumulation of assets and its impact on political and civic involvement which are considered instrumental as well as substantive characteristics of development becomes the most important criterion. Hence, whether or not privatisation programmes in developing countries have intrinsically addressed the broader issues of development depends crucially on whether policies and mechanisms to reduce social inequality informed privatisation policies; a consideration that was hardly necessary at the developed-country level and was difficult to find in the preceding analyses of privatisation in developing countries.

As a theory, then, privatisation in a post-Cold War world must not only define its features, but also seek to understand causality. It must evaluate outcomes not merely in terms of traditional economic results but more importantly in terms of its development effectiveness, specifically how the benefits and opportunities are shared among stakeholders in pursuit of pro-poor growth. In this approach, efficiency of the enterprise and in the allocation of resources, fundamental to orthodox economics, are made secondary to pro-poor growth considerations; and the diffusion of democracy seen more in terms of inclusive governance and promoting public participation in the monitoring and evaluative processes, with 'regime change' situated firmly in a foreign policy that is premised on leadership and is fully-supportable internationally, and then preferably achieved from within.

Failing such a holistic approach as described above, the poor will continue to be benefited disproportionately from FDI and even from development aid; socio-economic inequalities will continue to define developing countries, manifesting in civil strife and radicalisation of the disaffected.

It is a sad commentary on the notion of civilization that, even after 2400 years the dominant discourse continues to be: ' ... right must give way to might; the strong will do what they can, and the weak what they must' (Thucydidies). Hence, we need to be willing always to reflect upon our assumptions and the dominant discourse that informed them. Indeed, as Nietzsche counselled, we need to read slowly, deeply, and cautiously, with doors left open.

Bibliography

Adam, C. *et al.*, (1992), *Adjusting Privatization: Case Studies from Developing Countries*, (London: James Currey).

African Development Bank (1999), *African Development Report 1999*, (New York: Oxford University Press).

Amsden, A., (1989), *Asia's Next Giant, South Korea and late Industrialization*, (New York: Oxford University Press).

Baker III, J., (1987), 'Leadership and Cooperation', in Miljan T. (ed.).

Bang, N., (1990), 'Short-Term Money Markets in Korea: Reconstructions and Deregulation', in Gayle *et al.* (eds).

Bauer, P. (1991), *The Development Frontier: Essays in Applied Economics*, (Cambridge, Mass: Harvard University Press).

Baumol, W., *et al.* (1988), *Contestable Markets and the Theory of Industry Structure*, (San Diego: Harcourt Brace Jovanovich).

Berg, E. and Shirley, M. (1988), 'Divestiture in Developing Countries', *World Bank Discussion Paper 11*, (Washington, DC: World Bank, 1988).

Berry, R., (1997), *The Economy, in Eastern Europe and The Commonwealth of Independent States*, 3rd. Edition, (London: Europa Publications Limited).

Bhagwati, J., (1988), *Protectionism*, (Cambridge Mass: The MIT Press).

Blasi, J., and Shleifer, A., (1996), 'Corporate Governance in Russia: an Initial Look', in Frydman, *et al.* (eds).

Böhm, A. (ed.) (1995), *Privatization in Central & Eastern Europe 1994*, (Dunajska, Slovenia: CEEPN).

Borish, M. and Noël, M., (1996), 'Private Sector Development during Transitition: The Visegrad Countries', *World Bank Discussion Papers, 318*, (Washington, DC: World Bank).

Borrell, B. and Duncan, R. (1992), 'A Survey of the Costs of World Sugar Policies', The *World Bank Research Observer*, vol. 7, No 2 July 1992, (Washington, DC: World Bank).

Boycko, M. *et al.*, (1996), *Privatizing Russia*, (Cambridge, Mass: MIT Press).

Buchanan, P., (2002), *The Death of the West*, (New York: Thomas Dunne Books, St. Martin's Press).

Campbell, *et al.* (eds) (1976), *An Inquiry into the Nature and Causes of the Wealth of Nations*, vol. 1., (Oxford: Clarendon Press).

Campbell White, O. and Bhatia, A. (1998), *Privatisation in Africa*, (Washington, DC: World Bank).

Carson, R., (1997), *Comparative Economic System*, vol. 1. (2nd edn), (London: M.E. Sharpe).

Ceska, R. 1995 'Privatization in the Czech Republic – 1994' in Böhm, A. (ed.).

Chang, C. (2004), 'Telecommunications in Guyana: From state-ownership to de-monopolisation?', in Cook, P. *et al.* (eds).

—— (1997), *Privatisation as a Contributing Asset to Small Under-developed Countries*, Unpublished Doctoral Thesis.

Cook, P. *et al.* (eds), (2004), *Leading Issues in Competition, Regulation and Development*, (Cheltenham: Edward Elgar).

Csepi, L. and Lukacs, E. (1995), 'Privatization in Hungary – 1994', in Böhm, A. (ed.).

Chase-Dunn, C., (1989), *Global Formation: Structures of the World Economy*, (Cambridge, Mass: Blackwell Publishers, Reprinted, 1992).

Chunan, P. *et al.*, (1996), 'International Capital Flows: Do Short-Term Investment and Direct Investment Differ?', *Policy Research Working Paper 1669*, (Washington DC: World Bank).

Clawson, R., (1995), 'Post-Stalin Efforts to Reform the Soviet Industrial Economy, 1953–1985', in Logue, J. *et al.* (eds).

Covarrubias, A. (1996), *Lending for Electric Power in Sub-Saharan Africa*, (Washington, DC: World Bank).

Crewe, I. (1989), 'Values: The Crusade That Failed', in Kavanagh, D. and Seldon, A. (eds).

Dalton, G. (ed.) (1968), *Primitive, Archaic and Modern Economies, Essays of Karl Polanyi*, (New York: Anchor Books, Doubleday & Co.).

Davis, J. *et al.* (2000), 'Fiscal and Macroeconomic Impact of Privatization', *Occasional Paper 194*, (Washington, DC: International Monetary Fund).

De Melo, J. and Panagaryia, 'The New Regionalism in Trade Policy', *World Bank and CEPR Conference on New Dimensions in Regional Integration*, (Washington, DC: World Bank).

Desai, R. and Goldberg, I. (2000), 'The Vicious Circle of Control, Regional Governments and Insiders in Privatized Russian Enterprises', *Policy Research Working Paper 2287*, (Washington, DC: World Bank).

De Soto, H. (1989), *The Other Path: The Invisible Revolution in the Third World*, (New York: Harper & Row).

Dobek, M. (1993), The *Political Logic of Privatization: Lessons from Great Britain and Poland*, (Westport: Praeger).

Donaldson, T. (1989), *The Ethics of International Business*, (New York: Oxford University Press).

Dornbusch, R. *et al.* (eds) (1989), *The Open Economy: Tools for policymakers in developing countries*, (New York: Oxford University Press, 2nd printing).

Dzisah, M. (1996), 'Privatization sale hits snag', in *Africa Business*, February 1996 (London: IC Publications Ltd).

Ernst, M. *et al.* (1996), *Transforming the Core: Restructuring Industrial Enterprises in Russia and Central Europe*, (Boulder: Westview Press).

Ehteshami, A. (2003), 'Reform from above: the politics of the participation in oil monarchies', in *International Affairs*, vol. 79, January 2003, (Oxford: Blackwell).

Fadahunsi, O., (1996) (ed.), *Privatisation in Africa: The Way Forward*, (Nairobi: AAPM).

Ferreira, D. and Khatami, K., (1996), 'Financing Private Infrastructure in Developing Countries', *World Bank Discussion Paper No. 343*, (Washington, DC: World Bank).

Fletcher, C. (1995), *Privatization and the Rebirth of Capital Markets in Hungary*, (Jefferson, NC: Mc Farland & Company).

Frydman, R. *et al.*, (1996) (eds), *Corporate Governance in Central Europe and Russia*, (London: CEU Press).

——, (1993), *The Privatisation process in Russia, Ukraine, and the Baltic States*, (London: CEU Press).

Fukuyama, F., (1999), *The Great Disruption: Human nature and the reconstitution of social order*, (New York: The Free Press).

Galal, A., (1989), 'The Reform of State-Owned Enterprises: Lessons from World Bank Lending', *PPR Series, No. 4*, (Washington, DC: World Bank).

——, (1991), *World Bank Discussion Paper 119*, (Washington, DC: World Bank).

Gayle, D. *et al.*, (1990), *Privatization and Deregulation in Global Perspective*, (Westport, CT: Quorum Books).

Geggie, I. (1991), 'Designing Major Policy Reform: Lessons from the Transport Sector', *World Bank Discussion Paper 115*, (Washington, DC: IBRD/WB).

Glen, J. and Sumlinski, M. (1998), 'Trends in Private Investment in Developing Countries, Statistics for 1970–1996, *International Finance Corporation, Discussion Paper 34*, (Washington, DC: World Bank and IFC).

Goldman, M., (2003), *The Piratization of Russia; Russian reform goes Awry*, (New York: Routledge).

Gordon, L., (1987), *Eroding Empire: Western Relations with Eastern Europe*, (Washington, DC: The Brookings Institution).

Gorbachev, M., (1987), *Perestroika: New Thinking for Our Country and the World*, (New York: Harper & Row).

Goto, J., (1989), 'The Multifibre Arrangement and its Effects on Developing Countries, *The World Bank Research Observer*, vol. 4, No 2 July 1989, (Washington, DC: World Bank).

Gray, C., (1960), 'In Search of Owners: Privatization and Corporate Governance in Transition Economies', *World Bank Research Observer11, 2*, (Washington, DC: World Bank).

Greider, W., (1997), *One world, Ready or Not*, (New York, Touchstone).

Grootaert, C, & Braithwaite, J., (1998), 'Poverty correlates and indicator-based targeting in Eastern Europe and the former Soviet Union', *Policy Research Working Paper, No. 1942*, (Washington, DC: World Bank).

Halavàcek, J. and Mejstrik, M., (1997), 'The Initial Economic Environment for Privatization', in Mejstrik, M., (ed).

Hamilton, C., (ed.) (1990), *Textiles Trade and the Developing Countries, Eliminating the Multi-fibre Arrangement in the 1990s*, (Washington, DC: World Bank).

Helleiner, G. (1997), 'Capital Account Regimes and the Developing Countries', in

International Monetary and Financial Issues for the 1990s, vol. viii, (New York: United Nations).

——, (1992), 'The IMF, the World Bank and Africa's adjustment and external debt problems: An unofficial view', in *World Development Report, vol. 20, No.,* June 1992.

Hellman, J. *et al.,* (2000), 'Seize the State, Seize the Day: An Empirical Analysis of State Capture and Corruption in Transition', *Policy Research Working Paper 2444, World Bank Development Research Group,* (Washington, DC: World Bank).

Henry, R., (1990), 'Privatization and the State Enterprise Sector in Trinidad and Tobago: Market and nonmarket issues in a Plural Political Economy', in Gayle, D. *et al.* (eds).

Husain, I., (1994), 'Why Do Some Economies Adjust More Successfully Than Others?', *Policy Research Working Paper 1364,* (Washington, DC: World Bank).

Joffe, J., (1989), 'The Foreign Policy of the Federal Republic of Germany', in Macridis, R. (ed.).

Joskow, P. ,(1998), 'Regulatory Priorities for Reforming Infrastructure Sectors in Developing Countries', *Conference Paper, 10th ABCDE,* (Washington, DC: World Bank).

Kaldor, M., (2003), 'American power: from compellance to cosmopolitanism?', *International Affairs,* Vol. 79 No. 1, January 2003, (Oxford: Blackwell Publishing).

Kasekkende, L. *et al.* (1997), 'Capital Inflows and Macroeconomic Policy in Sub Saharan Africa', in *International Monetary and Financial Issues for the 1990s, Vol. VIII,* (New York: United Nations).

Katz, B., (1992), 'Introduction: Public Enterprises in Sub-Saharan Africa', in Rexford A. *et al.* (eds).

Kaufmann, D., et al. (2000), 'Governance Matters: From Measurement to Action', in *Finance and Development 37(2),* (Washington, DC: IMF).

Kavanagh, D. and Seldon, A., (eds), The Thatcher Effect, (Oxford: Clarendon Press).

Kay, J. *et al.,* (1986), *Privatisation and Regulation: The UK Experience,* (Oxford: Clarendon Press).

Kelly, M. *et al.,* (1992), *Issues and Development in International Trade Policy* (Washington, DC: IMF).

Kessides, C.,(1993), 'The Contributions of Infrastructure to Economic Development', *World Bank Discussion Papers No. 213,* (Washington, DC: World Bank).

Killick, T. (1995), *IMF Programmes in Developing Countries,* (London: Routledge).

Kirkpatrick, C. (2001), 'Regulatory Impact Assessment in Developing Countries: Research Issues', *CRC Working Paper Series, Paper No. 5,* (Manchester: Manchester University).

Koester, U. and Bale, M., (1990), 'The Common Agricultural Policy: A Review of its Operations and Effects on Developing Countries', in *The World Bank Research Observer, vol. 5, No 1,* January1990, (Washington, DC: World Bank).

Krueger, A., (1993), *Economic Policies at Cross-purposes: The United States and Developing Countries*, (Washington, DC: Brookings Institution).

Krugman, P., (1988), 'External Shocks and Domestic Policy Responses', in Dornbusch, R. (eds).

Krzysztof, P., (1995), 'Privatization in Poland', in Böhm, A. (ed.).

Kueczynski, P., (1982/1983), 'Latin American Debt', in *Foreign Affairs*.

Kumar, A., *et al.*, (1997), 'Mobilizing Domestic Capital Markets for Infrastructure Financing', *World Bank Discussion Paper No. 377*, (Washington DC: World Bank).

Letiche, J., (ed.) (1982), International Economic Policies and Their Theoretical Foundations, (New York: Academic Press).

Lewis, W., (1955), *The Theory of Economic Growth*, (London: Allen and Unwin).

Lewis, Peter, M., (1990), 'The Political Economy of Privatization in Nigeria', in Gayle, D. and Goodrich, J. (eds).

Lieberman, I. and Rahuja, S. (1995), 'An Overview of Privatisation in Russia', in *Russia: Creating Private Enterprises and Effective Markets*, (Washington, DC: World Bank).

Logue, J., *et al.* (eds) (1995), *Transforming Russian Enterprises: From State Control to Employee Ownership*, (Westport: Greenwood Press).

Macridis, R., (ed.) (1989), *Foreign Policy in world Politics: States and Regions*, (7th Edition), (Englewood: Prentice Hall).

Mairal, H. (1996), 'Legal and Other Issues in Privatization: The Argentine Experience', in *Privatisation in Asia, Europe, and Latin America*, (Paris, France: OECD).

Megyery, K. and Sader, F., (1997), 'Facilitating Foreign Participation in Privatization', *Foreign Investment Advisory Service, Occasional Paper 8*, (Washington, DC: World Bank).

Meier, G., *et al.* (eds.) (1984), *Pioneers in Development*, (New York: Oxford University Press).

Mejstrik, M., (ed.) (1997), *The Privatization Process in East-Central Europe*, (Norwell, Mass: Kluwer Academic Publishers).

Meltzer, A., *et al.* (2000), '*Report from the International Financial Institution Advisory Commission presented to the Senate Banking Committee in March 2000*', (On-line, http// www.csf. Colorado.edu/roper/if.Meltzer-commission-mar00).

Metcalfe, J., *et al.* (2004), 'Competition, innovation and economic development: the instituted connection', in Cook, P. *et al.* (eds).

Michalopoulos, C., (1987),'World Bank Lending for Structural Adjustment', in *Finance and Development*, June 1987 (Washington, DC: IMF).

Miljan, T. (ed.), (1987), *The Political Economy of North-South Relations*, (NY: Broadview Press).

Minogue, M., (2004), 'Public management and regulatory governance: Problems of policy transfer to developing countries', in Cook, P. *et al.* (eds).

Mladek, J., (1997), 'Initialization of Privatization through Restitution and Small Privatization', in *The Privatization Process in East-Central Europe*, (Norwell, Mass: Kluwer Publishers).

Moore, J., (1986), 'Why Privatise?' in Kay, J. *et al.* (eds).

——, (1986), 'The Success of Privatization', in Kay, J. *et al.* (eds).

Myrdal, G., (1969), *The political Element in the Development of Economic Theory*, (New York: Simon and Schuster).

Nankani, H., (1988), 'Methods of Privatization of State-Owned Enterprises', vol. II. *World Bank Technical Papers, No. 89*, (Washington, DC; World Bank).

Narayan, D., (ed.) (2002), *Empowerment and poverty reduction: A source book*, (Washington, DC: World Bank).

Nellis, J., (1986), 'Public Enterprises in Sub-Saharan Africa', *World Bank Discussion Paper no. 1*, (Washington, DC: World Bank).

Page, S. *et al.* (1991), 'The GATT Uruguay Round: Effects on Developing Countries', in *Overseas Development Institute*, (London: Blackwell Publishing).

Pannier, D., (ed.) (1996), 'Corporate Governance of Public Enterprises in Transitional Economies', *World Bank Technical Paper Number 323*, (Washington, DC: World Bank).

Park, Y. and Song, C., (1997), 'Managing Capital Flows: The Experience of the Republic of Korea, Thailand, Malaysia and Indonesia', *International Monetary and Financial Issues for the 1990s, vol. viii*, (New York: United Nations).

Parker, D. and Kirkpatrick, C., (2004), 'Economic regulation in developing countries: a framework for critical analysis', in Cook P. *et al.* (eds).

Poirson, H., (1998), 'Economic security, private investment and growth in developing countries', *IMF Working Papers 98/4*, (Washington, DC: IMF).

Polanyi, K., (1977), *The Livelihood of Man*, (New York: Academic Press Inc.).

——, (1944), *The Great Transformation*, (Boston: Reinhart & Company).

Prebisch, R., (1982), 'The Latin American periphery in the global system of capitalism', in Letiche, J. (ed.).

——, (1984), 'Five Stages in my Thinking on Development', in Meier, G. *et al.* (eds).

Rexford A. *et al.*, (eds) (1992), *Privatization and Investment in Sub-Saharan Africa*, (New York: Praeger).

Rohwer, J. (1995), *Asia Rising: Why America will prosper as Asia's economies boom*, (New York: Touchstone).

Rondinelli, D. *et al.*, (eds) (2003), *Reinventing Government for the Twentieth-first Century*, (Bloomfield CT: Kumarian Press).

Rostow, W., (1961), *The Stages of Economic Growth, A non-communist Manifesto*, (London: Cambridge University Press).

Rutland, P., (1997), (3rd edn), *The Czech Republic: The Economy in Eastern Europe and the Commonwealth of Independent States*, (London: Europa Publications Limited).

Sader, F., (1993), 'Privatization and Foreign Investment in the Developing World, 1988–1992', *World Bank Working Papers*, (Washington, DC: World Bank).

Sampson, G. and Takacs, W., (1990), 'Returning Textiles Trade to the Normal Workings of GATT: A Practical Proposal for Reform', in Hamilton, C. (ed.).

Sen, A. (1999), *Development as Freedom*, (New York: Alfred A. Knopf).

Serageldin, I., (1993), 'Making Development Sustainable', in *Finance and Development* December 1993, (Washington, DC: IMF).

Servén, L., (1997), 'Uncertainty, Instability, and Irreversible Investment', *Policy Research Working Paper 1722*, (Washington, DC: World Bank).

Sherrod, J., (ed.), *Privatization: A Source Book*, (Detroit: Omnigraphics Inc.).

Sigmund, P., (1988), *St. Thomas Aquinas on Politics and Ethics*, (New York: W. W. Norton & Company).

Sklair, L., (1995) (2nd ed.), *Sociology of the Global System*, (London: Prentice Hall Harvester Wheatsheaf).

Starr, P., (1989), 'An Academic Challenge to Privatization', in Sherrod, J. (ed.).

Starodubrovskaya, I., (1996), 'Russia', in Pannier, D. (ed.).

Stiglitz, J., (2002), *Globalization and its discontents*, (New York: W. W. Norton & Co).

Strange, S., (1987), 'Protectionism- Why Not?', in Miljan, T. (ed.).

Stromquist, N., (2002), *Education in a Globalised World*, (Maryland: Rowan and Littlefield).

Sword, K., (1997), 'Poland, the Economy', in *Eastern Europe and The Commonwealth of Independent States*, (London: Europa Publications Limited).

Tenev, *et al.*, (2002), *Corporate Governance and Enterprise Reform in China: building the institutions of modern markets*, (Washington, DC: World Bank/ IFC).

The West Indian Commission (1992), *Statistical Profile of the Caribbean Community CARICOM*, (Barbados, West Indian Commission).

Tobin, J., (1998), 'Financial Globalization: Can National Currencies Survive?', *Conference Paper, 10th ABCDE*, (Washington, DC: World Bank).

Thatcher, M., (2002), *Statecraft*, (New York: HarperCollins).

——, (1993), *The Downing Street Years*, (New York: HarperCollins).

Trela, I. and Whalley, J., (1990), 'Unravelling the Threads of the MFA' in: Hamilton, C., (ed.).

Tussie, D., (1987), *The Less Developed Countries and the World Trading System*, (London: Frances Pinter (Publishers)).

United Nations Development Programme (1999), *Human Development Report 1999*, (New York: UNDP).

United Nations Department for Development Support Management Services, (1995), *Performance Contracting For Public Enterprises*, (New York: UN).

US Government, General Accounting Office (2000), '*Report to the Chairman and the Ranking Minority Member, Committee' on Banking and Financial Services, House of Representative, GAO-01-8*, (Washington DC: U.S. Government).

Vassilyev, D. (1995), 'Privatization in Russia 1994', in Böhm, A. (ed.).

Vickers, J. and Yarrow, G., (6th Printing) (1995), *Privatization: An Economic Analysis*, (Cambridge, Mass: MIT Press).

Vuylsteke, C., (1988), 'Techniques of Privatization of State-Owned Enterprises, vol. 1, Techniques and Implementation', *World Bank Technical Paper Number 88*, (Washington, DC: IBRD/WB).

Walker, W., (1987), 'Trade Does Not Need Scapegoats' in Miljan, T. (ed.).

Wallerstein, I. (2005) (2nd edn), *World systems Analysis*, (Durham: Duke University Press).

——, (1974) *The Modern World System vol.1* (New York: Academic Press).

Wermuth, L., (2003), *Global Inequality and Human Needs*, (Boston: Alan & Bacon).

Williams, S., (1997), 'East Africa's tangled rail tracks' in *Africa Business*, February, 1997 (London: IC Publications, Ltd.).

World Bank, (1987), *World Development Report 1987*, (NY: Oxford University Press).

——, (1991), *World Development Report 1991*, (NY: Oxford University Press).

——, (1993), *Guyana, From Economic Recovery to Sustained Growth*, (NY: Oxford University Press).

——, (1993a), *Guyana: Private Sector Development, World Bank Country Study*, Washington, DC: World Bank.

——, (1996), 'Property Rights and Enterprise Reform', in *World Development Report 1996*, (Washington, DC: World Bank).

——, (1997), *World Development Report 1997*, (New York: Oxford University Press).

——, (1997a), *Helping Countries combat Corruption: The role of the World Bank*, (Washington, DC: World Bank).

——, (2000/2001), *World Development Report 2000/2001 – Attacking Poverty* (New York: Oxford University Press).

——, (2005), 'Annual Review of Development Effectiveness', *Operations Evaluation Department* (Washington DC: World Bank).

——, (2006), 'World Development Report, Equity and Development', (Washington, DC: World Bank).

World Health Organisation (1998), 'Life in the 21st Century: a vision for all', in *The World Health Report, 1998*, (Geneva: WHO).

Yin-Fang, Z. *et al.*, (2002), 'Electricity Sector Reform in Developing Countries: An Econometric Assessment of the Effects of Privatisation, Competition and Regulation', *Working Paper Series, Paper No. 31*, October 2002, (Manchester, University of Manchester).

Zayyad, H., (1996), 'Privatization and Commercialisation in Nigeria' in Fadahunsi, O. (ed.).

Index

economic system 163–4
Electricity Sector Reform Act 1999
191–3
Enhanced Structural Adjustment Facility
(ESAF) 171–2
ethnic polarisation 162, 168–9
external debt 166–7
extra-judicial killings 162
GDP growth 161
governance 159–62
historical background 163–71
import substitution 164
inequality 60
informal economy 167
Inter-American Development Bank 162
International Monetary Fund (IMF)
171–3, 176–7
migration 168
nationalisation 163–4
Parliament Reform Report 162–3
patrimonialism 181–2
Peoples' Progressive Party/Civic (PPP/
C) 174–5
private sector 160–61
Privatisation Policy Framework Paper
(PPFP) 187–8
privatisation since 1994 178–81
Privatisation Unit 176, 200
proceeds of privatisation 181
property rights 31, 32
Public Utilities Commission (PUC) 69,
190–91, 194–5, 196–7
public works projects 182
Quadripartite Agreement 191
railways 73
rate of return for investors 73–4
restitution of property 173
revenue sources 168
sale of assets 173–4
Social Impact Amelioration Programme
(SIMAP) 172
squatting 167
subordination of the state 172–3
sugar production 67, 169, 180
suspension of economic recovery programme 175–6
tax evasion 169
telecommunications 209
verandah effect 182

Guyana Electricity Corporation (GEC)
185–202 *see also* Guyana Power
and Light (GPL)
AC Power, selection of 189
accountability 190
bidding 188–9
management service contract 190
public participation 191
rate of return 191
regulation 190–91
transparency 190
Guyana Power and Light (GPL) *see also*
Guyana Electricity Corporation
(GEC)
accounts receivable 196, 201
board members 192
consumer charges 191–2, 199
disconnection 197–8
environmental protection 198
estimated consumption 197–9
external financing 195–6
governance 200
investor obligations 194–5
Licence 192–3
loss reductions 195
over-billing 197–9
pro-poor growth 197–8
rate increases 199
reconnection costs 198
regulation 192–3, 196–7
subsidies 199
supply 194–5
termination of joint venture 185–6
transparency 193
Guyana Sugar Corporation (GUYSUCO)
171, 173, 194

Hayek, Friedrich von 4–5
Helms-Burton Law (US) 35
Highly Indebted Poor Countries (HIPC)
Initiative 65
Hong Kong
currency intervention 35
voluntary export restraint (VER) 38
Hungary 10–11, 93–4, 134–5, 146–8 *see*
also EEC-3 countries
debt reduction 138
foreign investment 147–8
local ownership 147–8

Printed in the United States
by Baker & Taylor Publisher Services